Nature's Northwest

The Modern American West
Richard W. Etulain and David M. Wrobel, Editors

Nature's Northwest

The North Pacific Slope in the Twentieth Century

William G. Robbins and Katrine Barber

The University of Arizona Press   Tucson

The University of Arizona Press
© 2011 The Arizona Board of Regents
All rights reserved

www.uapress.arizona.edu

Library of Congress Cataloging-in-Publication Data

Robbins, William G., 1935–
    Nature's Northwest : the North Pacific Slope in the twentieth
century / William G. Robbins and Katrine Barber.
        p.   cm. — (The modern American West)
    Includes bibliographical references and index.
    ISBN 978-0-8165-2894-3 (hard cover : alk. paper)
    ISBN 978-0-8165-2959-9 (pbk. : alk. paper)
    1. Northwest, Pacific—History—20th century.
2. Regionalism—Northwest, Pacific. 3. Human geography—
Northwest, Pacific. I. Barber, Katrine. II. Title.

F852.R64 2011
979.5'03—dc22

                                        2010040204

Publication of this book is made possible in part by a grant
from the Franklin College of Arts and Sciences and the
Department of History at the University of Georgia.

16 15 14 13 12 11   6 5 4 3 2 1

Contents

Illustrations

Tables

Preface
Toward a Regional Narrative

During his tenure as director of the Center for the Study of Southern Culture at the University of Mississippi and continuing when he served as chair of the National Endowment for the Humanities in the 1990s, William Ferris championed the value of studying regional history and culture. Despite "interstates and national television programming," he insisted that distinct and unique voices, "rooted in the home and the community in which we live," continued to endure across the land. Historian Lawrence Levine agrees. The existence of long-standing divisions in the nation "by ethnicity, by region, by geography, by economics," he argued, has muted the cultural influence of big corporations and mass culture. That the United States was once a unified place, he contends, is largely a myth. Mark Crispin Miller, a professor with expertise in media studies, believes "there are still important regional differences in this country" despite the homogenizing influences of national culture.[1] We cite the testimony of Ferris, Levine, and Miller to underscore the shortcomings of arguments for singular national narratives of history and culture.

To better grasp the dizzying period of change in the twentieth century, the writer Garry Wills suggested that the previous one hundred years would be more understandable "if we can just get high enough in the waves to see the broad expanse of sea that carries us along."[2] This volume reflects an effort to ride the crest of multiple national and regional stories to conceptualize and write a selective history of the Greater Pacific Northwest in the twentieth century. We do not subscribe to the notion that there is a single national narrative that fits either the United States or Canada; nor is there a single regional chronicle that carries convincing thematic unity. Although this book provides some evidence suggesting congruent and common features to Northwest history, there is nothing natural about the political bounds to British Columbia or to the states of Idaho, Montana, Oregon, and Washington, the subjects of this book.[3]

While the American states and the province of British Columbia share common historical antecedents, their collective stories are also divergent and complex, and they sometimes differ sharply along racial and ethnic lines. The approach engaged in this narrative, therefore, will explore local and regional politics, economies, and cultures, but always with a wary eye to difference and to extraregional, national, and transnational influences. Our effort will attempt to frame a regional history that probes stories that transcend the border, especially those that interrogate issues of race, class, gender, and relations between states, provinces, and nation-state governments. Regions, we suggest, are appropriate forums for questions relating to extraregional significance.[4]

Deliberately transborder in scope, embracing southern British Columbia, Idaho, Washington, Oregon, and western Montana, this study references Alaska only in passing while acknowledging that a powerful argument can be made that historical ties of economy, culture, and passage require that it be considered an extension of the Northwest. California, an economic colossus in its own right, is not part of the formal structure of our "Greater Northwest," despite the fact that its economy, culture, and demographics profoundly influence the region. Because of the enormous size of its economy and population, California is truly the "elephant in the closet" for the American West and beyond. Historically, when the California construction industry slowed, loggers and mill workers in the Northwest suffered layoffs and plant closures. Furthermore, in the last quarter century or more, an exodus of "equity" refugees from California ("white flight," critics call it) has reshaped the landscape of virtually every adjacent state.

The narrative thread we pursue attempts to achieve some of Frederick Jackson Turner's objective that local history can be understood only in relation to the rest of the world.[5] In one sense, this is an account of diasporic ethnic populations—the descendants of French Canadian trappers, Scottish and English clerks, and Cornish miners, German, Irish, Scandinavian, Italian, Chinese, Japanese, Filipino, black, and Mexican immigrants—who brought with them cultural and social trappings alien to Northwest places. This study is grounded in the hard reality that immigrants constructed New World societies amidst the homelands of sizable numbers of Native people, whose presence, although diminished in numbers at the onset of the twentieth century, would become increasingly influential with the passing decades.

Historical context is important, because national and global forces persistently shaped and reshaped life in the transborder Northwest. Patterns of immigration, two world wars, the cold war, collapsing economies, the growing assertiveness of Native people, and the increasing capacity of humans to transform the physical environment reflect forces beyond simplistic notions of regional initiative. History is always contingent, in part a measure of human activity, success, and failure through time. Having some understanding of the complexities of the past holds potential for helping us live as imperfect humans in an unpredictable world.[6]

This book attempts to grapple with the full spectrum of human behavior, of ambition and accomplishment, of grasping and greed, of success, achievement, and failure. Even those labels, however, are oversimplified. Building dams, for instance, contributed in the long run to destroying salmon runs, but the dams also drastically reduced flood damage to cities, towns, and agricultural land. For nearly a century, dams in the Pacific Northwest have been producing relatively cheap electricity, a form of energy that has made life comfortable for generations of people.[7] Private utilities and federal, state, provincial, and urban governments built dams at particular moments in the past when there was overwhelming support for such projects. At this writing, private utilities are removing some early-twentieth-century dams, and a strong regional interest in restoring salmon runs is driving the discourse (and controversy) about removing four federal dams on the lower Snake River.

What we see across the present northwestern landscape reflects human activities and initiatives that have taken place in particular locales over decades and centuries. Although regional constructs are intellectual abstractions, since the early formulations of the Oregon Country in the 1840s, scholars have reckoned with the work of imperial mapmakers and national geopolitical pronouncements in Washington, D.C., London, and Ottawa. Political maps of the twentieth-century Northwest no longer reflected features common to Indian/First Nations people, when cultural divisions ran north and south rather than east and west. In terms of the region's long human history, therefore, international and nationally imposed state and provincial boundaries are recent developments.[8] While this book mostly employs natural features to define the Greater Northwest, we have no illusion that such a construction is completely satisfactory. Ambiguity, belief, and perception rest in the eye of the beholder and contribute to imprecision in discussing regions.

It is important for American and Canadian scholars to look beyond the more conventional, insular, and physically circumscribed discussions of history, literature, politics, and economics to geographies of greater scale.[9] Such an effort is challenging, especially for Americans who tend to conceive of the continent as if it were a *USA Today* weather map, ending abruptly at the forty-ninth parallel. While the "borders" between Canada and the United States are creatures of politics and history, they also serve as intellectual iron curtains of sorts that are at odds with common bioregional geographical features and global economic imperatives. Until very recently, scholars have largely failed to give significant meaning to the inscription carved into the Peace Arch, the monument to international cooperation at the border crossing in Blaine, Washington: "May These Gates Never Be Closed."[10]

The consequence of blinkered scholarly enterprises north and south of the border is an intellectually bifurcated Pacific Northwest that ignores larger landscapes of geography and human activity: (1) kindred north–south bioregional features,[11] (2) similar cultural and historical experiences among Indian/First Nations people, (3) common oceanic highways, and, for more than two centuries, (4) the integrative influence of a global capitalism that has been little bothered with international boundaries. A case in point is the Asian economic crisis of the late 1990s, which greatly affected the import-export trade in British Columbia and America's Pacific Coast states. Periodic slumps in the U.S. construction industry have contributed to layoffs in the woods and the closure of sawmills in the American Northwest and British Columbia. The North Pacific salmon industry's difficulties affect fisher communities along the North American coast, including Alaska as well as Asian nations such as Japan.

This book examines social, economic, political, cultural, and environmental change in the Greater Northwest, with special attention to Idaho, Oregon, Washington, western Montana, and southern British Columbia. Because common economies, resources, politics, and cultures transect the international boundary, we argue that the greater transborder region always represented more than a simple, politically circumscribed geography. The narrative also emphasizes an enduring theme— the persisting interactions through more than two centuries between the original occupants of the land and the newcomers who eventually came to dominate the region.[12] Since the Second World War, the increasing affluence and greater mobility of professional people as well as the accelerated movement of capital around the globe have provided a powerful and dynamic impetus to change in the region. At the outset of the twenty-first century, new classes of wealthy, less-place-bound people have been remaking many former resource-dependent communities into gentrified homelands with strikingly different sets of values.

At the beginning of the twentieth century, the Greater Northwest was ablaze with change and seemingly obsessed with progress, with boosters and developers emphasizing the expanding rail systems north and south of the international boundary.[13] But the promotional literature praising railroads, population increases, and the growing sophistication of urban living also ignored realities of poverty and ethnic and racial discrimination, especially in the United States. At the turn of the century, Michael Katz and Mark Stern write, "America had become . . . a land of extremes—of wealth and poverty and racial privilege and discrimination." The promotional narratives included alarming contradictions. The nation that took great pride in its political democracy and economic and technological advances still prohibited women (and virtually all people of color) from voting, holding public office, and most wage-earning employment.[14] Similar conditions existed in Canada.

Move forward one hundred years. Despite a dramatically broadened voting franchise, great strides in racial and ethnic relations, progress in the legal status for Indian/First Nations people, and significant advances in medical knowledge, persisting concerns linger, especially the continued volatility of resource economies and the increasing number of immigrants moving to the region. Katz and Stern argue that the transformation taking place across North America in the early twenty-first century is just "as profound as the one driven by the industrial revolution of past centuries." Although the great fault lines between the beginning and end of the twentieth century have shifted, one constant remains as potent as ever—inequality.[15] As this book goes to press, the dark clouds of a widespread economic recession have blanketed the region, the most severe economic downturn since the Great Depression of the 1930s.

Over the course of a century, the Greater Pacific Northwest has witnessed dramatic changes. In the early twentieth century, more than 50 percent of the population in Idaho, Montana, Oregon, Washington, and British Columbia lived in settlements with one thousand or fewer residents. At the onset of the twenty-first century, only 2 percent made their homes in such communities. The modal northwesterner who lived on a farm or in an isolated resource town now resides in a suburb. With the extraordinary growth and concentration of the Northwest population during the last century, governments at all levels have vastly extended their influences in daily life, regulating traffic, liquor, and minimum-wage scales and providing a myriad of social services unimagined in the early twentieth century. Although governments have not been all things to all people, they have been a positive force in providing modest social insurance programs, guaranteeing fair labor standards, offering limited protections for trade unions, and furnishing a range of health benefits.[16] The more activist role of governments accelerated during the Great Depression and reached a high point sometime in the 1970s. During the last three decades, two parallel trends have taken place on both sides of the border: growing inequality and insecurity and a move toward more punitive social and economic policies at the federal, state, and provincial levels.

Still another constant remains for the Greater Northwest—the wonderful natural abundance that still has a powerful hold on its people and culture. Although Microsoft, Intel, and other high-tech industries have surpassed agriculture, logging, mining, and fishing as the most visible economic indicators, what we might call "nature's industries" remain the centerpiece of much of the cultural landscape. Literary themes rooted in material and cultural worlds of resource extraction, along with related motifs associated with majestic backdrops of coastal headlands, mountains, cascading rivers, and desert landscapes, continue to inspire the best regional writers—Mary Clearman Blew, William Dietrich, Ivan Doig, Timothy Egan, David Guterson, Jack Hodgins, Ken Kesey, William Kittredge, Joy Kogawa, Craig Lesley, Sharon Pollock, Native American/First Nations authors Sherman Alexie, Eden Robinson, and Elizabeth Woody, and many others. Although declining species such as salmon and environmental restrictions have placed restraints on resource extraction, a new amenity-based appreciation for the region's magnificent natural treasures—the great outdoors, with its scenic splendors and recreational pleasures—continues to provide citizens with the opportunity to enjoy a wonderful natural inheritance.

In the last year of the twentieth century, Garry Wills remarked that people everywhere were "caught in a rushing flood of time that is difficult to measure in meaningful ways." By the end of the twentieth century, the world's population had tripled, and science had prolonged human life and advanced food production, especially in wealthy industrialized nations. As in the Greater Northwest, agricultural progress had changed humans everywhere "from being primarily rural to being primarily urban." It is our hope that this narrative offers sufficient perspective to better understand the turbulent currents of change that shaped the twentieth-century Northwest.[17]

Acknowledgments

Because a work of synthesis is necessarily derivative, this book reflects the accumulated research, insights, and knowledge of scholars representing a variety of academic disciplines. I am grateful to anonymous readers as well as series editors Richard Etulain and David Wrobel, who offered constructive suggestions for additional sources to consult and for bringing balance to this narrative of the long twentieth century. Thanks to Bob McDonald of the University of British Columbia for his guidance on recent books and articles on provincial history. Good friend Jeremy Mouat, Augustana Faculty–University of Alberta, was equally helpful in offering perceptive insights about past and present transborder issues. Copy editor Mary Hill effectively rescued the manuscript from some of its most serious stylistic lapses.

It was a special treat to work with Katrine Barber, who agreed to join this enterprise and assume responsibility for the cultural chapters. Katy, who first enrolled in one of my U.S. history survey classes in the early 1990s, has become a treasured friend. Finally, I am especially appreciative of the ongoing and singular friendships with former Oregon State University students Laurie Arnold, Karyle Butcher, Ron Gregory, Lindon Hylton, Nancy Swain, and Don Wolf, and current student Tina Schweickert.

—WGR

I am grateful to my colleagues in the Department of History at Portland State University and to the larger history community, academic and public, that have lent me support in this endeavor. I have been fortunate to count myself among Bill Robbins's many students. For nearly two decades I have depended on his thoughtful and generous counsel, and it was with sincere pleasure that I embarked upon this collaboration.

—KB

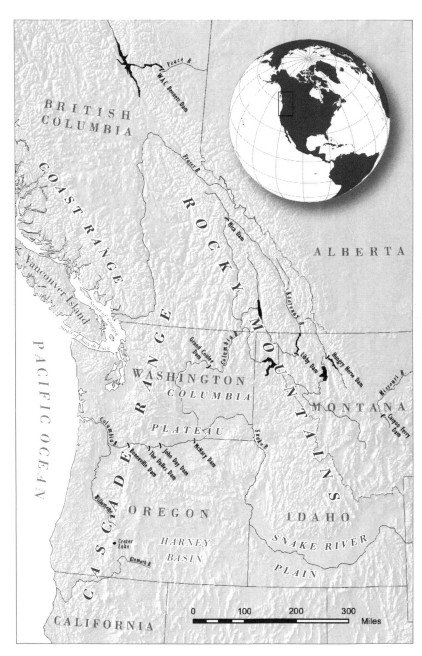

Physical map of the Greater Pacific Northwest

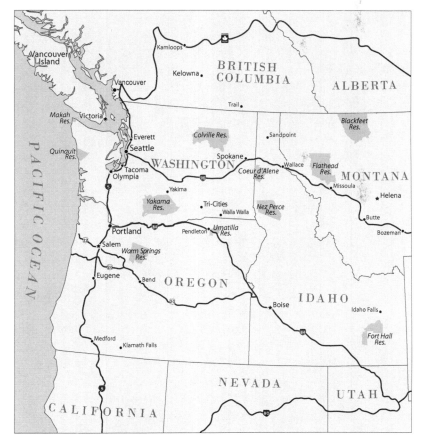

Political map of the Greater Pacific Northwest

Introduction
Mapping the Greater Northwest

In the long perspective of human cultural history, representations of the Pacific Northwest have enjoyed a relatively brief existence—a bit more than two centuries in the minds of imperial mapmakers. From the time the first explorer-adventurers began passing through the homelands of Native people in the 1790s, both geographical and material reference points have informed our understanding of the region—especially the flow of the Columbia River and its 259,000-square-mile watershed as well as the tangible realities of an abundant and generous landscape. As a great waterway that transects modern international boundaries, the Columbia River courses northwesterly through British Columbia and then southerly for five hundred miles before crossing into the United States. If we acknowledge, therefore, that common cultures, comparable resource development, and congruent technologies bridged the international boundary, the Greater Northwest should embrace both American and Canadian stories.

Regional definitions are inherently fuzzy, arbitrary, and fraught with exceptions.[1] For a general bounding to the Greater Northwest, the Rocky Mountains furnish a convenient eastern marker, with Helena and Butte, Montana, on opposite sides of the Continental Divide, providing urban markers to waters flowing east to the Missouri and west to the Columbia rivers. The Missouri is already a sizable stream when it flows through the Helena Valley on its plodding course across northern Montana to join the mighty Mississippi at St. Louis. In contrast, the turbulent Columbia offered up more difficult challenges for early-nineteenth-century adventurers Meriwether Lewis and William Clark, confronting them with experiences they had never witnessed.[2] Coursing downstream from the Snake River during three October weeks, the captains sketched a remarkable story of abundance, especially the large numbers of salmon caught by Native tribes and hung to dry on racks in preparation for trading with other tribes.

During their winter on the lower river, the captains also gave testimony to the region's forested landscape, reporting frustration with the tangled density of the vegetation and their impotence in the face of the elemental forces of nature. After the men fought their way through "intolerable thickets" and fallen timber to gain a vantage point from which to view the surrounding countryside, William Clark reported timber "more than 200 feet high & from 8 to 10 feet through at the Stump." When the Scottish botanist David Douglas visited the same area twenty years later, he measured the circumference of a fir tree at forty-eight feet.[3]

A fur-trading partner in the North West Company, Alexander Mackenzie, first revealed the mysteries of the interior Northwest to the outside world in 1793, when he led an overland trek from western Canada's Peace River to the mouth of the Bella Coola River, roughly midway between Vancouver and the Queen Charlottes. The tortuous route of Mackenzie's travels convinced him that the Columbia River provided a more promising commercial route for trafficking in furs. Mackenzie's partner, Simon Fraser, in search of the elusive Columbia, followed a major river from the western interior to the coast in 1808, only to find himself at 49 degrees latitude, well north of the Columbia. Fraser, in fact, navigated the river that now bears his name. It was North West Company partner David Thompson who first floated the entire course of the Columbia River in 1811.[4] Most striking in both the Canadian and American reports were the glowing descriptions of the region's natural wealth, including furs, fish, and timber—materials that could be turned to profit in distant markets.

Nature has provided the Pacific Northwest, with its big trees, big fish, numerous waterways, and expansive inland plateaus, with significant regional markers. From the time when Native people dominated the landscape to the present, salmon have been one of the defining symbols of the Northwest. Archaeological discoveries throughout the Columbia, Fraser, and other watersheds reveal the human consumption of salmon, with some of the sites dating to at least ten thousand years ago. The physical world of the Columbia system arguably provided the most productive fishery in all of North America and perhaps beyond. Indeed, Indians of the mid-Columbia so valued salmon that the Corps of Discovery purchased eight dogs to eat, with William Clark complaining to his journal: "The Indians not verry fond of Selling their good fish, compels us to make use of dogs."[5]

Anthropologist Richard Daugherty described Pacific Northwest Natives at the time Columbus made his voyage to the "New World" as "People of the Salmon." In this materialist interpretation, Indians—from the Columbia Plateau to coastal villages—were all consumers of salmon, the animal that stood at the center of their nutritional, social, spiritual, and artistic worlds. There is evidence to support the argument that the Northwest's indigenous population may have been part of a truly impressive series of regional associations.[6] Native people enjoyed special relationships with prime fishing locations on the mid–Columbia, Fraser, and Klamath rivers and in the extensive salmon-breeding habitats surrounding Puget Sound. The billions of dollars the federal government has spent since the mid-1980s to save anadromous fishes of the Columbia River and other waterways suggest the persistence of salmon as an iconic symbol.

The Columbia River that Lewis and Clark traversed in 1805–6 would eventually become the defining physical feature of the Pacific Northwest, an extensive drainage basin extending from Canada's inconspicuous Columbia Lake, 2,650 feet above sea level, to Astoria at ocean's edge. If the Great River of the West provides a descriptive metaphor for the region's boundaries, its multifaceted landscape of rivers, mountains, and climatic regimes also presents a host of problems. Born of ancient geologies of fire and ice, the waters of the Columbia fluctuated wildly between late spring and early summer, when melting snow brought the river to flood crest, and late autumn, when its flow dropped precipitously.

In their long, winding passage to the Pacific, the Columbia and its major tributaries slice through several different climatic zones, markedly contrasting ecosystems, and unique human populations. If understanding place begins at the intersection of geography and history, the Columbia River has been a powerful regionalizing influence for the Northwest, providing a connecting thread between temperate coastal rain forest and mostly semiarid interior. For the human communities that have occupied its diverse landscapes and climatic zones, the Columbia watershed presents special challenges and opportunities. In its present configuration, the river functions as a coordinated series of hydropower dams linking British Columbia, Washington, and Oregon into an integrated system to maximize the generation of electricity, protect against flooding, and provide river transportation more than four hundred miles inland.

As a regional construct, the Greater Pacific Northwest is an anomaly of sorts because it is relatively "new" to the American and Canadian imaginations, literally a distant corner of expanding empires gradually made known to its citizens over the course of the last two centuries. Until Alexander Mackenzie and Lewis and Clark trekked across the Continental Divide on their way to the Pacific, the region was beyond the reach—or at best on the periphery—of the great demographic and economic changes taking place in Atlantic centers of commerce. For the expanding United States, the captains turned what had been distant speculation about the Columbia River country into practical geography and with the passing years opened the floodgates to the ever-westering push of white Americans.

North of the forty-ninth parallel, the Fraser River gold rush marked the creation of British Columbia as a formal outpost of the British Empire with a rapidly growing immigrant population. Following the American Civil War, transnational economic and industrial forces overwhelmed the Northwest landscape in a very brief period. That very recent and dramatic historical transformation has provided archaeologists, anthropologists, historians, and other scholars with unique opportunities to explore with some precision the spectacular changes that have taken place over the last two centuries.

By the early 1840s, a half century or more after the onset of European American influences in the region, the Columbia watershed was widely recognized, if vaguely understood, as the Oregon Country—a geographic region extending from the forty-second parallel north to the Russian settlements in Alaska and east to the Rocky Mountains. Imperial negotiations between the United States and England (1846), a war of conquest with Mexico (1846–48), and subsequent congressional compromises in creating territories and states shaped the present boundaries of the American Northwest. At the core of the imperial strategies driving the work of American mapmakers was a preoccupation with international imperial strategies.[7]

To understand something about the physical landscape of the Greater Pacific Northwest and to know something about the human groups that have inhabited the region is to acknowledge that the Columbia, Fraser, Snake, and Klamath rivers have been significant forces in shaping history. The American Northwest (Oregon, Washington, Idaho, and western Montana) also shares historical traditions common to contiguous areas in western Canada: early economic development centered in the fur trade; similar stories about dispossessing Native people; the concurrent appearance of sawmills and then fish canneries; the extension of transcontinental railroads to Portland, Tacoma, and Vancouver, British Columbia;

technological adaptations in mining, logging, fishing, and agriculture; and shared immigrant/ethnic traditions. Dissimilarities exist too, especially in federal-provincial and federal-state constitutional relations.[8]

The great San Francisco publishing house of H. H. Bancroft drew attention early on to the relative absence of violence toward Indians north of the forty-ninth parallel compared with the seemingly open warfare that took place below the forty-ninth parallel.[9] Until the 1990s and 2000s, however, such cross-border comparisons have been rare, with most historical studies assuming the perspective of the nation-state. Historians of the United States and Canada have been more interested in comparing each nation's western parts with the East rather than comparing places north and south of the international boundary. Although recent studies tend to be exploratory, scholars like Elizabeth Jameson, Jeremy Mouat, and others are suggestive of major strides in comparative, transborder scholarship on the U.S.–Canadian Wests.[10]

From the mid-nineteenth century to the present, most residents of the Greater Pacific Northwest have been immigrants—in the words of British Columbia geographer Cole Harris, "occupiers of spaces that recently belonged to others." There are no lengthy pasts for most people in British Columbia, he argues, "and most ways have been brought from afar."[11] For the American Northwest, this was certainly true of the Finns and Chinese living in the early-twentieth-century fishing town of Astoria and for the Irish, Cornish (from Cornwall, England), Germans, French Canadians, Scandinavians, Welsh, Scots, and Chinese who made up the bulk of the working-class population in copper-rich Butte, Montana.[12] Most of the Caucasian immigrants to the western edge of North America were people imbued with notions of progress, bearers of civilization who would turn an abundant land into a good place for future generations. To achieve those objectives, they shoved aside with impunity and marginalized the original occupants of the land. In recent years historians have written more balanced narratives, examining with greater care the loud boasting and self-aggrandizement and condemning the slaughter of buffalo and relegation of Indian peoples to the margins.[13]

Native people did not pass quietly into the night, however, clinging instead to reserved legal stipulations in mid-nineteenth-century treaties and struggling against great odds to protect themselves from the powerful assimilative influences of federal, state, and provincial governments. This book will account for the experiences of the dominant immigrant groups in the Greater Northwest as well as the efforts of indigenous people, who continue to significantly influence life in the region. Mostly a twentieth-century story, the legal struggles of treaty Indians in the American Northwest did not achieve real success until Seattle Federal District Judge George Boldt handed down his famous 1974 decision guaranteeing treaty Indians the right to fish "in their usual and accustomed places." The Indian "New Deal," the termination policies of the 1950s, and the resurgence of tribal sovereignty since 1970 are also partner to that story.[14] In British Columbia, the rights of First Nations people moved more slowly, finally gaining momentum with the *Calder* case in 1973, the pathbreaking Canadian high-court decision upholding aboriginal rights to land.[15]

The Pacific Northwest exists in reciprocal proximity with other places. Before the coming of Europeans to the Northwest Coast, Kwakiutl, Tsimshian, and Haida villagers periodically raided Indian settlements from Puget Sound south to the Columbia River. Native people throughout the region also participated in extensive trading networks that reached from the Pacific Coast to buffalo country on the northern plains. With the onset of the maritime fur trade in the late eighteenth century, Atlantic-based trading ships began plying Northwest Coast waters, bringing with them exotic goods to exchange—and deadly pathogens that proved devastating to Native people. While the region had meaning primarily for the extraction of wealth in furbearing animals in the nineteenth century, beginning with the inrush of European Americans in the 1840s, the Northwest increasingly became a point of destination for people who viewed the region's landscape through a cultural lens reflecting opportunity for material advancement.[16]

It is impossible to understand the vast changes that have taken place in the Pacific Northwest without knowing something about the broader network of market-related, political, and cultural influences that have transformed the region. Regional stories, therefore, must be embedded in larger national and international events and circumstances. As city and countryside exist in relation to each other, regions exist in relation to more distant places. It is important to recognize that regional boundaries are historical, sometimes ephemeral, shifting with the needs and purposes of scholarly enterprise.[17] With its lived experiences in natural resource extraction (farming, mining, logging, and fishing), the Pacific Northwest provides an abundance of rich, sensuous stories of real people and real places. This wealth of historical material suggests the potential for scholars to engage the public in an interrogation of regional and national mythologies.[18]

Regional histories should be set in larger national and international movements of peoples, ideas, and goods and services. In that sense, British Columbia historians have produced a more critical body of literature than their American counterparts. The province's scholars long ago developed a conceptual framework that emphasized the significance and complexities of class, the existence of multicultural groups, the exploitation of natural resources, and economic ties to distant places. The one constant theme in the provincial story was the notion that British Columbia existed in proximity to other places and could be understood only by looking at the world around it. The province's best historians largely avoided the illusion that British Columbia's communities were at the center of the universe.[19] Until the writings of Dorothy Johansen in Oregon and Joseph Kinsey Howard in Montana, historians of the American Northwest fell short of that standard.

New research agendas on both sides of the border during the last three or four decades have brought increasing attention to formerly excluded groups and circumstances: Native Americans and First Nations, immigrant and ethnic minorities, workers in a variety of occupations, women's issues and gender relations, themes related to consumption and production, and new interpretive insights into popular culture.[20] Although Northwest historians usually work within national, state, and provincial political units, recent innovative studies suggest the potential for loosening national blinders through cross-border research and academic exchanges. The growing volume of research on labor, working-class, and transborder union movements indicates common occupational skills, organizing strategies, and ideological similarities that transcended borders and linked regional workers to a broader geographical canvas.[21]

While scholars debate the boundaries and breadth of what should be included in works of historical synthesis, those efforts should include the experiences of people missing from earlier histories. "Lived history," Thomas Bender writes, "is embedded in a plentitude of narratives," with the historian making sense of this welter of material through "a serious conversation between the historical experience of the present and the histories available in the past." It is not the purpose of critical history to subvert conventional or regional narratives but to reexamine how they related to alternative voices and hitherto silenced people.[22] For the Pacific Northwest, those questions should cross borders and boundaries and contribute to more fruitful analyses and stories with infinitely greater complexity.

For much of the twentieth century, the American Northwest has been a subordinate component of a global superpower, with national geopolitical strategies greatly influencing the region's economy and politics. The crisis of the Great Depression and subsequent transoceanic wars have influenced agricultural production, timber harvests, and river development in the Northwest. Water development advocates argued that building dams on the Columbia system would control flooding, improve inland transportation, provide storage reservoirs for irrigating the arid Columbia Plain, and—important to national defense—produce cheap hydropower for the region's aluminum plants and Seattle's aerospace industry. The Northwest's growing population, developers insisted, required an infrastructure appropriate to an expanding economy. Although fishers opposed some of those early projects, the great spurt of dam building during the 1950s and 1960s introduced dramatic new opportunities and problems to the region, issues that persist into the twenty-first century.

Similar to other western states with extensive holdings in federal lands, the twentieth-century American Northwest shares distinctive features that set it apart from the rest of the nation. With the imperial resolution of the Oregon boundary dispute with England in 1846, the new Oregon Territory (1848) was a creature of the federal government from the very beginning. U.S. Army contingents herded Native people onto marginal lands, and generous federal subsidies later spurred transportation and mineral development in the region. The federal government loomed large in the nineteenth-century Northwest, shaping its political boundaries and providing incentives to attract new people.[23]

The sizable federal estate in the American Northwest, the presence of large Indian reservations, and its extensive natural resource base have put the region at the center of contentious disputes involving logging, mining, and the ecological health of salmon-bearing streams. Because the federal government owns millions of acres of mineral, timber, and grazing lands and holds appropriation rights to much of the region's water, private claims to those resources were controversial and volatile issues throughout the twentieth century. From the initial withdrawal of the federal forest reserves in the 1890s through the early twenty-first century, northwestern states have struggled over issues involving private access to public lands. The region's public estate has been a battleground over a host of issues: national forest timber harvests, federal grazing rights, wilderness and national monument set-asides, and construction of hydropower and irrigation dams on waterways.[24]

Unlike the American Northwest, where large corporations made huge timberland purchases at the turn of the twentieth century, British Columbia's land-tenure system limited the opportunity for outright private ownership. Under the terms in which British Columbia joined the Canadian Confederation in 1871, provincial lands not already transferred to the private sector remained in public ownership. Until the province revised its land-tenure policies in 1912, the right to purchase or lease public lands was treated as a matter of patronage, with public figures amassing sizable holdings of valuable agricultural, grazing, and mineral lands. With approximately 45 percent of its 234 million acres in valuable old-growth forests, however, the timberland-tenure question would remain at the center of the province's often volatile politics.[25]

Following completion of the Canadian Pacific Railroad in 1887 and the emergence of British Columbia's lumber industry, the provincial government began offering generous timber leases, with thirty-year rentals for only a few cents an acre. Although the government subsequently tightened the restrictions to renewable twenty-one-year leases, those constraints did not slow the alienation of thousands of acres of Crown timberland in long-term lease arrangements. In his classic novel *Woodsmen of the West*, M. Allerdale Grainger described the wholesale graft involved: "A Man could go anywhere on unoccupied Crown lands, put in a corner post, compose a rough description of one square mile of forest measured from that post, and thus secure from the Government exclusive right to the timber on that square mile."[26] When the legislature ended the most flagrant abuses in 1912, approximately 80 percent of British Columbia forests had been committed in long-term leases, most of them to large corporations. With modifications during succeeding decades, British Columbia governments continued to view large, long-term lease arrangements favorably, valuing such agreements for the revenue they produced.

The time frame for this book, roughly 1900 to the early twenty-first century, encompasses more than a century of tremendous demographic, economic, technological, and cultural change in the Greater Northwest. At the outset of the twentieth century, the North American West came of age in the production of agricultural crops, Earl Pomeroy argues, adjusting to the limitations and opportunities of western climatic conditions and adopting innovative strategies to produce crops that better conformed to rainfall and temperature variations. More than other sections of the nation, the West had matured agriculturally by 1900, taking advantage of railroads that enabled farmers to overcome difficult topography and vast distances and to create functioning agricultural economies.[27] With its western window to Pacific trading routes and transcontinental rail links to eastern markets, the Northwest was a full partner in continental and global trading and investment networks at the onset of the twentieth century.

Persisting complaints of economic colonialism between 1880 and into the early twentieth century contributed to a series of insurgencies in the Northwest: agrarian and urban protests against railroad corporations and steamboat monopolies, organized labor's opposition to wage and working conditions in lumber mills and mining districts, and the emergence of truly radical third parties such as the Populist movement. Those late-nineteenth-century insurgencies spilled over into the twentieth century in the form of the Industrial Workers of the World, the radical industrial union whose syndicalist message appealed to loggers, miners, and harvest hands. After a decade of antiunionism and enforcement of the open shop during the 1920s, labor uprisings reemerged during the Great Depression on both sides of the border, especially among dock workers in major ports.[28] Organized labor made great strides during the late 1930s in most industries, enjoying nearly three decades of significant gains in better wages and working conditions. That period of relative strength for organized labor in the private sector began to erode in the 1970s and then went into a downward spiral that continues into the twenty-first century.[29]

This book will trace the "promise" of the Pacific Northwest, from the effusive narrative line pursued in early-twentieth-century promotional writings celebrating the region's limitless abundance and opportunity to the more restrained and sober assessments that began to appear as the region approached the end of the millennium. Slowly, imperceptibly, the notion that the Northwest offered everything the human imagination could conceive shifted to a more reflective temper as global conflicts abroad and social dissension at home contributed to more sober judgments about the region's prospects. If an overweening sense of hubris ushered in the twentieth century, the onset of the twenty-first century witnessed its opposite amidst warfare abroad, a problematic economy, and increasing divisiveness at home.

In the new millennium the Greater Northwest is beset with environmental problems that are shared worldwide—global warming, acid rain, polluted waterways, and a host of toxic landscapes. Seattle-based Northwest Environment Watch also points to other troubles: widening income inequality, heightened social segregation, a weakening of shared values, increased economic uneasiness, and an eroded social cohesiveness.[30] A burgeoning high-tech sector in the urban Northwest and a declining timber economy have contributed to a growing urban-rural divide, with the Cascade Mountains providing a crude geographic marker separating the rural eastern side from the more heavily populated western side. A large influx of newcomers to Greater Seattle, Portland, and Vancouver, British Columbia, further exacerbated tensions in the region. Writing for the *Portland Oregonian* on the last day of 1999, Gail Kinsey Hill underscored the region's growing sense of anxiety: "New people, new money, new technology, all rushing in without time for assimilation."

I
Into the New Century

1

The Years of "Exuberant Optimism"

At the age of seventy-eight, in 1912, she became Oregon's first woman voter, culminating a personal and courageous careerlong struggle for women's suffrage. Two decades after immigrating westward on the Oregon Trail with her family, thirty-six-year-old Abigail Scott Duniway launched *New Northwest*, a weekly publication that quickly became the most widely read suffrage newspaper in the Pacific Northwest and beyond. Duniway proved herself a tough-minded suffragette, despising the religious fanaticism of some of her colleagues, supporting direct-legislation measures (the initiative, referendum, and recall), and aligning herself with reform movements such as Populism. When Mary Elizabeth Lease campaigned in Portland in 1892 for Populist Party candidate James B. Weaver, Duniway introduced the Kansas firebrand to a large crowd.[1]

Abigail Scott Duniway was much more than a single-minded devotee of women's suffrage. Because of her agrarian background, Duniway admired pragmatic entrepreneurs, supported small-scale business enterprise, and despised anything that suggested aristocracy or injustice. Living through a period of dizzying social, economic, and cultural change, including the great age of railroad development, she was an unabashed booster of building rail lines and promoting settlements in the interior Northwest. In addition to her rural constituents, Duniway enjoyed the support of leading Portland businessmen, who assisted her suffrage work with interest-free loans.[2] She was born in 1834 when Andrew Jackson was president and died during Woodrow Wilson's first term in office. While her 1852 trek along the Oregon Trail took five months, when she died in 1915, four transcontinental railroads linked the American Northwest with the eastern United States, reducing the travel time over the same distance to about four days. As the longtime public face for women's rights in the region, Duniway was also at one with late-nineteenth-century conventions of regional boosterism.

The life experiences of another immigrant, British-born John Minto, provide another fitting individual profile for the turn-of-the-century

Abigail Scott Duniway (1834–1915). The most prominent advocate for women's rights in the Pacific Northwest and a person of national importance, Duniway was also a well-known writer and newspaper editor.

Northwest. The Britisher arrived on the lower Columbia River in the mid-1840s, when human, animal, and water power provided energy to accomplish most work tasks. First employed on a water-powered sawmill thirty miles east of Astoria, Minto worked at "rolling logs by hand to the saw." After a few months he moved to the Willamette Valley, where he did "the severest kind of labor—that of binding wheat in its own straw." A tireless promoter of modern agricultural practices, Minto served as editor of *Willamette Farmer*, a progressive weekly advancing the cause of scientific farming, railroad development east of the Cascades, and improving navigation on the Columbia River.[3]

When John Minto died in 1915, he left behind a legacy as a successful breeder of sheep, including a report that the secretary of agriculture solicited in 1909 on the sheep industry in the Northwest. Minto also gained renown as an orchardist and for carrying out original horticultural research. Like Duniway's, Minto's life spanned the entire settler era, lasting well into the age of railroads, including the completion of the Oregon Electric from Portland to Eugene in 1912. While he was a notable booster of the region, Minto wanted investors in Northwest resources to act with honesty and as good citizens. He was especially concerned with the timber fraud scandal that emerged at the turn of the century, reporting in 1908 that outside capitalists were hiring "agents to secure large bodies of timber." When he died at the age of ninety-three, Minto had lived through the "land fraud" prosecutions that placed the region in national headlines.[4]

Although the life of Montana's Samuel Hauser bridged a similar span of time, his experiences were markedly different from those of his Oregon peers. Like Mark Twain, Hauser "lit out for the territories" during the Civil War, in his case to new gold discoveries around the rough-and-tumble mining town of Bannock. Hauser moved quickly, forming a banking partnership in Virginia City and then in 1866 establishing the First National Bank of Helena, initiating a thirty-year career as Montana's leading banker. When his bank failed during the depression of the mid-1890s, Hauser seemingly had lost everything, including investments in several mining ventures. But in the midst of disaster, Montana's foremost gambler turned to hydropower development on the Missouri River. With the financial backing and prestige of copper magnate William A. Clark, for a time Hauser was able to successfully navigate his fledgling company away from Montana's expanding monopoly, the Anaconda Copper Mining Company.[5]

In his last business enterprise, Hauser's fortunes failed again when his Missouri River project, Hauser Dam, collapsed during a springtime flood in April 1908. Even then the tireless Hauser stalked through financial houses in New York in an effort to raise capital to rebuild the failed dam. In the end, the aging Hauser—a proprietary capitalist from a bygone era—lost out to John D. Ryan of the Anaconda Copper Mining Company and its subsidiary, the Montana Power Company. Hauser's story is an instructive one. When he died in 1914, he represented a dwindling generation of paternal capitalists who functioned as sole proprietors of their enterprises, dealing on a first-name basis with financiers, including those who controlled the Northern Pacific Railroad. Hauser's career marked the transformation of the American economy from individual enterprises to the modern bureaucratic corporate world of the twentieth century, a business environment that he never understood. The disintegration of his banking empire and his other business failures reflected larger changes in both Montana and the national economy.[6]

Born to Scottish immigrants, Robert and Joanna Dunsmuir, at Fort Vancouver in 1851, James Dunsmuir would be partner to his family's rise from crude log cabin beginnings on Vancouver Island to a life of palatial opulence, economic and social prestige, and enormous political influence. His patriarchal father, who situated the family's growing wealth in Vancouver coal-mining ventures, eventually took James and his brothers into his expanding business operations as partners. Following in his father's footsteps, James quickly gained a reputation as an uncompromising mine owner, intolerant of unions, who believed that talent and birthright were proper guides to business decision making. Living in his father's shadow until the latter's death in 1889, James worked relentlessly for the next several years to wrest control of the Dunsmuir financial empire from his mother and several sisters, an effort that he finally accomplished in 1902.[7]

The powerful Dunsmuirs used their great wealth to advantage in the business and political worlds, especially in their struggles with labor. During a prolonged strike between May 1890 and November 1891 over wage reductions and a push for the eight-hour day, James Dunsmuir convinced the provincial government to send in the militia to quell the strike. During a second major strike in 1903, Dunsmuir was part of an employers' association that resorted to strikebreakers, firings, and blacklists to destroy union activity. Like his father, James also entered politics in 1898 when he was elected to the provincial legislature, an experience that proved him ill suited for the give-and-take of politics. Filling a political

James Dunsmuir (1851–1920). Heir to his family's fortune in Vancouver Island coal, Dunsmuir was antilabor and a powerful spokesperson for the forces of capital in British Columbia at the turn of the twentieth century.

vacuum as political parties were realigning, Dunsmuir served a brief stint as British Columbia's premier between 1900 and 1902. As the richest man in British Columbia, James Dunsmuir, whose wealth and influence surpassed his father's, retired from the business world at the age of sixty-one and spent his remaining years fishing and hunting from his fifty-room mansion in Esquimalt.[8]

Abigail Scott Duniway, John Minto, Samuel Hauser, and James Dunsmuir were transitional figures, coming to the Northwest by horseback, wagon, or ship and departing life at the peak of railroad development. While Hauser and Dunsmuir were the only ones directly involved in railroad investment, all four viewed the expanding rail lines as physical representations of modernity—social, cultural, economic, and political. British Columbia geographer Cole Harris argues that capitalist enterprise, industrial production, and a belief in progress centered in technological advances in transportation and communication characterized the onset of the modern age.[9] Railroads remapped the region, reorganizing nodes of power, population, and trade; they realigned time, space, economy, and culture. The transcontinental roads intensified the need for more capital and prompted additional technological advances through the introduction of mechanical farm and mining equipment. Railroads meant higher land values, the transition from subsistence to commercial farming, the end of open-range grazing, and the sudden appearance of urban centers where none existed before.

As symbols of the industrial revolution, the transcontinental railroads rationalized market and production strategies across the Greater Pacific Northwest and invited effusive celebrations about the region's economic prospects. Completing a transcontinental line to the Northwest, the *Portland Oregonian* predicted in 1880, would open a "great natural channel of communication" that would develop commerce and redeem "the great northwest from its isolation." The individual who made it all happen was German-born American journalist Henry Villard, who represented German investors. Villard gained control of strategic railroad portages on the mid–Columbia River and then in a daring move formed a "blind pool" with eastern investors and purchased controlling stock in the financially troubled Northern Pacific. After an accelerated pace of construction, Villard joined dignitaries on September 8, 1883, to witness driving the last railroad spike at Gold Creek, sixty miles west of Helena, Montana.[10]

The three-hundred-strong elite group, including European bankers, diplomats, governors, and former president Ulysses S. Grant, filled four trains and traveled at the Northern Pacific's expense. From western Montana the excursion trains proceeded to East Portland, arriving on September 11 amid grand celebrations. A huge pageant that lasted into the evening greeted the trains, and the *Portland Oregonian* boasted that "a new destiny" would visit Portland now that the city was linked to the rest of the world.[11] Left unsaid in the local euphoria was the dark cloud of fiscal ruin settling on Henry Villard, with close associates predicting in the spring of 1883 that his financial collapse was near. Yet in the face of the precipitous depreciation in his railroad stocks, Villard continued his charade of optimism to the end. Only four months past his greatest achievement, Villard lost the presidencies of his companies and railroad properties. The ubiquitous banker J. P. Morgan and a committee of investors then proceeded to place the Northern Pacific under new management.[12]

Historian Dorothy Johansen has called the great railroad-building era between 1880 and 1910 years of "exuberant optimism," a feverish period of activity that witnessed the completion of four transcontinental lines linking the Greater Pacific Northwest to eastern North America. In

addition to the Northern Pacific, the new transcontinentals included another Villard venture, a branch road through the Blue Mountains, connecting with the Oregon Short Line at Huntington on the Snake River in
1884. From there the railroad crossed southern Idaho to join the Union
Pacific at Granger, Wyoming.[13] First the Northern Pacific, then the Great
Northern, and finally the Milwaukee Road all traversed Montana and
northern Idaho and then passed through the thriving city of Spokane en
route to points west. Of all the interior cities in the Pacific Northwest,
Spokane was the prototypical railroad town, a settlement, according to
Donald Meinig, "virtually created by the railroad." In the Inland Empire,
all roads led to Spokane.[14]

With word of pending railroad construction, Spokane's population
rose quickly to 350 in 1880, nearly 3,000 in 1885, close to 7,000 in 1888,
12,000 in 1890, and 30,000 two years later.[15] With its fissured basalt rock
underpinnings and jumbled topography, Spokane's unlikely setting gives
emphasis to historian William Cronon's remark that "geographical arguments do not explain" the location of cities, "only history and culture can
do that."[16] Until the emergence of auto travel in the 1920s, Spokane was
at the center of rail transportation for the Inland Empire, a vast area
reaching across northern Idaho to the Continental Divide in western
Montana, north into British Columbia's Rossland and Kootenay mining
districts, and south through the highly productive wheat country of the
rolling Palouse Hills.

As a strategic economic hub, Spokane's reach extended in every direction, providing banking, supply, transportation, and labor services linking very different extractive enterprises into an integrated unit. By the
late 1880s, Spokane gave meaning to the vast Inland Empire, a place,
Katherine Morrissey writes, "imbued with particular meanings, forged
through a set of historical circumstances." If railroads brought into being
the Inland Empire, wheat and minerals represented the material wealth
that attracted people and capital to the region.[17]

The growth of Puget Sound's two principal cities, Seattle and Tacoma,
was also closely tied to the coming of the railroads. Although the Northern Pacific named Tacoma as the western terminus for its line, construction on the eastern division of the road was put on hold in 1873, when
entrepreneur Jay Cooke's financial empire met disaster. When Henry Villard began gaining control of several transportation companies in the late
1870s, Puget Sound boosters were alarmed, fearing that the Wall Street

genius would favor Portland.[18] When he gained control of the Northern Pacific in 1881, the fears of Tacoma's leading entrepreneurs were confirmed. Although the city's boosters failed to achieve their immediate objective, a railroad directly across the Cascade Mountains, Tacoma benefited immensely via a rail link with Portland.

After Villard's failure—and with the Northern Pacific's Old Guard back in control—the company turned its attention to Tacoma and building the Cascade division line, an accomplishment that turned the city on Commencement Bay into a boomtown. The opening of the huge St. Paul and Tacoma Lumber Company Mill in 1889, with lush timberlands purchased from the Northern Pacific, was the key factor driving the local economy. When the company completed a second mill in 1900, St. Paul and Tacoma was the leading lumber producer in the world.[19]

With 17,500 residents, Portland was clearly *the* metropolitan center of the Pacific Northwest in 1880. Seattle, which would surpass Portland by the turn of the century, was still a fledgling stump community of 3,500. But Seattle's restless entrepreneurs were on the prowl, in the process of developing an infrastructure that would quickly push the city to the forefront in the region. While Tacoma's population boomed to 36,026 in 1890, Seattle—still without a transcontinental rail link—grew to 42,837 in the same decade. Before it had rail links to national markets, Roger Sale writes, Seattle's entrepreneurs signaled at a very early period an interest in economic autonomy, building a diverse infrastructure in retail stores, meat packing, foundries, small manufactures such as furniture making, and a waterborne transportation system that traveled to the far ends of Puget Sound.[20]

Mirroring Tacoma's initiatives, Seattle's business and political leaders invited the Northern Pacific to build a major terminal on the city's waterfront in 1873, offering handsome inducements in cash and bonds, six thousand acres of land, several thousand town lots, and nearly half the property fronting on Elliott Bay. Following the collapse of Jay Cooke's financial empire, however, the city's investors initiated two limited railroad projects that secured much of the Puget Sound hinterland for Seattle. With local businessmen Thomas Burke and Daniel Gilman leading the way, the city's leadership began making overtures in the mid-1880s to attract James J. Hill's Great Northern Railway to the Queen City.[21]

Burke, Gilman, and their financial backers created a waterfront road— Railroad Avenue—as a special attraction to the Northern Pacific, the Great Northern, and other large rail systems. With a wary eye toward the Hill interests, Burke and Gilman were willing to take any measure to attract the Great Northern. What Burke and Gilman forgot, however, was the railroad baron's great need for Seattle. From the Great Northern's base in St. Paul, Minnesota, Hill's construction crews moved slowly, efficiently, and relentlessly across the plains, but he had yet to determine the western terminus of his line. To do so he needed a person familiar with the local power structure. Thomas Burke was his man. Hill directed Burke to work with the city council to gain access to waterfront property. Following their initial meeting, Burke confided that Hill "knows what he wants and isn't afraid to ask for it, and I might add, generally gets it." When the first Great Northern train moved along the Seattle waterfront and stopped at a rough-hewn terminal in 1893, Hill was dissatisfied. What followed were years of wrangling among Hill, the Northern Pacific, and the city of Seattle. In the end, the Hill interests were able to build a tunnel under part of downtown Seattle to a spanking new terminal, open and ready for business in 1905.[22]

According to James J. Hill's biographer, Hill was a ruthless entrepreneur, a buccaneer who, on a whim, could make and unmake encampments, villages, and towns. From his Summit Avenue command post in St. Paul, Minnesota, atop a bluff overlooking the Mississippi River, Hill's mind swept westward to embrace a lucrative empire of farming, logging, and mining. Although the great railroad baron jostled with his peers for strategic positioning in the resource-rich region, it was not a struggle the shrewd Canadian immigrant would lose.[23]

Hill also gained full control of the perennially troubled Northern Pacific in the late 1890s. Although Edward Harriman's Union Pacific—and soon the Milwaukee and St. Paul—also had terminals on the Seattle waterfront, the Hill interests dominated the local railroad scene. The major competing lines, the Northern Pacific and Union Pacific, were quickly and shoddily constructed, in need of major repair, and burdened with a heavy debt load. In contrast, the Great Northern was carefully built, with gradual curves and gentle grades. Roger Sale believes that Hill's Seattle front man, Thomas Burke, was naively optimistic for assuming that the interests of the Great Northern and Seattle were the same.[24] If the turn-of-the-century standard for progress was measured in population numbers, Seattle—with 80,671 people in 1900 and 237,000 in 1910—was the clear winner among northwestern cities. Although Portland still held first place, with 90,426 residents in 1900, the city fell to second place in the numbers game in the first decade of the new century, with a population of 207,000.

North of the forty-ninth parallel, investors from central Canada influenced the federal government to finance a transcontinental railroad as a tool of economic development and as a geopolitical weapon to counter American influences in British Columbia. As part of Canadian premier John A. Macdonald's National Policy, Ottawa negotiated an agreement with the Canadian Pacific Railway Company (CPR) to complete a rail line to the Pacific. The generous terms of the arrangement included seven hundred miles of track, tax and tariff waivers on material purchases, $25 million in subsidies, and alternative square-mile sections of land up to a distance of twenty miles on each side of the track for a total of twenty-five million acres.[25]

The first through freight train reached Victoria—crossing Georgia Strait on a steamer—in December 1885. As British Columbia's largest city, with a population of eight thousand, Victoria's excitement was muted, however, because the CPR had already announced that its terminus would be on the mainland near the small village of Granville. While surveyors platted the new settlement, developers quickly incorporated the area as the city of Vancouver. Realtors engaged in a booming business in land sales, and construction gangs put up buildings along the southern shores of Burrard Inlet. Amidst much merrymaking, huge crowds turned out on May 23, 1887, to greet the arrival of the first Canadian Pacific train. In addition to building social infrastructures in schools, law enforcement, and fire protection, investors opened lumber and shingle mills, machine shops, and other manufacturing plants in the city. With its thirteen-mile electric street railway and electric light and telephone system, Vancouver was truly a modern city by the early 1890s.[26]

Vancouver was also a railroad town. Armed with a provincial land grant of six thousand acres and an equivalent federal land concession, the CPR emerged as Vancouver's largest landowner, strategically selling off its properties in targeted sales over the next decades. With its construction crews, mechanics, freight handlers, and other railroad personnel, the CPR was the city's largest employer. In the end, Vancouver provided the CPR with a spectacular and profitable venue for real estate promotion.[27] In retrospect, the extension of the Canadian Pacific Railroad to Pacific waters remapped British Columbia's economy and demographic profile, attracting investment, accelerating the extraction and processing of natural resources, and providing a transportation link to the rapidly developing prairie provinces east of the Rocky Mountains.

The extension of railroads to the Pacific Northwest linked regional geography and property relations into interdependent continental, even global, systems. Because the American and Canadian governments created favorable environments for economic development, there were few restrictions on the behavior of railroad companies or those who followed in their wake—investors in mining and timber properties and other extractive activities. This was especially true of the great Columbia Plain, where railroads affected almost every aspect of economic endeavor.[28] Because travel on the Columbia River was problematic, the Northern Pacific and other lines traversing the Columbia Plain were critical to the region's development, providing links to Pacific ports and to eastern industrial markets. The isolated Palouse Hills on the eastern edge of the plain, a country of rolling, bunchgrass hills intersected with small streams, provides an excellent example—a land, as it turned out, ideally suited to growing winter wheat.[29]

Although Walla Walla growers were shipping wheat to Portland in the late 1870s, the system of wagons, chutes, barging, and portaging was slow and laborious. With the completion of the Northern Pacific, however, construction crews built a spur road eastward through Washtucna Coulee across the Palouse River to Colfax. The Columbia and Palouse Railroad, completed in 1884, set off a frenzy of land purchases and an influx of immigrants attracted by the Northern Pacific's aggressive advertising campaign in the eastern United States, England, and Europe. The incoming settler population quickly set about converting bunchgrass country to growing wheat, and the Palouse quickly surpassed the Willamette Valley in wheat production.[30]

During the great wheat boom of the 1880s, settlers flocked to the Columbia Plain, with the most successful farmers working the deep, rich loess soils of the Palouse. Crisscrossed with railroads during the 1880s, southeastern Washington was producing more than 90 percent of the state's wheat output by 1890. Farmers also planted adjacent areas in northern Idaho and northeastern Oregon to wheat, but the total output in those areas paled in comparison with the Palouse. A Washington State University scientist reported that most of the arable land suited to wheat cultivation had been put to the plow by 1910, yielding record per-acre harvests.[31]

Separated at midsection by nearly impenetrable, rugged mountains, Idaho has been called the "residual state," with its boundaries carved from neighboring Oregon, Washington, Montana, and Wyoming. Different histories also separate the geographically ungainly state. Northern Idaho's Coeur d'Alene mining district developed into one of the nation's most heavily capitalized lead-silver operations when entrepreneur Daniel C. Corbin built a spur railroad from Spokane into the mineral-rich south fork of the Coeur d'Alene River in the mid-1880s.[32] Unlike the sagebrush desert in the southern part of the state, impressive forests and valuable mineral deposits characterized northern Idaho. With its large cadre of hard-rock miners, the Coeur d'Alene district quickly turned into a battleground between workers and mining companies, with violent clashes erupting in the 1890s.

History and industrial activity took a different course in the vast sweeping arc of southern Idaho's Snake River Plain, a largely arid region with rich soils and sizable streams flowing into the Snake from the mountainous north. Irrigation agriculture dates from the 1860s and the establishment of Mormon communities in the territory's far southeastern corner. Farther to the west, farmers in the Boise, Payette, and Weiser area also began diverting water to raise vegetable crops for nearby mining camps. The extension of the Oregon Short Line across southern Idaho attracted additional farmers, who claimed land under the Carey Act of 1894 and the Newlands Reclamation Act of 1902.[33]

With public and private promotion of irrigation agriculture in the next decades, the state's population rose to 161,772 in 1900 and 325,594 in 1910. Most of the expansion in irrigated agriculture took place on the Snake River Plain midway between the upper and lower valley. With a water-transport infrastructure of thirteen thousand miles of canals and ditches, some eighteen thousand farmers were irrigating roughly two million acres by 1920. Southern Idaho farmers produced a variety of crops, largely reflecting environmental factors, especially temperature differences between the upper and lower Snake River Plain. Whereas farmers in the Boise Valley (elevation 2,700 feet) enjoyed a 180-day growing season, the upper valley in the vicinity of the small town of Ashton (elevation 5,240 feet) had fewer than 90 frost-free days.[34]

Amid the boastful stories of population increases, expanding agricultural systems, and robust fishing and lumbering economies, Native people across the American Northwest continued to adjust, finding their way in a world not of their own making. After suffering through the U.S. government's treaty-making frenzy of the 1850s and removal to reservations, Northwest tribes endured decades of privation, malnutrition, disease, and extreme poverty. Because reservation life severely restricted hunting-and-gathering activities, enrollees began taking seasonal leaves to seek wage-labor jobs, especially during the harvest season. Reflecting the Indian Bureau's "Civilization Program," Indian children were required to attend reservation day schools, where Native dress, languages, and cultural practices were prohibited and where the curriculum focused on manual trades for boys and domestic instruction for girls. An even greater danger faced tribal members in the form of repeated federal threats to break up the reservations, to provide Indians with individual allotments of land, and to place "surplus" lands for sale on the open market.[35]

The idea behind allotment policy—embodied in the General Allotment Act of 1887—was to destroy the Indians' communal land base, turn them into independent farmers, and open vast areas of reservation land to non-Indian settlement. In the end, the federal government abdicated its trust responsibility to the tribes and permitted wholesale fraud, which resulted in huge transfers of land to non-Indians. Between 1887 and 1934, when the Indian Reorganization Act ended the practice, the federal initiative reduced the Indian land base by nearly ninety million acres. In the end, Indian lands in the American Northwest were severely eroded, with many reservations taking on the checkerboard appearance they exhibit today.[36]

In virtually every instance, influential non-Indians actively pursued the acquisition of valuable reservation land. The allotment policy drastically reduced the Yakama Indian Reservation, once embracing more than 1,371,918 acres, to 780,000 acres. Although 4,506 tribal members held 440,000 acres of allotted land in 1914, much of that valuable property also passed to non-Indian ownership through sale, fraud, or failure to pay taxes. Northern Idaho's Coeur d'Alene Indian Reservation underwent a similar loss of land. The 1873 executive order creating the Coeur d'Alene Reservation included 598,000 acres, but through the General Allotment Act and other federal laws, nearly 250,000 acres passed to non-Indian owners. Laura Woodworth-Ney contends that both Indians and non-Indians shaped the emerging Coeur d'Alene tribal world.[37]

Although Oregon's Confederated Tribes of the Umatilla Reservation enjoyed a treaty-secured land base, the growing non-Indian settlements around wheat-rich Pendleton pressured the Indian Bureau to grant white farmers access to land in the lower Umatilla Basin. The local newspaper, the *East Oregonian*, put the farmers' case bluntly in 1877: "We favor their [Indian] removal as it is a burning shame to keep this fine body of land for a few worthless Indians." Congress passed the Umatilla Allotment Act in 1885 to provide enrolled tribal members with eighty-acre allotments, to retain land for tribal use, and to put up for sale "surplus" reservation lands. Both the 1885 act and an 1888 amendment make clear the congressional intent to reduce the reservation's size.[38]

Historian Coll Thrush reminds us that Indians in the Greater Northwest also inhabited urban environments, places where large numbers of newcomers have ousted Native people, often from prime waterfront locations. "Every American city," he argues, "is built on Indian land." The subject of his study, the city of Seattle, acknowledges the Native presence in totems, bronze statues, the names of its ferries, and the community's namesake, a Duwamish/Suquamish leader, Seeathl. The problem, Thrush contends, is that academic scholarship has placed Indians and cities like Seattle as polar opposites in the American imagination: "The connections between urban and Indian histories—both in Seattle and across the nation—have yet to be made."[39] Thrush offers an important reminder that Portland, Tacoma, Spokane, Vancouver, British Columbia, and the region's lesser urban centers were *and still are* places of Indian habitation.

Although Canadian federal and provincial relations with First Nations people differed from those in the United States, there were parallel tensions involving title to land, treaties, and issues of sovereignty and self-government. Before he was appointed governor of the new colony of British Columbia in 1858, James Douglas had signed fourteen treaties, setting aside Indian land reserves during his governorship of Vancouver Island. But following his appointment as provincial governor, he created no additional Native reserves. Douglas's policy of creating Indian land reserves and granting Natives the same rights to land as whites exhibited a spirit of equity absent among most provincial administrators. After Douglas retired from public service in 1864, British Columbia politicians adopted policies that treated Native people as primitives, humans without a sense of landownership. Provincial authorities based their assumptions on the mythology that British sovereignty had turned a wasted and empty land to productive economic use. With the passing decades, however, Indian villagers from the coast to the interior began to assert specific demands—recognition of aboriginal title, treaty-guaranteed rights to land, and the ability to govern themselves.[40]

Under the new dispensation following Douglas's departure, and especially after the British North America Act of 1871, settlers and land speculators began appropriating Indian reserve lands on Vancouver Island and on the mainland. Under the British North America Act, Indian affairs became the responsibility of the federal government, with its guiding legal principles vested in the Indian Act of 1869 (with a major revision in 1880). Under the Indian Act, the federal Department of Indian Affairs acted in paternalistic, culturally destructive ways toward traditional practices, banning potlatch ceremonies and other activities. In the face of those indignities and the continued seizure of their lands, Indian villagers across British Columbia protested, petitioned, and confronted Indian Affairs officials in joint meetings. Although provincial and federal authorities failed to act in most cases, First Nations people were laying the basis for future challenges through litigation and negotiation that would eventually give them an increasing cultural and political presence in the twentieth century.[41]

With the forces of the Industrial Revolution penetrating the most distant recesses of the Greater Northwest, the region began to take on elements of a flawed but slowly modernizing society in the late nineteenth century. In the midst of those dramatic changes, the now dominant immigrant population held to deeply seated cultural values, including open discrimination against Native people and other nonwhite groups shoved to the margins of the regional economy. At the same moment, state and provincial governments denied the majority of women—toiling in the home and contributing mightily to the agricultural and resource economy—the right to participate in politics. Legislatures also passed miscegenation laws at very early dates, variously prohibiting marriage between whites and blacks, full-blood Indians, Chinese, Hawaiians, and other nonwhite groups.[42] Social and legal barriers existed in the American Northwest and in British Columbia, with the dominant whites relegating Chinese and Indian people to thoroughly marginalized status as low-wage day laborers prohibited from participating in the political process.

In British Columbia authorities denied Indians, Chinese, and other people of color (and all women) the right to vote in the 1870s. The annual provincial directories listing all adult males and heads of families made no accounting for Indians or Chinese. Although British Columbia's census enumerated some Indians and most Chinese, officials grouped the Chinese in identical occupations with ages rounded to zero or five and surnames listed with simple, two-letter identities. Anti-Chinese sentiment was rampant in British Columbia, as it was in the American Northwest, with only the actions of the federal government constraining provincial leaders. Even then, with virtually all of Canada's Chinese living in British Columbia, federal authorities banned Chinese from voting in 1885 and imposed a $50 head tax on new immigrants. The federal Parliament increased the tax to $100 in 1902 and $500 the following year. Mirroring earlier activities in California, white workers in Vancouver formed an Asiatic Exclusion League in 1907, engaged in acts of violence against the Chinese (and the growing Japanese population), and vented their hatred toward a people they perceived as threatening their jobs. Working-class Caucasians led the opposition to Asian immigration in the province.[43]

Anti-Chinese and later anti-Japanese agitation in the American Northwest followed patterns already played out in California, with Asians serving as pawns in struggles between capital and labor in railroad construction and the extractive industries. The California gold rush and the stories of "Golden Mountain" first attracted Chinese males to the Pacific Coast in the 1850s. They came in even larger numbers—most of them as contract laborers—to work on the Central Pacific Railroad. Following completion of the railroad in 1869, many Chinese drifted north for construction work on the Oregon and California Railroad (1870–73) and eventually to rail projects and mining activity all across the Columbia River country. Although California's Chinese dwarfed the number immigrating to the Greater Northwest, the persecution, discrimination, and violence in the region echoed those of the Golden State. White citizens' organizations and political parties—from Roseburg and Portland north to Tacoma and Seattle—passed resolutions condemning Chinese immigration "as injurious to the prosperity of the country, and the morals of the people."[44]

Sizeable numbers of Chinese also immigrated as individuals and groups to the gold fields of Montana and Idaho in the 1860s. The 1870 census lists the nearly two thousand Chinese in Montana, about 10 percent of the territorial population. Often working in small groups in abandoned placer deposits, the frugal Chinese extracted good quantities of gold; still others worked as servants or operated laundries or restaurants. Ethnic hatred was rampant in Idaho, where approximately four thousand Chinese comprised about 27 percent of the territorial population in 1870. Discriminatory territorial and then state laws subjected the Chinese to special taxes and property restrictions. With the exodus of Chinese miners returning to their homeland during the 1880s and 1890s, their numbers dropped to less than 1 percent of Idaho's and Montana's populations by the turn of the century. In the most infamous incident involving the Chinese in the Northwest, seven horse thieves attacked, tortured, and killed at least thirty-four Chinese miners in Hells Canyon on the Snake River in May 1887 in a brazen effort to steal their gold. Although the perpetrators operated on both the Idaho and Oregon sides of the river, a subsequent trial in Lewiston failed to convict anyone for the crime.[45]

Hiring what were deemed "cheap" Chinese laborers to blast tunnels and lay track in building the Oregon and California Railroad suggests the way certain occupational categories were racialized in the Northwest. The virulent anti-Chinese rhetoric appeared early, becoming especially noisome during economic downturns, pitting one segment of the working class against another, with the Chinese serving as a scapegoat for unemployed whites. Although most of the "Chinese Must Go" violence took place in Seattle and Tacoma in 1885 and 1886, lesser incidents occurred in virtually every Oregon town along the Oregon and California Railroad line.[46]

The most vicious anti-Chinese activity occurred around Washington's Puget Sound, especially in Tacoma and Seattle. Knights of Labor spokesmen told a Seattle crowd in September 1885 that if the Chinese were not removed, "riot and bloodshed" would ensue. Although there were few casualties, the Chinese suffered huge property losses in looted shops, stores, and homes put to the torch. In the wake of the disorder, the federal government sent 350 troops to Seattle, some of whom joined in beating the Chinese. Seattle Knights of Labor organizer Daniel Cronin shifted his anti-Chinese mongering to Portland early in 1886, urging business and labor leaders to rid themselves of the "yellow menace." Following several weeks of protests, street marches, and violence against the Chinese, the furor finally spent itself, with some of the Asians leaving for San Francisco's Chinatown.[47]

There is little nobility in the telling of this story. Oregon's leading suffragette, Abigail Scott Duniway, pointed out that business leaders were primarily interested in cheap labor, whether workers were white or Chinese. Chinese and white female workers, she observed, received less than half the wages paid to white males in local woolen mills. The hostility toward Indians, Chinese, and other people of color left a legacy of discriminatory legislation, including congressional passage of the Chinese

Exclusion Law in 1882, prohibiting further immigration for a ten-year period. With various amendments in the succeeding years, the law remained federal policy until 1943, when the United States permitted Chinese aliens to apply for citizenship. British Columbia, which also banned Chinese entry to the province, did not reopen immigration to the Chinese until 1947.[48]

Miscegenation laws were another form of discriminatory legislation across the region, with some remaining on the books well into the twentieth century. The Oregon legislature passed a measure in 1866 prohibiting "any white person, male or female, to intermarry with any Negro or Chinese person having one-fourth or more Negro or Chinese blood, or any person having more than one-half Kanaka [Hawaiian] or Indian blood." It did not repeal the legal ban on interracial marriage until 1951. Idaho adopted a miscegenation statute in 1867 directed against "Negroes or Mulattoes," and in 1932 it prohibited marriages between "the Caucasian and Asian races." Montana joined the parade in 1909, banning marriage between whites and blacks and Asians; it did not repeal the law until 1953.[49]

Despite its well-documented record of discriminating against Native people and Chinese immigrants, the state of Washington proved an anomaly in the American Northwest; it was the only state in the West and only one of eight in the nation without miscegenation laws. When proponents introduced miscegenation bills in the 1935 and 1937 legislatures, a coalition of progressive ethnic and labor organizations turned back both measures. Although interracial marriage might be disparaged in British Columbia, the province did not legally restrict miscegenation. The provincial registrar occasionally listed mixed marriages, but the numbers were usually small. There are also periodic references in the records of clergy refusing to marry interracial couples, but the legal context was not part of the objection.[50]

With some differences across the Greater Northwest, there is a remarkable degree of congruity on the suffrage question. When the Liberal Party came to power in British Columbia in 1916, voters approved a party-sanctioned referendum granting women the right to vote and hold elective office. Another ballot measure to prohibit the sale of alcohol failed. The franchise measure followed a lengthy struggle dating to 1871, when American suffragette Susan B. Anthony barnstormed through the Northwest, including a stop in Victoria, where she compared the condition of women to antebellum slavery in the American South. Following Anthony's appearance, the British Columbia legislature granted women property holders the right to vote in municipal elections—the first legislature to do so in Canada. Although a few labor organizations and the Women's Christian Temperance Union repeatedly petitioned to enfranchise women, the provincial legislature's only concession was to extend women the right to vote in school elections in the late 1890s. It took the crisis of the Great War, the increased activism of women's organizations, petition circulations, and numerous public meetings to finally bring the suffrage question to a successful vote.[51]

The fight for women's suffrage in the American Northwest was long and equally arduous, with Oregon's Abigail Scott Duniway its leading spokesperson from the 1870s until her death in 1915. As editor and publisher of the region's leading suffrage publication, *New Northwest*, from 1871 to 1887, Duniway enjoyed long, if sometimes contentious, associations with national leaders such as Susan B. Anthony. Traveling widely across the region, Duniway delivered more than two hundred lectures a year at the peak of her influence. In her campaigns through Oregon, Washington, and Idaho, Duniway warned against aligning the suffrage movement with temperance causes, fearing that such alliances would invite the brewery and distillery interests to oppose female suffrage. Following the sale of her newspaper in 1887, Duniway moved with her family to Idaho and was living in the state when voters amended the constitution in 1896 to extend voting rights to women. Ironically, Idaho, Wyoming, Colorado, and Utah were the only states granting women the right to vote in 1896. When the Duniway family returned to Portland in the mid-1890s, Abigail vigorously resumed her suffrage work, including serving as editor of *Pacific Empire*, a Portland weekly.[52]

Oregon and Washington were slow to enfranchise women, with voters turning back suffrage amendments several times. With the powerful assistance of Abigail Scott Duniway and organized labor, Washington suffragettes Emma Smith Devoe, Cora Eaton, and May Arkwright Hutton waged a successful effort in 1910 to amend the state constitution to grant women the right to vote, serve on juries, and hold elective office. Harvey Scott, Duniway's brother and the longtime editor and publisher of the widely circulated *Portland Oregonian*, adamantly opposed extending the suffrage to women. Although Oregon's male voters again defeated a suffrage amendment in 1910, two years later (the year of Harvey

Scott's death) the state joined the ranks of states granting suffrage to both men and women.[53]

In Montana the Populist Party of the 1890s left a legacy of broad-based reforms, including workplace improvements for labor and an effort to extend the voting franchise to women. Montana voters finally brought to fruition the thirty-year struggle for gender equality at the ballot box when they approved a constitutional amendment in 1914. Jeannette Rankin, a leader in the state's feminist causes after 1900, was also a prominent national spokesperson for equal suffrage, helping to organize Washington's successful 1910 campaign for women's right to vote. Rankin was preeminent among her colleagues in forming the Montana Equal Suffrage Association, the organization responsible for narrowly achieving passage of the suffrage amendment in 1914. Two years later, the newly enfranchised female voters helped elect Jeannette Rankin to Congress, the first woman nationwide to hold a congressional seat.[54]

With the advantage of hindsight, the period that Dorothy Johansen characterized as years of "exuberant optimism" (1880–1910) offered a mix of rascality, flawed political leadership, economies of greed, narrow-minded social agendas, and civic principles gone astray. Only in a material sense can those decades be deemed a period of great progress and forward movement. With limited innovative political and cultural initiatives and an absence of consistent and courageous public decision making, the early-twentieth-century story for the Greater Pacific Northwest falls far short of its boosters' claims. The egregious legal, economic, and cultural discrimination against Native American/First Nations people would persist—with little movement toward equity—deep into the new century. Although no longer considered a threat to the dominant society, Chinese people lived a marginalized existence, often skillfully surviving in their own communities and providing services to the non-Asians around them. Japanese immigrants, who began arriving in large numbers in the first decade of the twentieth century, would experience similar social and economic assaults.

Insurgent protests continued into the first two decades of the twentieth century, with people organizing to curb the excesses of railroads, mining companies, and other externally controlled corporations. The insurgents were people who stood athwart the grasping ambitions of those who saw in the Pacific Northwest little more than opportunities for profit taking. With antecedents rooted in the nineteenth century, the continuing protest movements largely responded to the region's full-fledged industrial activity: railroad construction, distant capital investment in mineral resources, and the struggles of small-time farmers to survive in the absence of state, provincial, or federal controls over volatile markets.

2
Reformers, Radicals, and the New Order

William D. "Big Bill" Haywood was the quintessential turn-of-the-century western radical, committing his lifelong work to promoting the interests of the working classes. Born in 1869 in Bingham Canyon, Utah, the year the first transcontinental railroad was completed, Haywood hired on as a hard-rock miner at age fifteen to support his mother and siblings. In his midtwenties, when he was working in a northern Idaho silver mine, he met Ed Boyce, an organizer for the Western Federation of Miners (WFM), the most radical union in the United States. From that point forward, Haywood rose steadily to leadership positions in the WFM and later became the most prominent figure in the Industrial Workers of the World (IWW), the syndicalist union organized in Chicago in 1905.[1]

The violence-torn depression of the early 1890s, when the nation teetered on the brink of industrial chaos and anarchy, nurtured Haywood's maturing radicalism. The WFM, founded in 1893, emerged from the smoking ruins of labor-management clashes in northern Idaho's Coeur d'Alene mining district the previous year. The social and economic circumstances of those who labored in the mines, lumber camps, and harvest fields shaped Haywood's ideological conviction that the conflict between capital and labor was irrepressible. Events between 1890 and 1920 provided ample evidence to support that argument, with the social and economic clashes that took place the most significant the region has ever witnessed.[2]

Haywood gained national, even international, fame when a bomb detonated and killed former Idaho governor Frank Steunenberg as he opened the front gate to his Caldwell home on a snowy December evening in 1905. Following Harry Orchard's sensational confession, the federal government indicted Haywood and two other WFM leaders for conspiring to murder the ex-governor. The so-called trial of the century in the summer of 1907 focused the nation's attention on Boise, where prosecutor William Borah (soon to be a U.S. senator) dueled with the nation's most famous defense attorney, Clarence Darrow. The jury ultimately acquitted Haywood and his colleagues. But the famous trial was one of a kind, according to J. Anthony Lukas, who authored the classic account of the case, providing insight to a point in time when labor and capital contested for the soul of America.[3]

The grievances of people in the Greater Northwest extended beyond the region's dangerous extractive industries to small producers, especially farmers, who were subject to sometimes wildly fluctuating agricultural prices. In addition to the worldwide explosion of commercial agriculture, farming acreage in the United States more than doubled between 1870 and 1900, expanding from 407 to 841 million acres, with the Great Plains and the Pacific Northwest accounting for most of the increase. Although railroads and steamships provided agricultural producers with better access to markets, inequitable railway rates, corporate abuses, extortionate interest rates, and unfair taxes plagued farmers.[4]

Beginning with the emergence of Grangers in the 1870s, the Farmers' Alliances in the late 1880s, and the Populist uprising of the mid-1890s and continuing with protest movements in the first two decades of the twentieth century, citizens sought strategies to counter a turbulent market economy. Because agriculture set the tone for much of the region's political life in the 1890s, farmers were in the forefront of western protest, accusing merchants and railroads of acting in collusion to raise shipping rates and attacking banking institutions for discriminatory lending practices. From the time the Patrons of Husbandry (the Grange) first appeared in the 1870s and continuing through the rest of the century, rural protesters pursued railroad regulation (even government ownership), greater equity in tax policy, the formation of marketing cooperatives, and a variety of other collaborative enterprises to shield themselves from volatile market conditions. When the United States descended into the industrial depression of 1893, agrarian reformers joined industrial workers in a common cause against the forces of capital, both identifying themselves as members of the "productive classes."[5]

Although agrarian uprisings varied in their objectives, a study of Lewis County in western Washington shows that farmers wanted protection from international economic cycles and corporate abuses. Because they believed in "a cooperative commonwealth" where producers enjoyed "the fruits of their labor," Lewis County agrarians supported the Populists in the early 1890s. In Progressive Era Oregon, farmers and urban laborers often cooperated because they believed that producers should reap the benefits of their labor. In southern Oregon's Jackson County, another center of rural discontent, farmers protested railroad and flour-mill monopoly, inequitable taxes, and the low prices they received for their orchard crops. Jackson County gave Populist James B. Weaver a plurality of the presidential vote in 1892 and overwhelmingly supported Democratic-Populist fusion candidate William Jennings Bryan in 1896.[6]

Washington and Oregon offered up ambivalent stories about the successes and failures of Populism, with Oregon the only Northwest state where William McKinley won a narrow victory over William Jennings Bryan in the presidential election of 1896. Despite McKinley's win, the insurgent forces in Oregon continued to pursue agendas similar to those in adjacent states. Although Farmers' Alliance chapters in Oregon and Washington differed ideologically, both protested the unregulated power of trusts and corporations, extortionate railroad rates, high taxes on farmland, and a short money supply. Oregon also had an ostensibly Populist governor when Democratic incumbent Sylvester Pennoyer converted to Populism in 1892. The most influential voice pushing the state's reformers was William S. U'Ren, who served only a single term in the state legislature but who lobbied successfully for a series of early-twentieth-century reforms known as the Oregon System.[7]

The depression of the 1890s in Washington provided the catalyst to bring together a coalition of groups under the banner of the People's Party. For a brief period, the reformers enjoyed considerable success, electing Populist John Rogers to the governor's office in 1896 and a Populist supporting cast to the legislature the following year. A visionary and the author of a utopian novel, Rogers had earlier gained legislative support for funding public education. Once he was in the governor's office, however, partisan infighting disrupted opportunities to pass other reform measures, including establishing a state railroad commission. When Washington's Populist influence dissipated around the turn of the century, local chapters of the Grange quickly assumed the mantle of agrarian reform, focusing on building coalitions to push Progressive Era legislation.[8]

Montana's Populist Party emerged in early 1892, when a group of laborites, proponents of Henry George's "Single Tax," miners, and aggrieved farmers met in Butte to seek remedies for corporate abuses, the use of strikebreakers, and the misdeeds of railroads. At the party's June nominating convention, reformers adopted positions that mirrored the national platform, but they also demanded that the federal government force the Northern Pacific Railroad to forfeit its land grant. Because silver mining was critical to Montana's economy, the state's Populists called for the "free and unlimited coinage of silver," a theme equally popular in Idaho.

The nationwide depression in 1893 and the collapse of the market for silver boosted the party's fortunes, and in 1894 Montana voters elected three Populists to the state senate and thirteen to the house. In the watershed national election of 1896, Democrat-Populist fusion candidate William Jennings Bryan carried Montana, while fusion candidates captured the governor's office and an overwhelming majority in the house. Although the party's influence quickly declined, Montana Populists left a significant reform legacy: mine-safety legislation, the eight-hour workday, the initiative and referendum, the direct election of senators, and the right for women to vote and hold office.[9]

With its significant dependence on silver mining and persisting agricultural troubles, Idaho became a stronghold for Populist influences. The party supported the graduated income tax, federal ownership of railroads and telegraph and telephone lines, and a return to the unlimited coinage of silver. Mine owners and workers viewed the silver issue as a way to boost the state's depressed silver-mining districts, and debt-ridden farmers viewed inflationary measures as a way to raise agricultural prices. In Idaho's first federal election as a state in 1892, voters supported Populist candidate James B. Weaver and gave the successful Democratic candidate, Grover Cleveland, only two popular votes *statewide*.

In the 1896 presidential election, both of Idaho's major political parties followed the fusionist principle, with silver Republicans and Democrats joining with Populists to support William Jennings Bryan. Voters also elected Populist-Democrat Frank Steunenberg to the governor's office.[10]

Agrarian unrest was largely absent in British Columbia because of its relatively limited arable land. However, the province shared with the American Northwest the social and economic factors common to other extractive industries. Under those conditions, labor radicalism in the Greater Northwest illustrates the cross-border movement of ideologies and union organizing that linked workers to larger worlds of capital and labor. An early union organizer along the western Canadian–U.S. border addressed that transborder reality: "There is no 49th parallel of latitude in Unionism. The Canadian and American workingmen have joined hands against a common enemy."[11] From the 1880s through the Great

Depression, the international boundary proved to be a permeable border, especially to the northward flow of American capital, entrepreneurs, labor, and ideas. Workers from south of the border followed in the wake of capital investments in railroad construction and mining enterprises in British Columbia, creating outposts of American influence in a nation always apprehensive about the aggressive designs of its southern neighbor. With the passage of time, a growing nationalist sentiment, writes Jeremy Mouat, convinced British Columbians that provincial resources "should be exploited for the greatest benefit to the region."[12]

Workers and their ideas passed easily everywhere across borders in the Far West. With shared work lives and ruthless bosses north and south of the border, workers fought for better wages and union representation. The American presence, especially in the Kootenay mining district, also provided Canadian corporate executives with a perfect foil when they confronted labor difficulties, blaming "foreign agitators" for their troubles. Vancouver Island coal miners, with few American influences, went on strike on several occasions to protest wage cuts and other on-the-job abuses between 1877 and 1901. In each instance, the powerful Dunsmuir family successfully appealed to provincial authorities to call out the militia to suppress labor uprisings.[13]

Vancouver Island and lower mainland workers did not passively accept sordid living conditions in company-owned hovels and horrendously unsafe work environments. The Dunsmuir employees and other British Columbia miners eventually developed a militant reputation and a propensity for radical politics. In 1898 miners elected Ralph Smith, one of their own, to the provincial legislature, where he was instrumental in pushing through a law establishing the eight-hour day for underground miners. In the early twentieth century, industrial disputes in British Columbia were more violent than anywhere else in Canada. From a very early period, labor exercised an influence in the legislature far beyond the number of its elected members.[14]

The first significant episodes of labor unrest in the American Northwest took place in Idaho's Coeur d'Alene mining district in the summer of 1892, when miners walked off the job to protest wage cuts. When local workers appealed to the Butte Miners' Union for assistance, mine owners brought in more than eight hundred immigrant strikebreakers to resume operations.[15] Violence broke out in July, when armed guards at the Helena-Frisco mine exchanged gunfire with the strikers. In the midst of the gun battle, strikers dynamited the four-story Frisco ore-processing mill. Idaho's Republican governor, Norman Willey, then ordered the Idaho National Guard to deploy at the mines along the North Fork of the Coeur d'Alene River; he also requested the assistance of federal troops. With 1,500 state and federal troops assembled in the valley, authorities arrested approximately 600 locals and confined them to warehouses surrounded by stockadelike fences. After more than two months in the infamous "bullpens," a few leaders were indicted and convicted by local officials on conspiracy and contempt charges; however, following a U.S. Supreme Court decision in 1893, the state of Idaho dropped all charges. The most significant consequence of the Coeur d'Alene strike was the formation in 1893 of the radical WFM in Butte.[16]

Labor violence flared again in the Coeur d'Alenes in the spring of 1899, when miners demanded union recognition and wage scales commensurate with mining districts elsewhere. Events quickly escalated when armed union miners dynamited and reduced to rubble the Bunker Hill concentrator and company office. This often-told story involved Idaho governor Frank Steunenberg's request for federal troops, the arrest of more than a thousand miners, and the conviction of ten men for interfering with the U.S. mail. Governor Steunenberg later testified for eight days in Washington, D.C., before a House investigating committee about the "troubles" in Coeur d'Alene.[17]

But the violence-torn story of the Coeur d'Alene mines was not finished. Bunker Hill quickly rebuilt its mill, constructed an uphill blockhouse providing a panoramic view of all approaches to its facility, and imported miners from Leadville and Cripple Creek, Colorado. The terms of employment required all miners to sign "yellow dog contracts," forswearing union membership. Led by Bunker Hill, the Mine Owners' Association contributed $25,000 to the Republican National Committee in June 1900, seeking assurances that federal troops would remain garrisoned in the area indefinitely. Despite detectives keeping tabs on workers in the district and despite the company's effort to build better relations with the community, the Coeur d'Alene district continued to send Democrats to the state legislature. In the end, Bunker Hill was unable to convince workers to vote against their own interests.[18]

When Frederick Pope and William Talbot sailed north from San Francisco in 1852 and built a sawmill at Port Gamble on Puget Sound, they set in motion an export-based lumber economy that has dominated production in the Greater Northwest for more than 150 years. Although rudimentary forms of ocean transport, distance from markets, and a limited technology restricted output, the introduction of steam technology in ships and logging equipment during the 1880s vastly increased production and the ability to deliver goods to markets. With the end of the extensive pineries in Michigan, Wisconsin, and Minnesota in sight, Great Lakes capitalists began indulging in a frenzy of speculation in Northwest timberlands, purchasing huge tracts of old-growth forest. The greatest timber-brokered deal of them all involved Frederick Weyerhaeuser's purchase of nine hundred thousand acres of prime Douglas-fir timber from the Northern Pacific Railroad in late 1899.[19]

Weyerhaeuser and other timber speculators maneuvered through federal and state land laws, engaged in questionable title transfers, and negotiated territorial deals with the railroads to concentrate ownership in the hands of a few operators. Those large properties—with consolidation continuing during the twentieth century—have cast a long shadow over the region's property relations. In the wake of those developments, the lumber industry quickly became the most important factor in the expanding regional economy. From a subregional perspective, the most prominent trees were several species of pine that thrived at higher elevations in southern British Columbia, Montana, and Idaho and in eastern Oregon and Washington. The center for the greatest volume of production, however, has been the Douglas fir, redwood, cedar, and spruce country that stretches from northern California to British Columbia.[20]

Washington led the nation in lumber production by 1910, a position it relinquished to Oregon at the onset of the Second World War. As a consequence, the state operated in a highly volatile economy that swayed erratically in concert with national cycles of prosperity and depression. Those market-related conditions depressed lumber prices, wreaked havoc in the woods because loggers wanted only the best timber, and invited militant worker protests in the face of wage reductions. From Coos Bay on Oregon's southern coast to Puget Sound and the coastal timber communities bordering the Strait of Georgia, unpredictable markets contributed to fiscal instability for mill operators and uncertain and insecure expectations for workers and their families.[21]

Although Northwest mills shipped lumber to eastern markets and Pacific Rim nations, the West Coast's own rapidly growing population fueled much of the wood-products industry. Even before the completion of the Panama Canal in 1913, coastal markets from British Columbia to

California provided the greatest boon for lumber sales. In the first decade of the twentieth century, Washington's population increased 120 percent, Oregon's 62 percent, and California's—by far the most heavily populated of the three states—more than 60 percent. Expanding West Coast markets, therefore, were the most important factor in sustaining the Northwest lumber economy through the 1970s.[22]

Beyond the booming coastal sawmills, small but vibrant milling centers operated in central and eastern Oregon, northern Idaho, and western Montana. Commercial investments in western Montana and northern Idaho forests followed the rails of the Northern Pacific Railroad to the interior country. By the second decade of the twentieth century, sawmills operated from Bonners Ferry in the Idaho panhandle to Boise on the northern edge of the Snake River Plain. Many firms, such as Potlatch, were linked directly or indirectly to the sprawling Weyerhaeuser empire. Western Montana's relatively small milling capacity served a limited domestic market, most significant, the state's mining industry. Although Montana and Idaho mills shipped some finished lumber to midwestern and eastern markets, more robust lumber sales would await the coming of the Second World War.[23]

The central Oregon community of Bend traces its beginnings to the arrival of James J. Hill's Oregon Trunk Line in 1911. In short order, two Great Lakes–based companies, Brooks-Scanlon and Shevlin-Hixon, purchased some of the finest ponderosa pine timber on the continent and then opened two huge sawmills on opposite sides of the Deschutes River in 1916. Weyerhaeuser did the same for Klamath Falls on the California border, purchasing rich stands of ponderosa pine and opening a state-of-the-art sawmill after the Southern Pacific Railroad extended its line in 1909 from Weed in northern California to Klamath Falls. Baker City on Oregon's far eastern side also owed its existence to railroads. Salt Lake City investors incorporated the Oregon Lumber Company in 1889 and opened a large mill in Baker City in 1890, establishing harvesting and milling operations that would last through the Second World War.[24]

While British Columbia's lumber industry functioned in a different legal environment, it shared many features in common with producers south of the border. With approximately 45 percent of the province's land in high-value timber, the industry quickly moved to the fore in the provincial economy. Chief Forester H. R. MacMillan estimated in 1914 that logging and processing of wood material employed more workers, distributed more paychecks, created more local demand for goods, and produced more provincial revenue than any other activity. British Columbia followed the American practice of selling off its landed estate until 1896, when it began granting generous and transferable twenty-one-year leases with options to renew for equivalent periods. A frenzy of speculation took place in the early years of the twentieth century, with American investors visible among the lessees, eventually holding nearly half the industry's capital assets by the outbreak of the Great War. Forestry revenues made up more than 40 percent of the provincial budget by 1910 and continued to provide the ballast that kept the province afloat for several decades.[25]

British Columbia's industries and politics were closely intertwined. In the midst of an environment rife with graft and political deal making, the province's forestry commission urged the government to exercise greater control over surveying and bidding on provincial timberlands. Although the legislature passed a modest reform Forest Act in 1912, ending the leasing system's worst abuses, approximately 80 percent of provincial timberland was already under lease, most of it to large syndicates. British Columbia's lumber export market had also shifted from ocean highways to railroads, with the province shipping 90 percent of its lumber eastward by rail at the onset of the First World War. Like their American counterparts, British Columbia loggers and mill workers labored for arbitrary bosses and in unsafe work environments, with logging the most accident-prone of all provincial industries.[26]

The episodes of violence that took place in Idaho's Coeur d'Alene mining district during the 1890s were similar to incidents elsewhere in the region's tumultuous, boom-and-bust extractive industries. The labor-management struggles in Pacific Northwest mining sectors had parallels in the region's timber-producing districts, where perpetually depressed lumber prices placed mill communities at risk. The early-twentieth-century lumber town of Everett, Washington, provides a striking case study. Lumbermen in Everett treated workers with paternal contempt and used their political influence to destroy unions. The city's waterfront mills engaged in a Darwinian competitive struggle that equaled that of Montana copper titans Marcus Daly, William A. Clark, and F. Augustus "Fritz" Heinz. To protect against unions and union organizers, operators threatened to close their mills before acknowledging that workers possessed the right to organize. In his classic study, *Mill Town*, Norman Clark observed that Everett's mills operated under conditions of "competitive plunder," with the roots of the infamous "Everett Massacre" of November 5, 1916, originating with a corporate leadership that "confused property with character." It was a system, Clark writes, in which the capitalist class was at war with itself and with the wage earners who made its wealth possible.[27]

Employment in agriculture and fish and vegetable processing paralleled wage labor in logging—mostly seasonal in nature and requiring intense work for relatively limited periods. Irregular work meant a high level of mobility for many laborers, circumstances that undermined the development of social institutions such as schools, churches, and community organizations. More developed company towns such as Ocean Falls, British Columbia, where Pacific Mills owned the land, houses and dormitories, commercial district, and recreational buildings, raised questions of an overweening paternalism.[28]

Conditions on the American side of the border were no different. Agriculturalists required a heavy seasonal workforce, with the peak occurring during late summer and early fall harvests. Racial and gender occupational categories also characterized the workforce in fish and vegetable processing, with certain groups relegated to specific tasks. The best examples were salmon canneries, which employed large numbers of Chinese until technological advances made them dispensable. Packing and canning salmon was profoundly a western industry, employing wage laborers segmented along ethnic and gender lines. Vegetable processing in the Puget lowlands and Willamette Valley was largely the province of women, who sorted, washed, cut, and packed cans ready for preserving.[29] But it was the built-in instabilities of the extractive economy that fostered most of the labor discontent across the Greater Northwest.

Born of the Butte Miners' Union, the Western Federation of Miners emerged as the most important hard-rock mining union in the Rocky Mountain region, successfully organizing locals on both sides of the international border within ten years of its founding. The WFM quickly turned militant, supporting labor insurgencies, endorsing socialism, and in 1905 providing the core leadership for the radical Industrial Workers of the World. The WFM was arguably the most militant mine union in American history, and for a time it attempted to organize all miners in the West. The union changed its name to the Mine, Mill, and Smelter Workers Union in 1916 and lived into the 1960s. During its early years the WFM reacted to the aggressions of transcontinental mining companies and their efforts to foster class war in the mountain West. In less than a decade, the union had become the nation's most militant and radical labor organization.[30]

The WFM's aggressive doctrines appealed to workers in southeastern British Columbia's Kootenay mining region, where sharp class divisions divided workers and managers. Because of similarities in mining technology and the WFM's card-identification system, union members found it easy to take mining jobs on either side of the border. F. Ross McCormack estimates that shortly after the turn of the century, approximately half the miners in the Kootenays were from the United States, many of them refugees from the Coeur d'Alene troubles. With WFM agents working both sides of the border to organize hard-rock miners, corporate managers in the Kootenay district engaged in a variety of union-busting activities, accusing "foreign agitators" of causing unrest. "The accusations of 'foreign domination' . . . in British Columbia," Jeremy Mouat argues, "proved groundless." With the help of provincial authorities, however, mine owners obtained injunctions when workers walked off the job in protest. The owners were successful in breaking such labor stoppages, dealing significant setbacks to the WFM.[31]

By all estimates, the Indian/First Nations population in North America reached a low point sometime around 1900. At the same time, non-Native numbers were moving dramatically in the opposite direction, with the United States alone growing from sixty-three million in 1890 to more than seventy-five million at the turn of the century. The Indian population slowly recovered after 1900, the most striking increases taking place after 1950. An additional element in the recovery equation was "biological migration," children born to Indian and non-Indian parents. The United States census for 1910, the first tabulation to reflect data on full-blood and mixed-blood Indians, shows 56.5 percent listed as full-blood, a percentage that dropped to 46.3 percent in 1930. While use of the term *blood* is problematic, the Indian Bureau employed the designation for several decades to distinguish among Indians. Although changing census procedures—who should be counted as Indian—explain some of the population increase, improvements in Indian health and living conditions contributed to a marked rise in life expectancy and increased birthrates as the century advanced. Population recovery among Native groups, however, was uneven, with some groups remaining stagnant.[32]

The experiences of the Confederated Tribes of the Umatilla Indian Reservation during the first half of the twentieth century show static population numbers, the continued erosion of treaty rights, forced assimilation, and tribal efforts to survive through practicing traditional seasonal rounds and hiring out to non-Indians as agricultural workers. According to the official tribal history, the enrollment for 1910 was at an all-time low, with Umatilla numbers at 272 and Walla Wallas (which likely included the Cayuse) listing 397 members. Official Indian Bureau enumeration policies listed the reservation's principal bands as "full-blooded Indians," even though they might carry both Umatilla and Walla Walla bloodlines.[33]

The Umatilla people lived amid the drastic effects of the General Allotment Act, a federal initiative that contributed to the massive transfer of land to non-Indian ownership. The measure left the reservation a patchwork quilt of collective Indian, individual Indian, and non-Indian ownerships. At the same time, Indian Bureau acculturation programs forced children to attend agency schools that forbade the use of Native languages and other cultural practices. In the face of such adversity, tribal members continued their traditional ways, traveling to the Columbia River to fish "at their usual and accustomed places" and moving about the reservation on seasonal rounds, digging bulbs, berrying, and hunting deer and elk. Like other reservation Indians, literally existing in two worlds, tribal members left the reservation for agricultural labor in the Willamette, Hood River, and Yakima valleys. Despite a major U.S. Supreme Court decision upholding treaty guarantees to reserved water rights (*Winters v. United States*, 1908), non-Indian farmers continued to pump water from the Umatilla River as if it were exclusively their own.[34]

The lucrative hops-growing industry in western Washington provides an intriguing story about the participation of Indian/First Nations people in seasonal harvest labor. Large numbers of Native people, literally in the thousands, came from distant places (including British Columbia) to work in the hop fields around Puget Sound. Although earning wages was a motivating factor, picking hops was also part ceremony, during which Indians engaged in rituals of aboriginal politics and culture and exchanged valuable information. When aphid infestations destroyed western Washington's hop fields, the industry and its Native harvesters moved across the mountains to the irrigated fields in the Yakima Valley. Although entire families participated in the hop harvests, women made up the largest segment of the workforce.[35]

At the far corner of the American Northwest, the remote Makah Indian Reservation at Neah Bay harbored a people whose lives had traditionally

Roy Bishop, Pendleton Woolen Mills, and Jackson Sundown, champion bronco rider, at the Pendleton Roundup (date unknown). Nez Perce–born Jackson Sundown (1863–1923) became a skilled horseman and legendary rodeo rider who participated in competitions across the American and Canadian Wests. At age fifty-three he was named World Champion Bronco Rider at the famous Pendleton Roundup.

been oriented toward the sea—whaling, sealing, and fishing for halibut. With an average annual precipitation of more than one hundred inches, the twenty-three-thousand-acre Makah Reservation was ill suited for agriculture, the Indian Bureau's favored assimilationist program. With steep forested mountains surrounding their homeland, the Makah looked to marine resources for sustenance. Distance from the nearest canneries in Port Angeles, however, placed the Makah in a vulnerable situation in their efforts to obtain a fair price for halibut. Although diminishing marine resources would eventually test the resiliency of the Makah people, the tribe managed to remain remarkably independent into the early twentieth century, remaining free of most federal assistance programs.[36]

The Lummi, located between Bellingham and the international boundary, had subsisted on anadromous fishes in northern Puget Sound for centuries. Reduced in population to fewer than five hundred people by the late nineteenth century, surviving Lummi hired on as wage laborers or in supplying fish to nearby non-Indian canneries. Using reef netting to intercept sockeye salmon as they migrated toward the Fraser River, the Lummi prospered until cannery-owned fish traps severely restricted the area for reef-net fishing. Between 1900 and the 1930s the fish traps virtually excluded the Lummi from the commercial fishery, and to exacerbate the tribe's difficulties, Washington law-enforcement officials arrested Lummi for fishing off the reservation or during state-imposed closed seasons. The sharp contraction of their fishery forced many Lummi to seek work as migrant laborers in eastern Washington or in the lower Fraser River Valley.[37]

The story of First Nations people in southern British Columbia parallels the experiences of Indians in the American Northwest, with one notable exception: in British Columbia authorities made no effort to force Native villagers to move to reservations. Into the twentieth century, most people lived in permanent villages and moved about during the spring, summer, and fall months to pursue wage work or to participate in seasonal rounds. In the Okanagan and Kamloops areas, Natives worked on farms and ranches at harvesttime. While pursuing traditional activities such as hunting and fishing, they served occasionally as packers and in other types of wage labor. The most difficult circumstances for British Columbia Natives were health conditions, with reasonably accurate Canadian records in the mid-1890s indicating that Native birthrates were roughly comparable to those of the general population. The death rate, however, was much higher, especially among children. At the outbreak of the Great War in 1914, many Native children did not live to adulthood. Temporary encampments near agricultural fields or fish canneries provided ideal environments for contracting diseases, which people carried back to their distant villages, far removed from medical care.[38]

Canadian/British Columbian assimilation policies also shared similarities with initiatives in the United States. Residential and mission schools, with English-language instruction required, were the norm for socializing children. Beyond the school environments, educated Indians also faced discrimination and outright hostility when they sought employment in the provincial labor market. But the residential and mission schools also had unintended consequences—socializing Native students into a larger awareness of their identity as Indians. This awareness of mutual interests reflected their collective experiences in English-language schools. Provincial attacks on other aspects of Native culture included suppression of the potlatch, prohibitions that prompted practitioners to seek more subtle ways to carry on the activity. It also indicated the manner in which Native people were making accommodations with the larger society on their own terms.[39]

The agrarian discontent of the 1880s and 1890s carried over into the new century in a reform spirit known as the Progressive movement. Reformers and politicians who joined Progressive Era causes varied widely in ideology, from the truly radical, such as Oregon's William S. U'Ren, to Idaho's U.S. senator, William S. Borah, a nationally renowned Progressive who held that reputation without offending influential mining corporations in his home state. Progressive legislation manifested itself across the American Northwest through a variety of measures: electoral reform, railroad commissions, employer-liability and workers' compensation laws, women's suffrage, Prohibition, child-labor legislation, the eight-hour day for women in certain occupations, and a wide range of other social and economic reforms.

The most radical manifestations of regional change took place in Oregon. Urban scholar Carl Abbott challenges those who describe Portland as staid and conservative. Such interpretations, he argues, "served only the interests of corporations and the propertied classes." Another study of Progressive Era Portland points out that Oregon's electoral reforms generated a host of "utopian democratic visions." Although antidemocratic, nativist, and racist impulses sometimes evolved from these reform measures, historians should examine the Progressive Era with greater care to better understand the roots of modern democratic politics.

Dorothy Johansen, historian of an earlier generation, maintained that Oregon served as "a glass-walled laboratory of political experimentation."[40]

William S. U'Ren, the architect of the Oregon System, was the ideological standard-bearer for a host of "direct legislation" electoral reforms—the initiative, referendum, and recall; a direct primary law; and the direct election of U.S. senators. After brief stints in the Colorado mines as a young man, U'Ren studied law, worked as a newspaper reporter, and then made his way to his parents' ranch in eastern Oregon. After reading Henry George's *Progress and Poverty*, he became a convert to the single-tax cure for poverty, believing that direct legislation would enable citizens to enact laws and policies to suit their own interests. The most important matter, he wrote on one occasion, "was to restore the law-making power where it belonged—into the hands of the people. . . . Once given that we could get everything we wanted—single tax, anything."[41]

U'Ren quickly became immersed in Oregon's reform politics and served a term in the Oregon House of Representatives as a Populist in 1896 (his only electoral office). He shrewdly aligned himself with politically influential and wealthy Jonathan Bourne to push through initiative and referendum amendments to the Oregon Constitution (1902), a direct primary law (1904), corrupt-practices legislation (1908), and a recall amendment (1908). U'Ren made occasional moves to run for statewide or national office between 1905 and 1910, only to withdraw in lieu of various lobbying efforts on behalf of popular government. His campaign for governor of Oregon in 1912 turned into a humiliating defeat: he finished fourth behind the winner, reform Democrat Oswald West. His campaign platform was truly radical, however, including a requirement that the state provide employment for every citizen who demanded work.[42]

If Oregon was a pacesetter in creating a model for a democratic polity, Washington, Idaho, and Montana were not far behind. With Washington's growing reputation for insurgent politics, the state's progressive reformers followed William U'Ren's guiding spirit, enacting the most significant direct legislation measures—the initiative, referendum, direct primary, and recall. But Washington surpassed Oregon in establishing a railway commission (1905) to serve as a watchdog over the abusive lobbying practices of the Great Northern and Northern Pacific railroads. Washington also enacted the Workmen's Compensation Law (1911), a national model of its kind, which held employers liable for employees injured on the job. Employer groups charged that the Workmen's

Compensation Law was state socialism, but the Washington Supreme Court upheld the state's power to regulate industry.[43]

Washington's progressive legislative agenda included restrictions on child labor, limiting the workday for women in certain occupations, and prohibiting the sale of alcoholic beverages. At the local level, several communities established municipal ownership of transportation and utilities. The Reverend Mark Matthews of Seattle's First Presbyterian Church became a major proponent of nurturing a proper urban environment through establishing public parks, hospitals, and juvenile court systems. Matthews contended that it was less expensive to build quality social infrastructures than it was "to support a standing army, hundreds of policemen, jails, penitentiaries and asylums for inebriates." Grounded initially in the Social Gospel movement, Matthews grew increasingly conservative with the passing years, eventually allying himself with Seattle's downtown elites.[44]

Montana and Idaho progressives confronted powerful mining corporations in their efforts to regulate mines and to ameliorate conditions for workers. Adopting women's suffrage (1905) well before the other northwestern states, Idaho legislators pressed for social regulatory measures such as Prohibition in lieu of passing mine-safety legislation and other measures to assist rank-and-file workers. The state did not have a workers' compensation law until the reoccurrence of labor troubles in the Coeur d'Alene mines prompted legislators to act in 1917. However, Idaho followed Oregon and Washington in adopting a direct primary law in 1909 and the initiative, referendum, and recall two years later.[45]

Montana's reform politics of the 1890s carried over to the new century, during which the insurgent spirit burned white hot until it ran aground amid the superpatriotism and repression associated with the First World War. Reformers who had demanded direct legislation since the heyday of the Populist influence achieved their objective when voters approved a constitutional amendment in 1906, adding the initiative and referendum to the state constitution. Following Oregon's example, Montana also adopted a mechanism for the direct election of U.S. senators in 1911, two years before the passage of the Seventeenth Amendment to the U.S. Constitution. Following copper baron William A. Clark's wholesale bribery of the Montana legislature in 1899 to get himself elected to the U.S. Senate, the direct election of senators was not a hard sell.[46]

In virtually every legislative initiative, Montana's progressives had to confront the power, influence, and financial might of the Amalgamated

Copper Company. Two separate political clashes illustrate this point. When incumbent Republican senator Joseph M. Dixon issued broadside attacks on railroads and the company in his reelection effort in 1912 as a Teddy Roosevelt, Bull Moose/Progressive, the Amalgamated supported a less hostile progressive, Democrat Thomas J. Walsh. Dixon, who chaired the Progressive Party's Chicago convention that year, also served as Roosevelt's campaign manager. The Montana Progressive Party's stationery was directly confrontational: "Put the Amalgamated out of Montana Politics." Because of the company's all-out effort to defeat Dixon, Democrats gained a large majority in the legislature, and Walsh easily made it to the Senate. The company also fought Progressive efforts to pass a workers' compensation law, and when the legislature finally passed such a law in 1915, it was a modest measure.[47]

Although Montana progressives were unable to curb the influence of the company, they were more successful in passing humanitarian/social-reform measures and in expanding the public's ability to participate in politics. Voters passed a constitutional amendment in 1904 raising the minimum legal age for employment in the mines to sixteen, a measure extended to other industries in 1907. Lawmakers also enacted a compulsory school attendance measure and created a juvenile court system to offer counseling to delinquent children. Reflecting labor's strength in politics, voters also rejected a 1911 measure that would have enhanced the governor's ability to call out the state militia.[48]

The American Northwest also produced several nationally renowned progressive leaders. Idaho's William Borah was a progressive leader in Congress and chief sponsor of two important amendments to the U.S. Constitution, the direct election of senators (1913) and the income tax (1916). Tennessee-born Miles Poindexter, elected to the House of Representatives from eastern Washington in 1908, earned a reputation as a leading House insurgent, distinctions that elevated him to the U.S. Senate in 1910. During his first term, Poindexter joined Teddy Roosevelt's short-lived Progressive Party and supported the direct election of senators, women's suffrage, and a graduated income tax. During his second and last term in the Senate, he turned away from progressive politics and became increasingly isolationist in foreign policy matters.[49]

Montana voters elected three U.S. senators who achieved national acclaim as progressives: Joseph Dixon (1907–13), Thomas Walsh (1913–33), and Burton K. Wheeler (1923–47). Despite his liberal reputation, Walsh helped author two of the nation's most repressive civil liberties

measures, the Espionage Act of 1917 and the Sedition Act of 1918. Serving through the conservatism of the 1920s, Walsh and Wheeler gained
national fame for investigating corruption in the administration of President Warren G. Harding. Known to the eastern press as the "Montana
mudgunners," Walsh and Wheeler were different personalities, the former moderate, brilliant, and aloof, the latter a Populist radical who loved
progressive causes. Wheeler ran for vice president with Robert La Fol-
lette on the Progressive Party ticket in 1924 and later led the opposition
to President Franklin D. Roosevelt's "court-packing" scheme in 1937. One
other Montana progressive, Jeannette Rankin, a feminist, pacifist, and
radical, gained widespread recognition for her work with the Montana
Equal Suffrage Association. She became a national figure when constituents elected her to Congress in 1916, the first woman to hold office
in the U.S. Congress. In her two terms in Congress (1917–19 and 1941–43),
she gained fame for opposing American entry into both world wars.[50]

Although its congressional progressives did not achieve the stature
of Montana's Thomas Walsh or Burton Wheeler, Oregon sent reform-
minded Democrat George Chamberlain to the U.S. Senate in 1909, where
he supported progressive legislation during Woodrow Wilson's first administration. In his second term, Chamberlain criticized Wilson's prosecution of the war, backed repressive measures restricting civil liberties,
and opposed American membership in the League of Nations. In a letter
to Treasury Secretary William Gibbs McAdoo, *Oregon Journal* editor
C. S. Jackson complained that Chamberlain was too worried about Oregon's conservative Republican majority, believing that he needed such
support in his reelection campaign. Jackson concluded: "He was always
half-Republican-reactionary and privileged."[51]

Although he is largely neglected as an Oregon reformer, Harry Lane
gained a reputation for citizen activism in Portland, sufficient to put him
in the mayor's office in 1905. As a three-term reform mayor, Lane ended
the intimate ties between the city's business establishment and its elected
leaders and brought decency and civic integrity to the office. Elected to
the U.S. Senate in 1912, Lane supported most of President Woodrow Wilson's New Freedom reforms. He also endorsed Wilson's reelection in
1916 but broke with the president when the administration moved closer
to war with Germany in early 1917. Lane joined five other senators in
opposing Wilson's declaration of war measure in April, with the president famously referring to the group as "six willful little men." Although

Jeannette Rankin (1880–1973). A Montana native, Rankin was the first woman to be elected to the U.S. House of Representatives (and the U.S. Congress). A lifelong pacifist, she voted against American entry into the First and Second World Wars.

Lane was vilified as a traitor at home, his death the following month marked the close of a remarkable reform interlude in Oregon's politics.[52]

At the height of Theodore Roosevelt's Bull Moose/Progressive Party campaign for the presidency in 1912, British Columbia's *Victoria Daily Colonist* confidently declared: "We [already] have what the Progressive Party seeks to obtain for the people of the United States." With that bit of provincial sophistry, the *Colonist* suggested that British Columbia— and Canada for that matter—had no need for the kind of political, social, and regulatory initiatives taking place south of the border. Although there may be substance to that argument, when the Liberal Party defeated Conservative Party premier Richard McBride in 1915, it pushed through a credible slate of reform legislation: guaranteeing payment of wages every two weeks in major industries, establishing a workers' compensation system and a department of labor, and limiting miners to an eight-hour workday.[53]

The outbreak of war in Europe in August 1914 slowed the reform spirit, first in British Columbia and then in the American Northwest. The war revitalized the region's moribund economy, providing an immediate boost to lumber and wheat prices. In British Columbia, Great Britain's declaration of war against Germany altered every aspect of provincial life, with patriotism becoming the watchword of the day.[54] The war and its aftermath ultimately proved detrimental to organized labor in both Canada and the United States. When the American nation declared war against the Central Powers in April 1917, the Northwest states witnessed widespread strikes, which prompted unprecedented federal intrusion into labor-management relations. The most notorious effects of the war on both sides of the border, however, were the flagrant violations of the civil liberties of American and Canadian citizens.

II
Extraregional Conflict and Economics

3
War and Peace
The Politics of Reaction

When German armies marched into Belgium in August 1914, the European continent descended into a maelstrom of violence. Linked at the hip to the British Empire, Canada, including British Columbia, joined the fray on behalf of the Allies, England and France. By war's end in 1918 the province had the highest per capita volunteer enlistment in all of Canada. For the American Northwest, the European demand for foodstuffs and other items reversed a depressed economy, boosting prices for lumber, wheat, agricultural products, and minerals. Ottawa and Washington, D.C., policy makers also successfully linked the remote reaches of both nations to a world at war, making unprecedented demands for valuable war-related raw materials.[1]

Subsidies to the United States Emergency Fleet Corporation turned both Seattle and San Francisco into shipbuilding centers on the Pacific Coast, with jobs at Puget Sound construction sites rivaling those in the lumber-producing districts. Buoyed by guaranteed prices, wheat farmers in Washington's Palouse increased production to more than 6.5 million bushels by the end of the conflict. The Great War also ushered in a super-patriotism that played havoc with the region's politics, providing industrialists and business interests with the opportunity to initiate loyalty crusades to curb the demands of labor. The repression at home, lasting into 1919 and 1920, witnessed unprecedented violence, repressive private associations and state institutions, and spontaneous mob action. Dozens of people were killed and thousands were temporarily detained, most of them on trumped-up charges.[2]

The First World War and its aftermath initiated spectacular changes to the entire Pacific Coast. No section of the United States experienced such dramatic adjustments between 1916 and into the next decade.[3] The economic boom during the war was truly impressive, with strong export markets, high prices, easy credit, and substantial advances in industrial and agricultural production. Because of the high demand for wood products, agricultural goods, and critical minerals from northern Rocky

Skinner & Eddy Shipyard, Seattle, July 26, 1918. The steel-hulled cargo ship SS *West Elcasco*, under construction in Seattle, was built for the U.S. Shipping Board's emergency wartime program. The ship served with the U.S. Navy during the First World War and as an army transport during the Second World War.

Mountain mining districts, the Pacific Northwest prospered during the Great War. The city of Seattle provides a striking story of a dramatically expanding productive base where employment in manufacturing industries increased from 12,429 in 1914 to 40,843 in 1919. A people who were neutral at the outset of the conflict clearly prospered through selling their goods in war-stimulated markets.[4]

Although shipbuilding explains much of Seattle's economic growth during the First World War, the sudden demand for ships concealed potential weaknesses in the industry, especially with the return to peacetime. During the war Seattle's economy boomed through the construction of ships in its big yards and numerous spin-off industries. The Port of Seattle yearbook for 1918 lists fifty thousand industrial workers in the city, with thirty-five thousand of them employed in the shipyards. Through the war years and for a few months following the Armistice, Seattle's major problem was the shortage of labor. Even as the city moved toward full employment, however, Seattle's labor-management relations remained volatile, with several longshore strikes and walkouts, most of them attributed to the intransigence of the Waterfront Employers' Association of the Pacific Coast.[5]

In Vancouver, British Columbia, the Great War reenergized a depressed economy and marked the onset of dramatic changes to all facets of provincial life. Federal subsidies stimulated shipbuilding industries in Vancouver and Victoria, and with large numbers of enlistees marching off to war, the province confronted a labor shortage. Older, marginally employed citizens and women joined the wage-labor force in large numbers. With staple commodities like lumber and fish important to the war effort, Vancouver moved toward full employment. While volatile prewar labor-management relations moderated during the first years of the conflict, workers eventually protested modest wages in the face of inflationary pressures. The federal government created more unrest when it required young men to register for the armed forces in 1916 and followed with a conscription law in August 1917. Ottawa also continued its schizoid and ambivalent labor policies when it granted workers the right to organize in July 1918 and—in the same decree—prohibited strikes and lockouts.[6]

In Anaconda-dominated Montana, soaring copper and zinc prices pushed Butte's population to an all-time high of approximately one hundred thousand during the war years. Heeding inflated prices for agricultural crops and the slogan "Wheat Will Win the War," farmers accelerated their effort to turn eastern Montana's semiarid plains to growing grain crops. The U.S. decision to go to war in April 1917 caused more dissension in the West than in any other region of the nation, and nowhere was opposition more strident than in Montana. Labor and agrarian radicals in the West, with its large German, Irish, and Scandinavian populations, either favored neutrality or outright opposed an alliance with Great Britain. Following the declaration of war, patriotism burned hot in Montana and other western states, with politicians focusing their heaviest rhetoric against critics of the war. Writing in the *Journal of American History*, Christopher Capozzola observes that the First World War marked a high point for federal and state repression of civil liberties, private violence against individuals, and the detainment of thousands of people on trumped-up charges.[7]

By war's end nearly 10 percent of Montana's population—forty thousand men (and a few women)—had enlisted in the European conflict, a per-capita figure 25 percent greater than any other state. Montana also led in the percentage of casualties, with 939 citizens losing their lives in the conflict. At the same time, sizable numbers of Montanans opposed the war—people of German and Irish ancestry, Scandinavian farmers, those sympathetic to the Industrial Workers of the World (IWW), and socialists of varying ideologies. At the Wilson administration's request, Governor Sam Stewart created the Montana Council of Defense, which, with its county affiliates, proceeded to zealously pursue a superpatriotism that trampled on citizens' civil rights and incarcerated innocent people. To carry out its mission, the council pressured the legislature to pass the Montana Sedition Law, a measure later copied verbatim at the federal level in the Sedition Law of May 1918.[8]

For the Canadian and American governments and employers, the greatest problem at the outset of the Great War was the IWW, the radical syndicalist union with special strengths among workers in extractive industries. Although the IWW conducted sensational textile strikes in Lawrence, Massachusetts, and Patterson, New Jersey, migratory workers in the American Northwest's extractive industries, especially harvest hands and loggers, provided the setting for its greatest success and influence. In its confrontations with rabidly antiunion employers, the IWW fought both company bosses and the trade-centered American Federation of Labor (AFL).[9] Once the United States entered the war, federal and local authorities set out to destroy the union because of its militancy and willingness to take on the employer class.

For the American Northwest, the Great War marked a turnaround in commodity markets, with purchases of lumber and wheat sending prices soaring to three and four times prewar levels. The region's lumber trade expanded, especially in milling structural materials for building army cantonments and spruce for use in airplane construction. The lightweight, tough spruce was an ideal material for building aircraft wings. Spruce production eventually involved direct federal intervention because it was deemed an essential war material. The creation of the U.S. Spruce Production Corporation placed federal authorities in charge of all phases of production, from felling timber to milling lumber and, most important, controlling labor relations. By the summer of 1918, twenty-seven thousand soldiers were at work in the logging camps and mills of western Washington and Oregon.[10]

The Spruce Production Corporation was directly related to the region's lumber industry and its perennial labor problems. Shortly after the U.S. declaration of war in April 1917, loggers and mill workers began striking for higher wages, a shorter workday, and better food and living conditions in logging camps. IWW organizers in the Inland Empire led the initial strikes and walkouts, workforce interruptions that quickly spread from the pine districts to the big coastal production centers of Oregon and Washington. The rapidly expanding strike swiftly spread across the wood-producing districts of the Northwest until the industry was operating at about 15 percent of capacity. Although the AFL had established a few locals in the Northwest, the more aggressive IWW organizers galvanized both the loggers' and mill workers' unions into an unprecedented organizing drive. The strikes in the region's logging camps and sawmills in the summer of 1917 were the most spectacular up to that time.[11]

Twenty thousand workers in western Washington logging camps and lumber mills walked off the job in mid-July, with their chief objective the eight-hour day. Led by the AFL but with the strong support of the IWW, longshoremen also joined the strike, refusing to handle lumber produced in ten-hour mills. Although AFL union leaders coordinated the strike, Seattle's Chamber of Commerce fingered the IWW as the culprit, accusing it of disloyalty and interfering with the war effort. Prominent lumberman Edwin Ames, while acknowledging difficulties with the IWW, also warned AFL locals that their actions would not influence the industry's decisions. Carlton Parker, retained by the government to insure that the strike did not interfere with production, wired Secretary of War

Newton Baker toward the end of July about the lumbermen's demands: "They have patriotically agreed to the very serious sacrifice of granting the eight hour day . . . if the Federal Government agree in turn to suppress the agitation and strike activity of the I.W.W."[12] From that point forward, federal authorities worked in collusion with industry leaders to bring an end to the strike.

The federal government and employers countered the strike on two levels. Collaborating with the leading lumber companies, federal officials formed a quasi–company union, the Loyal Legion of Loggers and Lumbermen (4-L), to enforce the eight-hour day, improve living conditions in logging camps, and provide workers with higher wages. That achievement, most contemporaries agree, reflected IWW militancy and progressive AFL locals, not the 4-L. A logger who worked on Oregon's south coast remembers that the "IWW scare" brought clean bed sheets, deloused and warmer bunkhouses, better pay, and more attention to injured men. For the duration of the war, the eight-hour day became a regular feature of sawmill and logging camp employment, and the local business community was unstinting in its praise of workers who joined the 4-L.[13] Once the war ended, however, those improved working conditions and wage scales quickly eroded.

To counter radical union influences, federal, state, and local authorities also initiated a full-scale offensive against any group or individual suspected of militant labor activity, especially anyone affiliated with the IWW. The region's businessmen used every opportunity to link patriotism to profits and union workers to treason. Gray's Harbor logging boss Alex Polson offered a solution to the IWW problem in August: "The state or federal authorities will have to take a strong hand in suppressing the I.W.W.'s. It seems from every indication that they are backed by German influence." Polson urged the government to close all IWW meeting halls to break the strike. Lumbermen and their corporate counterparts elsewhere also engaged in a rash of exchanges with federal district attorneys, encouraging a systematic suppression of the IWW and associated fellow travelers.[14]

Well in advance of the federal crackdown in early September, employers, loyalty leagues, citizens' groups, and local vigilantes were already at work exacting "justice" through beatings, mass deportations (in Bisbee, Arizona), and occasional lynchings, as in the case of IWW organizer Frank Little in Butte, Montana. In early 1917 the Idaho legislature enacted the first criminal syndicalism law in the nation, making it a criminal act for citizens to advocate terrorist methods to achieve their objectives. Those events were mere preface to the U.S. Justice Department's action on September 5, 1917, raiding the offices and homes of Wobbly officials and confiscating potentially incriminatory documents. A Chicago grand jury subsequently indicted 166 IWW members on several charges of interfering with the war effort. The raids and the prosecution of the Wobblies destroyed much of the IWW infrastructure. Former leaders of the IWW drifted into other walks of life, including membership in the new Communist Party, with the union's indicted leader, William D. Haywood, serving a year in prison and then, in ill health, fleeing to the Soviet Union, where he led a lonely existence until his death in 1928.[15]

The most infamous suppression of civil liberties in the American Northwest took place in Montana, home to Anaconda Copper and the company's "kept" newspapers. Will Campbell of the *Helena Independent* proved the most hysterical of Montana editors, praising the vigilante hanging of Frank Little in Butte: "Good work: Let them continue to hang every I.W.W. in the state." Montana public officials used the state's draconian sedition law against members of the Nonpartisan League. When farmers assailed railroad monopolies for manipulating short- and long-haul rates, the Anaconda Company accused the protesters of being unpatriotic and sympathetic to Bolshevism.[16]

Because the Nonpartisan League sought stiffer regulations on railroads, state-owned grain elevators, producer cooperatives, and federal ownership of the telegraph, Montana's corporate superpatriots singled out league members as special targets. In their mindless search for scapegoats, Montana authorities brought approximately 130 sedition cases against individuals, most of them trivial in nature and involving blue-collar workers and farmers. More than 50 percent of those sentenced to prison were European born. It is interesting to note that Butte and Silver Bow County—a bastion of ethnic radicalism—accounted for only seven of the sedition cases. Most of the convictions involved the sparsely populated, heavily agrarian southeastern part of the state. Nearly ninety years would pass before Montana governor Brian Schweitzer issued posthumous pardons in May 2006 to the seventy-eight people convicted of sedition during the virulent anti-German hysteria of the First World War. "Across this country," Schweitzer declared, "it was a time in which we had lost our minds." Speaking in the rotunda of Helena's capitol, the governor continued: "It is not the American way for Americans to spy on neighbors. And today, we ask that we never forget the mistakes that we have made so that we don't make them again."[17]

Two major and related events, one Canadian and one American, set the tone for the immediate postwar era in both nation-states. Although low-level labor unrest in the United States persisted during the war, inflationary living costs in cities like Seattle prompted workers to press for long-deferred wage increases with the return to peacetime. Seattle's shipyard workers led the charge when they struck for higher wages in February 1919, burnishing anew the region's reputation for radical politics. When other unions joined in solidarity, the Seattle Central Labor Council called for a general strike, and in early February sixty-five thousand workers walked off the job. Despite conservative mayor Ole Hanson's histrionics ("the life stream of a great city has stopped"), strike leaders had already mandated that essential services—hospitals, milk deliveries, and electrical power—would be maintained.[18]

Following in the wake of Russia's Bolshevik Revolution, the Seattle general strike raised fears that a similar upheaval stood at America's western doorstep. The strike, however, was brief, peaceful, and uneventful, and it ended after three days amid unfulfilled objectives. Labor's failures in Seattle set the stage for a decade of antiunion, open-shop environments and conservative political leadership in local and state offices.[19] With the Seattle strike still a recent memory, Americans were then greeted with headline news that bombs had been sent to prominent individuals, including Mayor Hanson. May Day disturbances in eastern cities further intensified citizen anxieties, and then came the bombing of U.S. Attorney General A. Mitchell Palmer's house in Washington, D.C. The great Red Scare of 1919 was in full bloom.[20]

In British Columbia and the city of Vancouver, inflationary pressures, conscription, and the suppression of strikes during the war hardened class lines and helped shape future relations between labor and management. With inflation nearly 10 percent higher than the rest of Canada, union membership in British Columbia increased more than 20 percent in the months following the Armistice. Two overlapping events served to galvanize labor activism in British Columbia: the emergence of the One Big Union across western Canada and the Winnipeg general strike of May 1919. Buoyed by the Seattle strike earlier in the year, sympathy walkouts quickly spread through logging camps and mining towns in British Columbia's interior. In Vancouver twelve thousand workers struck in solidarity with their Winnipeg brethren. The British Columbia/Vancouver version of the general strike was never solid, however, because men and women slowly returned to work with each passing week.[21]

In Winnipeg federal authorities aggressively supported the employer class and worked with local officials and the North West Mounted Police to crush the strike. It is evident that the anarchist bombings in the United States precipitated the Canadian decision to take repressive measures. With the Manitoba insurrection coming to an end, Vancouver shipyard, factory, and street railway workers called off the local strike after twenty-five days.[22] Like their counterparts in the United States, Canadian workers would confront a decade and more of open-shop relations with management and persisting conflicts with conservative provincial and federal governments.

From the First World War through the early years of the Great Depression, the U.S. government vigorously pursued "civilization" programs on Indian reservations across the American West. As part of this strategy, the Bureau of Indian Affairs continued to favor off-reservation boarding schools as the most viable assimilation initiatives. Because most reservations were in isolated settings, the Indian agency treated the schools as laboratories of sorts where educational strategies would lead to cultural and linguistic change. To promote the policy, reservation day school instructors prohibited children from speaking indigenous languages or wearing Native clothing. Wartime conditions and Indian experiences at the boarding institutes and reservation day schools also quickened the hopes of those who wanted to advance assimilation and grant Indians full citizenship. Congress first granted citizenship to Indian veterans of the First World War, and then in 1924 President Calvin Coolidge signed a bill extending citizenship to "all noncitizen Indians born within the territorial limits of the United States." The Indian Citizenship Act of 1924, Brian Dippie writes, marked "the symbolic high point of the assimilationist era."[23]

Despite the move toward full citizenship, federal wardship status persisted in the American Northwest, including the many small treaty tribes around Washington's Puget Sound. In the decade following the First World War, federal policy in western Washington continued to be arbitrary and paternal. Despite Indian requests for federal intervention to protect access to traditional fishing grounds, Indian Bureau officials urged the tribes to abide by state fishing regulations. Puget Sound Indians,

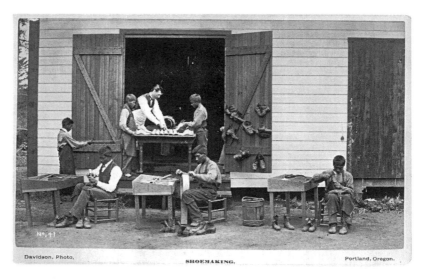

Davidson. Photo,   SHOEMAKING.   Portland, Oregon.

Forest Grove Indian Training School. The Forest Grove Indian Industrial
and Training School was the first off-reservation boarding school in the
American West. Established at Pacific University in 1880, the institution
was moved to a new site (Chemawa) north of Salem when the Forest
Grove buildings suffered a major fire in 1885.

however, were becoming increasingly convinced that the 1850s treaties
would eventually determine their relationships with the larger society.
The spokespersons for this new collective identity were tribal members
who had attended reservation or off-reservation schools. Although the
full realization of treaty-guaranteed rights to fish lay in the future, the
Northwestern Federation of American Indians emerged as the most important regional Indian organization fighting to clarify treaty rights.[24]

Oregon's coastal Indians went through a period of forced assimilation
and adaptation that had little relation to federal policy. On the allotment-
ravaged Siletz Reservation, the Indian Bureau operated both boarding
and day schools until the boarding school closed in 1908. The reservation
day school operated for another ten years before it also closed and agency
officials directed students to attend public schools. As the heavily tim-
bered Siletz Reservation diminished in size, individual Indians sought
work in sawmills, logging camps, and salmon canneries and as agricultural laborers. The effect of allotment on the Siletz was made clear in
an Indian agent's observation in 1931 that land patents issued to Indians

usually found their way to non-Indian owners. A similar story played out at the nearby Grand Ronde Agency, where allotments left only remnant plots of land for the tribal cemetery, Catholic church, and agency buildings.[25]

The General Allotment Act affected Montana's seven reservations unevenly, with the small Rocky Boy's Reservation remaining largely intact. Mixed ownership patterns emerged on other reservations, with half the Blackfeet, Crow, and Fort Belknap reservations allotted to individual Indians. But on the Flathead (Salish-Kutenai) Reservation, 45 percent of the lands remained tribally owned, while most of the 55 percent of allotted lands passed into non-Indian ownerships. On Montana's seven reservations today, the percentage of tribal control ranges from full ownership on Rocky Boy's to approximately 25 percent on the Blackfeet, Crow, and Fort Peck reservations. Persisting efforts to turn tribal peoples into farmers and stock raisers did little to improve the health and welfare of Native people, with Indians continuing to struggle with poverty, dietary deficiencies, and disease.[26]

Because of the isolated location of northeastern Washington's Confederated Tribes of the Colville Reservation and the difficulty of transporting students to government schools, the Indian Bureau's educational initiatives did not begin until after 1900. Although the Indian Bureau established day schools for the Colville, retaining teachers proved difficult, and attendance was haphazard for several decades. The Colville's greatest struggle, however, was federal pressure to relinquish the original 2,825,500-acre executive-order reservation. The House Committee on Indian Affairs initiated a move to reduce the size of the reservation in 1891, believing that "well-ordered white communities" nearby would benefit the Colville.[27]

Although the reservation's "north half" was open to non-Indian settlement in 1900, Congress did not pass a purchase agreement until 1906, a move the Colville called a "land steal." The government promised that land sales from the north half would be placed in a fund for the "education and civilization" of the Colville people. To the present day the government continues to deny compensation for the ceded land. Elsewhere on the reservation, allotment proceeded apace, with a 1916 presidential decree opening the remaining 417,841 acres of "unallotted and unreserved" lands to non-Indian settlement.[28] With the advantage of hindsight, it is clear that federal Indian policy between 1910 and 1930 was moving through a slow transition from the arbitrary and forced assimilation policies of the nineteenth century to President Franklin D. Roosevelt's more benign New Deal programs under Indian Commissioner John Collier.

In the early twentieth century, a new generation of leaders emerged among British Columbia's First Nations people, many of them educated in mission schools and fluent in English. Like the Nisga'a from the North Coast, who formed the Nisga'a Land Committee in 1907, these people became vocal leaders in the struggle to protect aboriginal land claims. In cooperation with other coastal groups, the Nisga'a organized the Indians Rights Association in 1909 and hired a lawyer to represent them in provincial and dominion affairs. The Nisga'a Land Committee also petitioned London, declaring the right to reserve a permanent land base for their own use.[29]

With the passing years, the Nisga'a petition simmered below the surface in First Nations relations with provincial and dominion officials. The federal government's announcement in 1914 that it would refer land issues to the federal court if Indians would agree to reduce the size of their reserves angered Native villagers. Natives then formed the Allied Tribes of British Columbia to press for a resolution of the land question. The issue, however, dragged on until 1927, when the Canadian Parliament added Section 141 to the Indian Act, a measure that removed the legal standing of any organization pursuing First Nations land claims. Indians remember Section 141, according to Paul Tennant, for its draconian, heavy-handed paternalism and denial of Native rights. The Allied Tribes organization disbanded after the passage of Section 141.[30] From the government's point of view, the First Nations land question seemed settled for all time.

The Northwest's huge export markets and high prices during the frenzied wartime production boom came crashing down within a few months of the Armistice. Collapsing commodity prices hurt farmers in Montana, Idaho, and eastern Washington and contributed to an exodus of people, especially from Montana and Idaho. The 1920s and 1930s marked a significant transition in western American agriculture—fewer farmers, larger acreages, and vastly accelerated mechanization. For the state of Idaho, the Great Depression of the 1930s simply extended the economic disaster that followed the First World War. Because of plummeting prices for wheat, potatoes, and sugar beets, Idaho farmers began to default on loans by 1921, conditions that explain Idaho's second-place ranking in out-migration among western states during the 1920s.[31]

A prolonged drought and downward spiraling agricultural prices had an even greater effect in Montana. The two-decade-long homestead rush to the state's eastern counties reversed after 1920, with the exodus of farmers placing Montana at the forefront of western states in population loss. The immediate postwar years marked a turning point for the state— the end of homesteading and the onset of two decades of drought and increasing poverty. Before the war's end, drought began taking its toll, with eastern Montana wheat yields falling to 2.4 bushels per acre in 1919. Those conditions convinced discharged veterans and young homesteading families to settle elsewhere, dramatically altering the state's demography. Rotting privies, boarded-up schoolhouses, drifting dust, and rusting fence lines were left, Joseph Kinsey Howard writes, "to tell the story of the '20s, Montana's disastrous decade."[32]

Montana's tragedy included mortgage foreclosures, millions of acres of abandoned cropland, and about half the state's farmers going out of business. Montana's economic problems extended to the timber-dependent western sections of the state, where depressed lumber prices caused sawmill closures and high unemployment. Although precipitation returned to normal in the mid-1920s and wheat prices were close to prewar levels by 1929, Montana's large cast of marginal farmers had moved elsewhere. With its control of the state's newspapers and its legendary lobbying influence in Helena, the Anaconda Copper Mining Company also held the upper hand in state politics, killing tax increases on its properties and contributing mightily to the defeat of gubernatorial candidates who refused to do its bidding.[33]

During the 1920s Washington and Oregon agricultural counties shared common problems: depressed prices for wheat, cattle, wool, and other goods. West of the Cascade Range the perpetually glutted market for lumber was the most troubling issue. The Northwest's preeminent industry continued to struggle with its perennial bugaboo—glutted markets and too many mills producing too much lumber for marginal profits. When Kansas City lumberman R. A. Long opened a huge, state-of-the-art sawmill at the newly planned community of Longview, Washington, in 1924, the Long-Bell Lumber Company and a new Weyerhaeuser mill nearby worsened the industry's production crisis.[34]

On Oregon's south coast, the sprawling Coos Bay Lumber Company operation—linked to a financial and trading system stretching from Tokyo to New York to London—provides a fitting case study for the region's lumber economy. The commercial viability of that increasingly global network greatly influenced distant production centers that processed food, minerals, and construction materials marketed in metropolitan centers. With its still impressive stands of commercial timber and its dependence on logging and sawmilling, the Coos Bay area prospered and suffered within that worldwide system, its mills alternately closing and reopening in accord with market conditions. In truth, the Great Depression came early to the region's timber manufacturing centers, with lumber production in the United States in steady decline beginning in the mid-1920s.[35]

In coastal British Columbia, where employers vigorously opposed union shops after the Great War, a prolonged recession forced sharp declines in union membership. On the other hand, isolated sawmill towns and logging camps provided better living conditions and began to afford modest recreational facilities. When the recession lifted in 1923, British Columbia's southern mainland experienced dramatic economic growth, with the city of Vancouver expanding its waterfront docks and warehouses to handle the growing volume of trade with oceanic markets. Continued population growth on the Canadian prairies also provided good markets for the province's wood-products industry. Vancouver prospered in other ways, with wages increasing 12 percent between 1922 and 1928, a rate twice that for the rest of Canada. The capital city of Victoria, in contrast, witnessed a reversal of fortunes during the 1920s: an exodus of working-class people that left the city with a higher percentage of people over sixty-five than any other Canadian city.[36]

Despite booming Vancouver and the southern mainland's vibrant economy, British Columbia remained a place of "hewers of wood and drawers of water." Products from the lumber mills, mines, and coastal fisheries powered the provincial economy. Its persisting focus on resource extraction and the relative absence of secondary processing underscored British Columbia's dependence on external markets. Using the Panama Canal (completed in 1913) to strategic advantage, the province increased its exports to Atlantic markets during the 1920s, with less than 20 percent of those goods winding up in eastern Canada. Pacific markets, on the other hand, were less favorable, with international politics eventually closing trade with Japan and the Soviet port of Vladivostok.[37]

Although there were progressive accomplishments in the American Northwest, undercurrents of racism periodically burst forth, most notably during the 1920s, when citizen groups began to use direct legislation to discriminate against religious and racial minorities. The far western states—ostensibly models of progressive reform on the surface—became centers of reactionary, repressive politics. With the entrance of the Ku Klux Klan into Northwest politics, states enacted criminal syndicalism laws and adopted measures prohibiting Japanese immigrants from owning land. The Klan touched virtually every corner of western politics, with the region's congressional delegation supporting federal initiatives to prohibit immigration from southern and eastern Europe and Asia. There was something fundamentally American about white supremacist movements, especially their links to conservative ideologies and the invocation of sacred American ideals that bridged rural and urban environments and social classes.[38]

Nativist strains—expressed most conspicuously through the rise of the Ku Klux Klan in the early 1920s—ran deep through parts of the Midwest and West. Those strains of fundamentalist, 100 percent Americanism enjoyed considerable success in the Pacific Northwest, where conservative and nativist views prevailed in the midst of a largely homogeneous population with a tendency toward social, cultural, and religious conformity. Kenneth Jackson offers the following figures as "personal estimates" of Klan memberships between 1915 and 1944: Oregon, fifty thousand; Washington, twenty-five thousand; Idaho, five thousand; Montana, three thousand; California, fifty thousand; and British Columbia, thirteen thousand (this figure may be exaggerated).[39]

The sudden increase in Klan membership should be placed in the context of the Northwest's relative isolation from the enormous social and cultural changes following the European conflict: voting rights for women, Prohibition, the Bolshevik Revolution in Russia, increased discussions about sex, and the region's economic struggles. Conservative, tradition-bound citizens blamed those distractions on the growing acceptance of libertarian and licentious activities, the increasing use of automobiles, and the emergence of jazz. Ethnic prejudices, especially toward immigrants from southern and eastern Europe, added to nativist invective and derogatory commentaries.[40]

With its largely homogeneous ethnic and religious population, nativist sentiments were especially strong in Oregon, where the American Protective Association, the Federation of Patriotic Societies, and the Ku Klux Klan enrolled sizable memberships during the 1920s. Billing themselves as the guardians of traditional American institutions and values, Klan organizers made considerable progress recruiting members beginning in 1921. Within two years the Klan was instrumental in electing eastern Oregon cattleman Walter Pierce to the governor's office, gained considerable influence in the state legislature, and supported Kaspar K. Kuble (with appropriate initials) as speaker of the House of Representatives. Although Pierce remained silent on the Klan issue, recent research reveals that he was a dues-paying member of the organization.[41]

Nativist factions in the Oregon legislature used direct legislation to push their social agenda, with their most infamous effort, the Compulsory School Bill, a measure referred to voters in 1922. Supported by nativist organizations, the ballot measure required all children between the ages of eight and sixteen to attend public schools. The bill played to deeply rooted prejudices against parochial schools, specifically targeting Roman Catholics, who made up about 8 percent of the state's population. Although voters approved the measure in the fall election 115,506 to 103,685, Portland-based Sisters of the Holy Name immediately challenged its constitutionality. The Oregon Supreme Court declared the law in violation of the state constitution in 1924, a decision sustained in the U.S. Supreme Court.[42]

With the support of agricultural organizations and the American Legion, the Klan-influenced Oregon legislature passed the Alien Property Act in 1923, a law prohibiting noncitizens from owning landed property. Directed at Japanese immigrants in Portland and the Hood River Valley, the act reflected Governor Walter Pierce's request that the legislature restrict Asians from purchasing or leasing land (California and Washington enacted similar laws). The same session of the legislature banned sectarian dress from public schools and petitioned Congress to restrict Asian immigration. Although the Klan quickly faded from Oregon public life, its racist, nativist values continued to resonate with the state's citizenry. As for the conflicted Walter Pierce, he went on to become an ardent supporter of Franklin D. Roosevelt's New Deal and served five terms as a progressive congressman from eastern Oregon.[43]

Although homogeneity provides one explanation for the success of generally conservative governments in the Greater Northwest, the story is much more complex.[44] Nativist groups such as the Ku Klux Klan enjoyed sharp increases in membership, especially in Oregon and Washington, while failing to gain comparable traction in Montana and British Columbia. The Klan's virulent anti-Catholicism had less appeal in Montana industrial towns such as Butte and Anaconda, both with sizable foreign-born populations, many of them Catholics. With Butte as its dominant urban center, Silver Bow County's 1920 population was evenly divided between "native whites of native parentage" (17,644) and "native whites of foreign parentage" (17,147). With ethnic enclaves of Irish, Cornish, Italian, Finnish, and Slavic peoples, Butte may have been the prototype for a diverse western community. Despite Butte's Catholicism, the white-robed KKK succeeded in establishing a short-lived local Klan in 1923.[45]

The peripatetic Klan also sent organizers north of the border into several Canadian provinces, including British Columbia, where nativist hostility flared during the mid-1920s. Klan organizers established the Kanadian Knights of the Ku Klux Klan in British Columbia. Although Klan organizers on the prairie provinces were generally more successful, the Kleagles (organizers) were active in spreading the group's virulent brand of racist and ethnic xenophobia among receptive people in British Columbia.[46] While the Klan had largely spent its energies south of the border by 1926, the Invisible Empire maintained its strength in the Canadian provinces into the early 1930s.[47]

More than any other polity in the Greater Northwest, Washington exemplified the conservative mood in regional politics during the 1920s. Almost completely under the control of the Republican Party, with many of its members opposed to the reform statism of Theodore Roosevelt, the legislature and the governor's office focused on efficiency and cost reduction, dabbled in the occasional enforcement of Prohibition, and engaged in sometimes bizarre politics. Republicans handily won the governor's office in 1920, 1924, and 1928, with Governor Roland Hartley setting new standards in efforts to dismantle state agencies and departments that he could not directly control. With the support of the Federated Industries of Washington, the vindictive Hartley targeted University of Washington president Henry Suzzallo for removal from office. Suzzallo's sin? When he served as a federal arbitrator during the war, Suzzallo had ordered an eight-hour day in Hartley's Everett lumber mill. He had also reputedly expressed interest in statewide elective office. The governor stacked the Board of Regents with his friends, and in a bruising and ugly confrontation, the regents fired Suzzallo in October 1926. The president's dismissal, Hartley argued, helped rid the state university of "special interests."[48]

If the 1920s were reactionary, as some historians argue, then Roland Hartley is a fitting political symbol for the decade. In a biting assessment of the governor, historian Norman Clark points out that Hartley "detested prohibitionists, social workers, suffragettes, direct primaries, direct leg-islation[,] . . . radicals, agitators, internationalists, pacifists, unions, taxes, and progressive education." And he was proud of it all! Clark argues that Hartley, who promised to run the state with the same frugal practices he demanded in his mills and logging camps, "never understood the differ-ences between government and primitive capitalism." With the stock mar-ket crash and the nation's descent into economic chaos in the early 1930s, Hartley persisted in issuing irrelevant clichés in the face of strikingly different realities.[49]

As for Oregon's governor, Walter Pierce, he lost nearly all of his Dem-ocratic support in the state legislature to the Republicans in the Novem-ber election in 1924. Nevertheless, he struggled on with his progressive ideas, pushing for public power, a state hydroelectric commission with the ability to organize public utility districts, and a more equitable re-distribution of the state's tax burden. In the face of the overwhelming Republican majority, Pierce vetoed thirty-one bills, and his own initia-tives died in the legislature.[50]

Notable progressives of both parties represented Idaho and Montana in the U.S. Senate during the 1920s—while Republicans controlled the legislative roosts at home. Idaho Republican William E. Borah, elected to the U.S. Senate in 1907, served until his death in 1940. One of the most prominent senators in the nation, Borah chaired the powerful Commit-tee on Foreign Relations from 1924 to 1933 and promoted the diplomatic recognition of the Soviet Union. Borah broke with his party and refused to support Herbert Hoover for reelection in 1932 because the president opposed direct federal relief to alleviate hunger and want during the early days of the Great Depression. Montana's two Democratic senators, Thomas Walsh and Burton Wheeler (the more radical of the two), led Senate investigations of corruption in President Warren G. Harding's adminis-tration. But conservative politics reigned supreme at home in Montana, especially following the defeat of moderate Democratic governor Joseph Dixon in 1924. Following Dixon's loss, Republicans vanquished liberal and progressive forces to political oblivion, with the Anaconda Copper Mining Company largely exercising its will in state politics.[51]

In British Columbia politics followed a similar trajectory, with the reformist Liberal Party replacing the long-serving Conservatives and Pre-mier Richard McBride during the First World War. Although the Liberal governments of John Oliver and John Maclean began with lots of reform-minded energy, the party's energy dissipated in the 1920s. There was some forward movement, however: woman's suffrage in 1917, pensions for mothers and deserted wives, efforts to regulate public utilities, and initiatives to improve health and education. But with Conservatives gathering momentum, reform slowed with the passing of time. Following the party's attempt to increase royalties on timber harvests, British Columbia's powerful forest products industry played a key role in the Liberals' demise. The Conservatives returned to office in 1928 with Simon Fraser Tolmie as premier, a person ill suited by temperament and ideology to confront the social and economic chaos of the Great Depression.[52]

In his acceptance speech to the Republican National Convention in 1928, Herbert Hoover voiced the hope of the progressive managerial class that would guide American economic life into "a new era" of "prosperity, peace, and contentment." Shortly after his inauguration in March 1929, the activist president convened a special session of Congress to address the farm crisis. Lawmakers responded with the Agricultural Marketing Act to create "stabilization corporations," which would purchase farm surpluses to stabilize commodity prices. Shortly before the stock market crash of October 1929, Hoover also commissioned a committee of social scientists to gather information about American society to provide "a basis for the formulation of large national policies looking to the next phase of the nation's development." Although the economic and social firestorm that followed made a mockery of the committee's findings, *Recent Social Trends in the United States* provided rich insights into pre-Depression America.[53]

Hoover's social scientists observed that the bonanza stories about the growing wealth of Americans during the 1920s were horribly skewed because the benefits went disproportionately to the wealthy. Moreover, increases in production came at a cost—the technological displacement of workers. Although nonfarm income far outpaced agricultural income, industrial workers lacked insurance for protection against the perils of unemployment. The findings in *Recent Social Trends* reflected the stark reality for commodity-dependent regions like the Pacific Northwest, where the lumber industry—accounting for half the wages earned in Washington and Oregon—had experienced steadily declining prices since 1923. Wheat farmers across the Northwest also witnessed increasing crop surpluses and falling prices throughout the decade, with a bushel of wheat bringing $0.38 in the fall of 1929. Well before the crisis years of the early 1930s, unemployment, underemployment, and failing banks were everyday realities in the region.[54]

4
Shaping a Regional Culture, 1900–1930

In the summer of 1905, Portland's visitors and residents planned their trips to the exhibits, rides, and educational lectures of the city's Lewis and Clark Centennial and American Pacific Exposition and Oriental Fair. Arts-and-Crafts-style advertisements portrayed the fair as forward looking, modern, and *the* place to be. For the price of admission, visitors could wander the exhibit halls of twenty-one different countries. They could explore the Forestry Building, the "largest log cabin in the world," and as they wound their way through the building's timbers, they could take in the three hundred Edward Curtis prints of the West's Native people. Visitors could traipse down the Trail, a midway of thrilling rides, the Temple of Mirth, and the W. H. Barnes Exhibit of Educated Animals. And after a long, hot day, visitors could unwind at the thirty or so taverns that had sprouted just outside the fairgrounds in anticipation of large, thirsty crowds.[1]

The city of Portland planned its exposition at a time when fairs were a "virtual mania" in the United States and around the world. Spurred by promoters and business investors, fairs and expositions leave historians with rich texts in which to explore the tenor of the times, the hopes and anxieties that people shared regarding the places in which they lived. The Lewis and Clark Exposition preached a triumphalist narrative about Americans venturing west to successfully dominate a new land. Portland, assured the town's boosters, was not the isolated outpost that eastern visitors might expect; rather, it was an urbane midsized city on the brink of economic prosperity, thanks to a resource-rich hinterland. The *Pacific Monthly* reported that Portland was "in every respect an eastern city." At the same time, those jerry-built taverns—outside of the carefully controlled fairgrounds—and the pickpockets, pimps, and con artists attracted by fairs were a source of anxiety for the cities that hosted them.[2]

By nearly every measure, the Lewis and Clark Exposition was a success despite lingering concerns about crime. More than 1.5 million visitors paid to enter the fairgrounds. Nonpaying visitors—reporters, dignitaries,

Lewis and Clark Exposition catalog cover, Oregon State Library. On the Lewis and Clark Exposition catalog cover, Meriwether Lewis and William Clark stand sentry over the fruits of American expansion, a prosperous and peaceful entrance into the twentieth century, with no visible evidence of the human or environmental violence wreaked by conquest.

workers, and so on—accounted for nearly another million visits during the four-month event. Oregonians connected the state's postfair prosperity to the event, which brought tens of thousands of dollars into the regional economy in hotel rentals, restaurant and bar receipts, and entrance fees to other local attractions such as the new Portland Art Museum building and the Oaks Amusement Park, both opened in 1905 to take advantage of fairgoers. Although the fair touted the city of Portland as every bit an eastern city, most of those who attended were from Oregon and Washington, with only 10 percent of the fair's visitors from east of the Rocky Mountains. A full 74 percent of fairgoers were from Oregon and Washington, with an additional 16 percent hailing from other western states.[3] Nonetheless, the Lewis and Clark Exposition neatly divided "Old Oregon" from a new, modern American state. Historian Carl Abbott claims that "before the exposition was a month old, Portlanders were certain that it marked the beginning of a new era."[4]

Four years after Portland boosters crafted their exposition narrative, Seattle would take a crack at its own world's fair, with the same positive spin about life on the West Coast. Seattle's Alaska-Yukon-Pacific Exposition was similar to Portland's Lewis and Clark Exposition, and both followed the general model for world's fairs. Seattle's fair boasted more visitors—about seven hundred thousand more than attended the Portland event. Seattle borrowed from French Renaissance architecture, while Portland had used design elements from the Spanish Renaissance, but John Charles Olmsted designed both sites. The Portland fair occupied Guild's Lake, a swampy area that later became an industrial and residential district, but Seattle's planners used the University of Washington's new campus site as the fairgrounds, with buildings and other infrastructure improvements reverting to the university, "providing a ready-to-use campus after the exposition closed." Carl Abbott's description of the Lewis and Clark Exposition easily extends to the Alaska-Yukon-Pacific Exposition as well: both represented "community enterprise in an age of confidence." The events also indicate the region's primary cities at this early point in the twentieth century. Spokane would not host a world's fair until 1974, with Vancouver, British Columbia, following twelve years later. Montana and Idaho have yet to host such an event, though the popularity of fairs has waned over the last century.[5]

More than simply exciting ventures, these early fairs reflected the cultural currents of the Greater Pacific Northwest from the onset of the new century to the Great Depression in the 1930s. The fairs celebrated the "frontier" qualities of their host cities—the stereotypical tenacity that for many characterized westward expansion in the American and Canadian Northwest. While still claiming those positive qualities, planners placed the settlement period of Washington and Oregon, and by extension the rest of the region, squarely in the past. Despite embracing a "pioneer era," planners claimed a sophisticated and modern present in which the Pacific Northwest was intimately tied to the political, economic, and cultural life of the eastern United States and Canada and, indeed, with the rest of the world.

By highlighting the experiences of settler society, fair narratives erased the violence waged against the region's Native peoples and the environmental disturbance that was integral to the American and Canadian conquest of the Pacific Northwest. Nonetheless, fair developers, like many artists and writers, borrowed imagery from Pacific Northwest Indian people to express a deep-rooted nativeness while simultaneously drawing from classical European design to suggest common cultural roots with the East Coast. Actual Native Americans at the fairs occupied dual roles. They represented the past, as seen in the romantic Edward Curtis photographs, but entrepreneurial Indians from the Umatilla Reservation also came to Portland to sell their handicrafts at a vendor spot just outside the midway's entrance.[6]

Exhibits that highlighted modern amenities and inventions—such as the infant incubators that made an appearance at so many of the world's fairs of the time—reflected Progressive Era faith in science, reason, and technology to tackle manifold social and economic problems. Club women, artists, writers, and suffragists joined boosters and politicians and used the fairs as a forum to publicize their own agendas. Fairs reflected a tangle of cultural forms and meaning within the region. Inheritors of those expressions find connections to Native cultures, reflections of the American and Canadian migrations, as well as contentious responses to westward imperialism and anxiety about the present role of the Pacific Northwest in the nation-state, whether the United States or Canada.

At the turn of the century, the region's cities increasingly invested in cultural and educational institutions such as libraries, high schools, museums, and performing arts centers. Some of those institutions had roots in nineteenth-century efforts, such as Portland's public library, which has antecedents dating to 1864. Montana Territory boasted the first historical society west of the Missouri River when the Montana Historical

Society was established in 1865. But an expanding population in the twentieth century meant more money, larger audiences, and a better-developed infrastructure, making cultural endeavors more viable. Improved roads and more people explain why northwesterners directed their energies toward building museums and libraries and collecting materials to fill them during the first half of the twentieth century. The region's leading architects carefully designed permanent buildings to house collections of paintings, sculpture, and classic literature, a rejection of the rough-and-tumble stereotype of the Pacific Northwest.

Another important explanation for the public interest in cultural and educational organizations lies in the distress that Americans and Canadians felt about the social effects of industrialization. Concern about industrialization was reflected in the multipronged Progressive movement. Librarian and historian Cheryl Gunselman notes that Progressive Era libraries were "agencies of opportunities, providing individuals with tools for economic and social upward mobility and shaping a nation of good citizens." Simultaneously, "the public library also served as a tool for social control." The same could be said about the growth of public schools and museums, which offered residents the opportunity to enrich their lives. Those institutions were also the standard-bearers of appropriate behavior and taste.[7]

Moreover, some of those institutions sought to enrich the region by importing outside cultural forms. Art museums, theater companies, and opera houses often focused their productions on the classics or on national themes rather than reflecting regional identity or talent. Historian Jean Barman writes: "For culture to be truly high in British Columbia during the 1920s, almost by definition it had to originate elsewhere." Nonetheless, there was room for the expression of regional identities; artists and writers often attended to what was close at hand, and citizens founded historical societies with the intent to memorialize a place-specific (and sometimes nostalgic) past.[8]

Many of the region's formal institutions of higher education originated before the turn of the century, and public school systems were legislatively in place by 1900. Nonetheless, a focus on informal and formal education—Chautauqua meetings, tax-supported libraries, and public schools—reveals an active citizenry concerned about the state of child and adult education in the region. Key issues included access, quality, and cost. Remote towns and communities that developed and sometimes foundered around single industries such as mining and timber posed tremendous problems to providing state- or provincewide services. In British Columbia, access to education plagued politicians, reformers, and individual families and culminated in important innovations in correspondence courses. Concerns of access were linked to questions regarding the level of quality in education and educational services. As with other professions in the early twentieth century, teaching and librarianship underwent revolutions in training and professionalism. This nationwide trend in Canada and the United States was felt throughout the Pacific Northwest. Moreover, efforts at cross-border fertilization were important to this movement. Cost had long been an issue, with Oregon officials engaging in significant debates about the merits of state-supported high schools in the nineteenth century. Along with much of Canada and the United States, the region valued free public libraries and began putting significant municipal, county, provincial, and statewide systems into place.

Adults throughout the Pacific Northwest gathered periodically for lectures, reading and study groups, debates, and other forms of informal education. This drive for self-education was rooted in nineteenth-century clubs, lyceums, debate clubs, and reading rooms, many of which were organized by women. Chautauqua meetings, events that historian Sheri Bartlett Browne calls "a community enrichment experience unparalleled in American history," originated in upstate New York in 1874 and emerged in the region by the turn of the century as "the greatest effort in organized adult education in the Pacific Northwest." In Oregon, Eva Emery Dye and her husband, Charles, founded the Willamette Valley Chautauqua Association in 1894. The association sponsored annual Chautauqua meetings at Gladstone Park between Portland and Oregon City. For thirty years, thousands of people came to Gladstone Park each July to spend a week camping, listening to lectures, engaging in discussions of contemporary events, playing baseball, and listening to music. Dye viewed those weeks as critical to the cultural and educational development of her adopted state: "College men and women, long cut off from old privileges, come here to renew their youth; aspiring men and women who never had any advantages come here to get inspiration. Worn-out farmers' wives, grown old with toil, count as the season comes, on the lectures of Chautauqua." Although the Gladstone Park events were the largest on the West Coast and the third largest in the nation, Idaho's Spirit Lake and Washington's Vashon Island in Puget Sound also hosted large annual Chautauqua gatherings.[9]

The women who spent their free time organizing such endeavors also turned their attention to other important social institutions, such as the creation of libraries. Club women throughout the region, as historian Sandra Haarsager found, directed their energies to collecting books for public consumption and to developing physical sites dedicated to reading. Women founded reading rooms, sometimes explicitly as alternatives to saloons and in other cases simply as places where working-class and middle-class people could gather for edification. By the turn of the century, social activists were agitating for public support of libraries to foster lifelong learning. The women who comprised the "first professionally trained librarians in the West shared a vision of the library as a powerful educational agency that could preserve democracy and eradicate social ills." Although Progressive Era club women assumed that an educated citizenry was essential for the future of democracy, libraries and reading rooms were also measures of social control, places where proper behavior could be encouraged and suitable knowledge gained.[10]

The region's first libraries originated in the mid-nineteenth century with the Hudson Bay Company (whose library dated to 1833), territorial, or university efforts. When the U.S. Congress granted territorial status, it often allocated funds for territorial libraries, as it did in Oregon and Washington but not in Idaho or Montana. Reading rooms and traveling and subscription libraries filled the gap until the turn of the century, when the American states and British Columbia began to allocate funds for permanent buildings, collections, and professional staff. With state or county funds and an application to the Carnegie Foundation, brick and mortar replaced traveling cases. In the early part of the twentieth century, library buildings suggested permanence and progress. According to Haarsager, "the physical construct of a public library, with its open-ended access to what was believed to be the best the western tradition had to offer in a setting of order, was the ultimate self-improvement opportunity. And, for those who valued measures like opera stages and statehood, a good library was the standard-bearer in community validation."[11]

At the end of the nineteenth century and beginning of the twentieth century, several historic trends in reform and education coalesced to create the library systems we recognize today. The Pacific Northwest benefited from the earlier experiments in older states and provinces. Key reforms in library work were rooted in Progressive Era ideals and included the professionalization of staff and public support. Club women often had a hand in organizing libraries in whatever form they took—

from private traveling trunks of books to full-fledged systems housed in permanent buildings. These women also wrote and lobbied for legislation supporting free libraries accessible to everyone. According to historian Thomas Augst, "by 1933, some three-quarters of the [United States'] public libraries owed their origins to the fundraising and organizational work of women's clubs."[12]

A year after achieving statehood in 1890, the Washington legislature allocated funds to support public libraries. British Columbia passed a free libraries act in 1891, and Oregon and Idaho followed suit in 1901. In Oregon the Portland Women's Club spearheaded the legislation after garnering support from women's clubs across the state. Club members, including suffragist Sarah A. Evans, worked with University of Oregon historian Joseph Schafer to lobby state politicians. Those efforts illustrate the close ties between women's activism (which often included agitation for Prohibition and suffrage), the educational community, and informal adult education, ties that were common elsewhere in the United States and Canada. As one historian wrote, many women in the Pacific Northwest were politically active despite prohibitions on their voting. The combination of agitation, legislation, and Carnegie funds led to an explosion of libraries throughout the Pacific Northwest. Between 1900 and 1920 Washington built forty-four new Carnegie libraries, Oregon thirty-one, Montana seventeen, and Idaho ten. While Carnegie funds made their way into Canada, only three Carnegie libraries were built in British Columbia.[13]

The Progressive Era urge to professionalize and make public schools more uniform matched the promotion of professional standards in libraries. School systems across the United States and Canada came under scrutiny at the turn of the century, but those in the West were particularly underfunded compared to the East and Midwest. Substandard buildings, curricula, and teacher's pay as well as a lack of qualified teachers plagued public school systems in the Pacific Northwest. These problems were the result of the remoteness of many students and funding structures that relied on property taxes to support numerous small districts. Individual schools varied widely in curriculum offerings and in the length of the academic year. Schools on Indian reservations and the educational opportunities afforded the region's African American students were the most troublesome. Progressive reformers viewed education as a panacea for the rapid social and economic changes brought by industrialization, with public schools, according to education historian Timothy Dunn, "the most potent institution to deal with disorder." Tax-supported schools would also equalize access to economic opportunities in the West; it was not by accident that both child labor and compulsory school attendance laws were passed in the first decades of the twentieth century.[14]

More than any other challenge, the scattered nature of the region's communities made providing educational opportunities difficult. In British Columbia administrators had to deliver services to towns and cities stretched over 360,000 geographically diverse square miles. There were other problems. Communities dependent on extractive industries appeared and disappeared—as did their students—with the alternating booms and busts that characterized much of the region's economy. Moreover, some schools closed when students left to work in nearby agricultural fields. Vast distances and difficult terrain led to the development of many small districts until improved roads and motor vehicles made traveling to consolidated schools possible. By the 1920s, Idaho boasted 1,771 school districts that served about 115,000 students, and Montana was home to 2,500 one- and two-room schoolhouses. To reach its distant students, British Columbia pioneered correspondence education, enrolling by the mid-1930s approximately 20 percent of the province's students in correspondence courses, the precursors of today's distance learning courses. By the Second World War, the region would begin the process of consolidating its public school system and bussing students to larger, centralized schools.[15]

Access to education was even more complicated for the region's African American students. Communities in at least two states barred black students from attending schools with their white counterparts. The Montana legislature passed a law in 1872 that, in part, required that black students be educated separately from white students; the legislature reversed course in 1883. Oregon towns such as Coos Bay on the southern coast, Vernonia west of Portland, and Maxville near La Grande segregated African American students in their public schools in the twentieth century. Regardless of education, for many of the region's African Americans limited employment options meant that a high school or college diploma did not hold the value that it did in white communities. Many black college graduates labored at menial posts, unable to break into the trades or the professions until the Second World War. In a post–World War Two survey, Seattle's black community expressed satisfaction with the school system despite having low high school and college graduation rates compared to the rest of the city. More education simply did not mean better economic opportunities.[16]

If the region's African American children had sometimes limited access to education, the United States and Canada implemented policies that coerced Native American and First Nations families to enroll children in government-approved schools. Both nations enforced assimilation through education for aboriginal children. By the early twentieth century, British Columbia had turned away from removing Indian children from their homes and placing them in boarding schools in favor of less expensive day schools. Canada's First Nations children attended 221 day schools in 1900 in contrast to the 40 boarding schools in which they had been taught. According to historian Roger Nichols, however, in the United States boarding schools were still operating "under a full head of steam at the turn of the century."[17]

Schools, less formal educational venues, and libraries extended opportunities to most of the region's people. At the same time, those opportunities were often meant to instruct the masses in norms of behavior and taste. Arguments regarding whether librarians should purchase novels with public funds, for example, illustrate concerns over the reading habits of a town's residents and a willingness to allow "experts" to proscribe books. Moreover, at the very time that many politicians and social activists were attempting to organize school districts in the farthest reaches of the region, some excluded African American and Native students or advocated only vocational curricula for them, thereby limiting their educational experiences and denying them the full benefits of residency.

Just as railroads knit the Pacific Northwest to the rest of North America, the region's museums, symphonies, opera houses, and elite theaters connected its residents to the cultural tastes and predilections of the United States, Canada, and Europe. In many ways, the cultural transfer was one-way, with local institutions bringing in the best of the world beyond the Northwest that they could appropriate. For many, true culture was made elsewhere. To house, perform, or exhibit culture reflected a region moving toward maturity. The Vancouver Art Gallery opened its doors in 1931 with an initial collection drawn from European artists. Historian Jean Barman writes that the museum "ignored not only British Columbian artists' work but that of almost all Canadian painters."[18]

There were exceptions to the rejection of locally created culture. Anthropologists and archaeologists collected Native-created stories and material items that would eventually form collections in natural history and anthropological museums and become part of the holdings at art museums as well. Novelists and poets gravitated toward themes that reflected the landscape and history around them. And organized groups formed historical societies to tell the region's history to visitors and to remind future generations of northwesterners of their shared past.

Nineteenth-century settlement and economic patterns meant that Portland would build the region's first art museum in 1895 in the city's downtown library building. A new building nearby was opened in 1905, coinciding with the city's Lewis and Clark Exposition. Unlike Vancouver's museum, the Portland Art Museum had a dual mission: to expose Oregonians to high-quality art in exhibits originating outside the region and to encourage the productivity and visibility of regional artists. An art school associated with the museum opened in 1909, with some of the students contributing to exhibits of regional art beginning in 1911. Washington launched its first art museum in 1927, when the Henry Art Museum opened in Seattle, and Idaho opened the Boise Art Museum in 1931, the same year that the Vancouver Art Museum opened in British Columbia. Although the Montana Institute of the Arts would not open until after the Second World War, the Montana Historical Society Museum often showcased artwork from Montana and beyond.[19]

If libraries, museums, and adult education brought extraregional culture to the Pacific Northwest, the region's elite founded historical societies to reflect state and regional identity. Residents initially established historical societies to collect the stories and relics that celebrated white settlement. Heroic narratives of ordinary people surviving an overland journey of thousands of miles and then civilizing the wilderness preoccupied the founders of those stateside institutions, while avocational historians in British Columbia focused on the province's distinctiveness from the rest of Canada and its links to Great Britain.

Montana established the first historical society west of the Mississippi River in 1865, one that is still extant. Washington and Oregon established societies in 1891 and 1898, respectively, with Idaho forming its museum in 1910. As historian David Wrobel demonstrates in his study of pioneer associations, state historical societies constructed narratives that often celebrated a past rooted in the struggle to overcome "wilderness" and "savagery" and fashion new civilizations in the continent's farthest corner. These narratives justified American and Canadian expansion, obscured the violence directed at Indian and First Nations people, and erased the struggles of the region's many nonelite groups. They also provided a common past linking citizens to the emerging American and Canadian regions.[20]

The Northwest's cultural institutions often shared a contradictory relationship with the region they served. One kind of collecting that joined museum curators, owners of small businesses, tourists, and amateurs in a common endeavor, however, was the amassing of Native American and First Nations "artifacts." Northwesterners and those outside the region channeled tools, carvings, jewelry, clothing, and even intellectual property such as songs, prayers, and family stories into their collections, divorcing them from their original community-embedded meanings. Collecting Native knowledge—represented in the careful carving of small argillite pipes or in the mythological stories that generations of people used to teach their children—was complicated business. Collectors sometimes stole items, surreptitiously cutting house totem poles at the base to carry them off to museums, but many also fostered friendships with Indian people, who found new outlets for their baskets and other items.

From first contact, American and European entrepreneurs and the nations that supported them and vied for control of the Pacific Northwest collected information about Native people with whom they sought to trade. Anthropologist Kathleen S. Fine-Dare argues that the Lewis and Clark expedition was the "first major expedition organized to collect objects of American 'natural' history," including Native American artifacts. A market in curios, masks, and baskets developed alongside that of animal pelts. Simultaneously, imperial governments began the process of categorizing tribes and their allies and enemies. By the mid-nineteenth century, governmental bodies in both the United States and Canada had collected information about Northwest Indians to assist in the implementation of federal Indian policies—in the United States, treaties and reservations; in Canada, small reserves that set aside resource sites such as fishing stations. Anthropology and archaeology arose in part in North America as a way to document the Native cultures that many assumed would give way to the onslaught of immigration, with its farms, railroads, and cities.[21]

The completion of the Canadian Pacific Railroad brought the person many consider the father of American anthropology, Franz Boas, to British Columbia, where he studied the Native peoples in the province for more than ten years. Boas wrote multiple reports based on his research that became critical reading within federal agencies and compelling reading for many people. One such reader was Joseph E. Standley, the proprietor of Ye Olde Curiosity Shop on Seattle's waterfront. According to historian Kate Duncan, the most important source for Standley's understanding of Native cultures in the Pacific Northwest was Boas's 1897 report, *The Social Organization and the Secret Societies of the Kwakiutl Indians*. Founded in 1899, Standley's shop became a sort of museum for Seattle residents interested in curiosities and in Native cultures in Washington and Alaska. Joseph Standley's collections were extensive and his knowledge of Indian material culture was significant, but his influence in shaping Seattle's Native "look" was unparalleled. Standley encouraged Native carvers and weavers to re-create the items pictured in Boas's book and lent the text to organizers of the Alaska-Yukon-Pacific Exposition. Doing so made Standley an "agent to new hybrid styles that would become significant in the development of Northwest Coast tourist art." Moreover, portions of his collections became part of the permanent holdings at Manhattan's Museum of the American Indian (now a Smithsonian museum), the Royal Ontario Museum, the Newark Museum, the Horniman Museum, the Burke Memorial Washington State Museum, and the Portland Art Museum.[22]

Franz Boas, James Teit, George Hunt, Edward Sapir, and many other ethnographers, anthropologists, and linguists became renowned for the stories, dictionaries, histories, and genealogies they collected among the Northwest's Native population. For Native and non-Native historians today, these texts form the foundation of knowledge of Native people undergoing tremendous cultural, political, and economic transformation. Lucullus Virgil McWhorter, a rancher born in West Virginia who moved to Washington's Yakima Valley as an adult in 1903, spent his free time collecting archival and photographic materials and, perhaps most important, interviews with Indian people of the Columbia Plateau. His work with Nez Perce and Yakama Indians aided in the documentation of the Plateau and Nez Perce Indian wars as well as the federal government's treatment of Indian people during the reservation period. The Yakama Nation formally adopted McWhorter in 1909 to honor him for his diligence in documenting Native history and for his kindness to Indian people.[23]

Nearly two decades later, McWhorter was instrumental in having the first novel authored by a Native American woman published. Cristal McLeod (Mourning Dove, or Hum-ishu-ma), an Okanogan woman who carted her typewriter from one migrant camp to another as she labored in hop fields and apple orchards, wrote most of *Cogewea, the Half-Blood: A Depiction of the Great Montana Cattle Range* (1927). For twenty years McWhorter encouraged Mourning Dove in her writing, much of which was based on the traditional stories of the Okanogan. Their correspondence reveals a close friendship and collaboration, leading one commentator to note that "neither Mourning Dove nor McWhorter could have written the book without the other." Hailed by Dexter Fisher as "a man of the utmost integrity whose genuine interest in Indian history and culture became the center of his work and publications," Mc-Whorter was dedicated to collecting information about the lifeways of the region's Indian inhabitants and documenting their mistreatment at the hands of federal agencies and white landowners. After McWhorter's death in 1944, his papers became part of the archival holdings at Washington State University, where the region's Indian and non-Indian scholars continue to examine them.[24]

Another collector was Lee Moorhouse, an amateur photographer in Pendleton, Oregon. From his late forties through his midsixties, Moorhouse photographed nearly nine thousand images, including hundreds of photographs depicting Native Americans. Moorhouse was a Pendleton businessman who held various appointed political positions, including his appointment as the Indian agent at the nearby Umatilla Reservation (1889–91). His photographic subjects included agricultural activities, Indian boarding schools, tribal leaders such as the Nez Perce Chief Joseph, and the Pendleton Round-Up, a rodeo founded in 1910.

Moorhouse carefully posed Indian people, adorning them with accessories from his own curio collection. In doing so, his work reflects the kinds of culture-laden alterations that other photographers made, including Edward S. Curtis, to create images that reaffirmed consumer beliefs about Indian people. Moorhouse's romantic images became the visual basis for advertising an "authentic" inland Northwest to local residents and outsiders alike. One of his postcards boasting an image of two Cayuse infants sold 150,000 copies, while Pendleton Woolen Mills used Moorhouse's images to sell blankets and marketed copies of the images themselves. The Pendleton Round-Up also used Moorhouse's photographs to advertise its western-themed entertainment.

Moorhouse viewed himself as an artist rather than as a documentarian. Even so, he was unique among his contemporaries in that he named his Indian subjects. He understood, as one commentator put it, that "he was photographing people." One of the women whom he repeatedly photographed was Anna Kash Kash, a woman he described as "well educated, a graduate of the Carlisle Indian school" who had taught Indian pupils at Carlisle and in Oklahoma. Although Moorhouse wrote about some Indian subjects complaining about being photographed, curator

Steven Grafe points out that "the frequency with which Moorhouse photographed specific individuals and events suggests that he enjoyed a level of familiarity with his Indian neighbors."[25]

The legacies of collectors such as Joseph E. Standley, Lucullus Virgil McWhorter, and Lee Moorhouse are certainly contested ground. By purchasing and sometimes stealing the material wealth of Indian people for private or public purposes, collectors removed items from their cultural context, often making them part of new narratives of conquest that physically and politically displaced Native people and relegated them to a distant and romantic past. Moorhouse published fifty of his posed images of Indian people in a book titled *Souvenir Album of Noted Indian Photographs* (1906). He alternated photographs with his poems, one of which related "the story of the race; / Vanquished by too great odds."

Because these material items, images, and intellectual property entered the marketplace, collecting was often tied to efforts to re-vision goods to fit preconceived ideas about what was "authentically" Indian. Non-Kwakiutl (Kwakwaka'wakw) carvers copied Kwakiutl designs because Standley found them marketable; McWhorter encouraged Mourning Dove to turn her attention to fiction rather than record the folklore of her people; and Moorhouse used props to turn Indians who normally wore store-bought clothes into the Noble Savages who could sell postcards. Nonetheless, collectors also played an important role in documenting the region's Native cultures, however imperfectly, efforts that are reflected in the work of contemporary historians and seen around the world in museum collections.[26]

Emily Carr's (1871–1945) modernist paintings captured British Columbia's fecund forestlands and the majestic totem poles of coastal First Nations villages in broad, colorful brush strokes. In another corner of the Northwest, Charles M. Russell (1864–1926), "Montana's Cowboy Artist," realistically depicted the sparse windswept plains of the interior as well as the horsemen who traveled them, the musculature of man and animal rendered precisely. Friendly contemporary critics of both artists described them as documentarians, capturing a vivid earlier period or quickly disappearing time when Native people dominated a wild land; their work came to represent the promise of the West but also its passing. Historian Brian Dippie, an authority on Russell, writes that "Russell's romanticism rested on his belief that things were best left in their natural state; improvement invariably meant decline, the artificial in place of the natural."

A critic writing about Emily Carr's solo show in Victoria in 1930 contended that her work illustrated "a migrant, vanishing race . . . a land of vast loneliness brooding over the forgotten relics of the Red Man."[27]

The land and its original inhabitants guided Carr and Russell as they composed their work, although their paintings are very different in style. Rather than simply documenting what they saw, however, they and other early twentieth-century writers and artists articulated narratives about the place and its people. Artists like Carr and Russell prodded their viewers to recognize the beauty of Native lands and cultures as well as the costs of colonization and modernization. Their artistic techniques often revealed broad, international training and the influence of their contemporaries, while their subjects remained rooted in the region. Carr studied in Paris, while the self-taught Russell spent time in New York, where he carefully studied the techniques of other artists. Many Northwest artists were drawn to Europe's artistic centers in Germany and France, while visiting artists, such as New York impressionist Childe Hassam, inspired local enthusiasts and popularized Pacific Northwest landscapes in their own work.

Individual artistic enterprise often reflected national and international trends. With roots in Europe, the international artistic and aesthetic Arts and Crafts movement valued good design, careful craftsmanship, and connections to place. Adherents of Arts and Crafts values in the Northwest founded societies to meet and celebrate those aims in nearly every city in the region. The movement made an indelible mark on the architecture, art, and print culture of the region beginning in the late nineteenth century and lasting into the mid-twentieth century. According to art historians Lawrence Kreisman and Glenn Mason, supporters of the Arts and Crafts movement discovered in Native crafts such as baskets and wood carvings the foundational ideals of beauty, simplicity, and good design. That appreciation of Native arts spread so that the inclusion of Indian handcrafted items became suggestive of an appreciation of local beauty. "American Indian objects became part of the expected décor," the historians suggest, "in the lobbies of many early rustic lodges, inns, and hotels not only nationally but also in the Cascade Range and Olympic Mountains, along Puget Sound, or on the shores of the Pacific Coast."[28]

Unequal access to artistic opportunities due to gender, race, and class inequalities persisted despite sketch clubs, professional training in distant places, and the artistic crosscurrents that modern communication and transportation technologies such as the railroad and telegraph

Emily Carr, *Totem Poles, Kitseukla*, Vancouver Art Gallery. Many contemporary critics credited Emily Carr with capturing the remnants of a quickly vanishing period in her paintings that depict Native material culture.

Charles Russell, *Sun Worship in Montana*, Amon Carter Museum. Historian
Ginger Renner has pointed out that Russell's paintings of Indian women
honor a capable domesticity. This painting's unnamed subject is physically
strong and nearly ceremonial in a pose that celebrates motherhood.

brought to the region. Despite common themes within their work, Carr and Russell lived very different lives. Charlie Russell married Nancy Cooper, who distinguished herself as a promoter of her husband's paintings. Her labor increased Russell's visibility in the American West and in the East, where collectors with deep pockets underwrote his thirty-three-year career as an artist. Carr remained unmarried, and though she would be recognized as an important Canadian artist within her lifetime, she struggled to make a living. At various times, according to art historian Sonia Halpern, Carr "conducted art classes for children, ran her own boarding house, grew and sold fruit, raised hens and rabbits, bred dogs, and sold pottery and rugs that she had made herself."[29]

Historian Jean Barman points out that while most of the students at prewar art schools in British Columbia were women, most of their teachers were men. Professional art was seen largely as the domain of men, with one of her critics telling Carr that "women can't paint; that faculty is the property of men only." The careers of women such as Anna Belle Crocker stand in stark contrast to the stereotyping critics. As the curator of the Portland Art Museum and head of the Museum Art School from 1909 to 1936, Crocker championed local artists and introduced museumgoers to art from around the world. Despite prejudice, many women, like their talented male counterparts, made their mark in the region's burgeoning art world.[30]

Some early commentators worried that Northwest writers were at best saccharine and at worst derivative. The women and men who attempted to describe the region's glorious landscape—sublime in its beauty, fraught with danger, and overwhelming in its massive scale—too often resorted to purple prose. Adell Parker, president of the University of Washington alumni association, urged his alma mater to focus on developing a vigorous regional culture in 1894: "Something wild and free, something robust and full will come out of the West and be recognized in the final American type. Under the shadow of those great mountains a distinct personality shall arise, it shall adopt other fashions, create new ideals, and generations shall justify them." Other observers did not share his confidence. Even into the 1980s, journalists assured Northwest readers that "we have more good books than you might think." The region's authors could be grouped in various ways—by their gender, by their roots in journalism and teaching, and by whether they favored poetry or prose, memoir or fiction. The most important division in early-twentieth-century

Northwest writing, however, was between those writers whose prose and poetry were sentimental and those who favored realism. Like many of the region's artists, writers wove the landscape into their work and borrowed from the rich Native cultures of the region.[31]

Nineteenth-century regional writing tended toward sentimental narratives that followed the development of the American or Canadian Northwest, a trend that continued into the early twentieth century. The most popular regional novel at the turn of the century was Frederic Homer Balch's historical romance *Bridge of the Gods*, written when he was twenty-six years old. First published in 1890, the book would go through twenty-nine editions by 1935 and to this date has not been out of print. *Bridge of the Gods* focuses on Native people in the Columbia River gorge and a minister who sought to Christianize them. Like Balch, Eva Emery Dye popularized the region's past through historical romances. Dye wrote several popular books, including *McLoughlin and Old Oregon* (1900), *The Conquest: The True Story of Lewis and Clark* (1902), which introduced readers to the role of Sacajawea in the expedition, and *McDonald of Oregon: A Tale of Two Shores* (1906). Sidney Warren, a mid-twentieth-century critic, described Dye's novels as "not as trite as most of the romantic fiction written by her contemporaries, and they did help to make Easterners aware of the Northwest." *The Conquest* became a play performed in New York's Belasco Theater to coincide with the opening of the Lewis and Clark Exposition in 1905.[32]

Eva Emery Dye at times felt constrained by the expectations placed upon her by local boosters who desired a literature that would promote the region. According to Sidney Warren, Dye "complained that Oregonians were interested in having native authors treat only with indigenous subjects and were reluctant to see them branch out." Other writers sought to break free from romance as a genre when it came to treating the region's subjects. In 1927 Oregon writers H. L. Davis and James Stevens self-published about two hundred copies of a short pamphlet, "Status Rerum: A Manifesto, Upon the Present Condition of Northwestern Literature Containing Several Near-Libelous Utterances, Upon Persons in the Public Eye." The pamphlet decried the state of regional literature, claiming that "the Northwest—Oregon, Washington, Idaho, Montana—has produced a vast quantity of bilge, so vast, that few books which are entitled to respect are totally lost in the general and seemingly interminable avalanche of tripe." The realism that Davis and Stevens advocated reflected the American school of naturalism represented at the turn of the century by Theodore Dreiser, Frank Norris, and Stephen Crane.[33]

Davis, Stevens, and Idaho's Vardis Fisher all wrote about regional subjects in ways that contrasted starkly with the romanticism of previous writers. Hardworking and hardscrabble loggers, farmers, and day laborers who were not so much inspired by the West's oversized landscape as overwhelmed by it replaced heroic pioneers, missionaries, and early statesmen. Fictional characters came to know the land through the work they performed, most of it hard physical labor related to the region's extractive industries: picking hops, running riverboats, working on green chains (sorting lumber before it dries), and sheepherding. According to historian Harold Simonson, "both Davis and Stevens interpreted the Northwest in terms of people who lived hard because living was hard." Fisher turned his pen to describe the difficult life of Idahoan farmers. His novels were "critical of Idaho frontier life and the Puritan rigidity of his family and [Mormon] church standards." All three authors drew from their own personal experiences in their writing.[34]

Harold Lenoir Davis was born near Roseburg, Oregon, at the turn of the nineteenth century. As an adult he labored at various jobs while he honed his skills as a poet, short story writer, and eventually novelist. His most important book was the Pulitzer Prize–winning *Honey in the Horn* (1935). Many have compared the novel to Mark Twain's *Adventures of Huckleberry Finn* for its broad cast of characters, including thieves and lynchers, meandering plot, and young protagonist, Clay Calvert. Davis would be remembered for drawing national recognition to Pacific Northwest literature as well as for being "a cantankerous rowdy and hard-drinking roustabout."[35]

James Stevens grew up in Idaho and worked in numerous labor-intensive jobs—road building, mining, and logging—from the time he was fifteen. Stevens resurrected and popularized Paul Bunyan, the larger-than-life logger, in *Paul Bunyan* (1925). In *Big Jim Turner* (1948) his protagonist "knew the adversities of the 72-hour work week, aching muscles, freezing winters, and blazing summers." Both Davis and Stevens celebrated what they viewed as the tough-as-nails characters that comprised and in many ways were products of the region they inhabited. Theirs were masculine stories in which men fought the land and each other in exhibitions of strength and endurance. One chronicler called it "culture with caulk boots"; another described it as "aggressive realism."[36]

Vardis Fisher, who was born in Annis, Idaho, in 1895 on an isolated homestead, held a doctorate from the University of Chicago and spent the early part of his career in universities. His fiction, like Dye's, was often historical. One novel addressed the tragedy of the Donner party (*The Mothers: An American Saga of Courage*, 1943) and another focused on the history of the Mormons (*Children of God*, 1939, winner of that year's Harper Prize in fiction). As director of the Works Progress Administration's Idaho Writers' Project (1935–39), Vardis wrote *Idaho: A Guide in Word and Picture* (1937), which became the model for other WPA-sponsored state guidebooks. In all, he wrote thirty-eight books, including a twelve-volume fictional human history series, Testament to Man. Although he was prolific, critics judged his work as uneven, praising some novels while panning others. Above all, Fisher earned a reputation as an exceptional regionalist, a designation he shared with Davis. Both men chafed at the perceived limits of such a designation. Moreover, Fisher believed that northeastern publishing houses—what he described as "the emotionally immature, intellectually sterile, and morally bankrupt literary establishment"—sought to undermine the burgeoning tradition of western literature of which he was a part.[37]

Regional realists located authenticity in those who worked in extractive industries, labor that characterized much of the Northwest economy. Most of the time, realists favored the rural and out-of-doors over the urban, the working class over the gentry, and male protagonists over female ones. But just as men participated in the sentimental myth building of Victorian era fiction, twentieth-century women wrote about the region in stark and uncompromising ways. Annie Pike Greenwood, who published her memoir *We Sagebrush Folks* in 1934, described life on a new irrigation project near Twin Falls, Idaho, in ways that reflected the difficulty of farm life before the Second World War, especially for women isolated in their homes. Two earlier works, Sui Sin Far's collection of short stories, *Mrs. Spring Fragrance* (1912), and Ella Higginson's novel, *Mariella; of Out-West* (1924), addressed the region's racism and classism, respectively. The stories of Sui Sin Far (Edith Maud Eaton) took place in the Chinatowns of Seattle and San Francisco and highlighted issues of assimilation and the anti-Asian hysteria so prevalent on the West Coast for much of the early twentieth century. Higginson was better known as a poet (she was Washington's poet laureate) and short story writer, but her only novel took up similar themes addressed in her other work: the poverty and isolation associated with farm life.

One commonality among all of these writers was their contributions to regional and national newspapers and magazines. The poems and short stories of the Northwest's writers appeared in *Harper's, Overland Monthly, McClure's,* and *American Mercury,* providing them with national exposure. Regional outlets were also important. Harold G. Merriam at the University of Montana greatly influenced the development of regional literature when in 1920 he founded the *Frontier,* a student literary journal. In 1927 Merriam revamped the publication into a regional literary magazine in the hopes of strengthening a Northwest literary identity. In his memoir he recalled being "conscious of the necessity . . . of getting the Pacific Northwest states . . . to realize their common culture. It seemed as if the region had no sense of being a unit. If possible I hoped that *The Frontier* might help to establish some such unity in literary matters."[38]

Col. Ernest Hofer, a former newspaper editor for the *Salem Capital Journal,* was less concerned about place-based literature when he founded the *Lariat* in 1923, but the pamphlet provided an important forum for the region's writers. The publication eschewed "modern" poetry in favor of the sentimental literature identified with the Victorian era and, in many cases, printed what Hofer's daughter, the poetry editor, deemed "terrible." In their diatribe Davis and Stevens singled out the *Lariat* as one of the reasons why literature in the region did not compare with the high quality of literature in other places. Though founded a bit later, British Columbia's *Contemporary Verse: A Canadian Quarterly* also published the works of regional writers as well as "virtually every modern Canadian poet between 1941 and 1951."[39]

At the onset of the twentieth century, the Lewis and Clark Exposition celebrated the region's authors with Western Author Week. The Portland Art Museum, which opened a new exhibit space to coincide with the fair, showcased local artists alongside others from around the world, "final confirmation that civilization and culture now extended all the way to the Pacific Coast." Eva Emery Dye, one of the founders of the Women's Club of the Lewis and Clark Exposition and of the Sacagawea Statue Association, spoke at the unveiling of the statue on the Portland fairgrounds, tying the romantic art and literature of the region to one of its hottest turn-of-the-century events. Boosters were just as eager to promote the region's cultural products as they were its wheat, apples, wool, and timber.[40]

Despite the moving pictures and other technological innovations high-lighted at the exposition, many northwesterners joined their counter-parts across Canada and the United States who worried about the pace and costs of modernity. Boosters loved fairs, but these same events split host communities because many people feared that the events loosened common moral ties. The taverns that greeted fairgoers as soon as they left the grounds at Guild's Lake concerned Portlanders who viewed the bars' out-of-town owners as ne'er-do-wells who cared little about the city's welfare. Developers refused to allow the midway concessions to operate on Sundays and instead brought in preachers to minister to Sun-day's crowds, practices that were later banned by court order. To curb the exploitation of young female visitors, the Portland Traveler's Aid chapter sent volunteers to greet them, offering them job and housing tips that had been vetted for safety by the organization. One of these volunteers, Lola Baldwin, became the first municipally paid policewoman in the United States.[41]

Similar fears regarding moral corruption linked to modernity could be found in the efforts to develop library and school systems, to curb the growth of dance halls and movie theaters, and to promote optimistic images of the region. Related fears infused cultural institutions and ex-pressions. Popular amusements attracted diverse people—lower- and middle-class visitors, black and white families, and young men and women who dodged parental supervision to clutch one another on rollercoaster rides. Part of the thrill of new amusements was the ability of visitors to shirk contemporary constrictions despite the policing of amusement parks, natatoriums, and theaters.

Historian Sara Paulson has traced the advertising campaigns for Oaks Park, an amusement park and skating rink in southeast Portland. The ads attempted to assure Portland residents that the park was suitable for middle-class families despite a popular reputation for sexualized rowdi-ness. The amusement parks that brought young single women and men together for rides and dances were likely to separate out people of color, especially from the parks' swimming pools, restaurants, and dance halls. Washington Water Power, owner of Spokane's Natatorium Park, was the first city agency in Spokane to be sued for discrimination when the park's restaurant denied service to Emmett Holmes in 1900 (he lost his case). Segregation in the region's amusement sites, often unstated in official policies but understood by visitors, continued well into the twentieth century.[42]

The personal and organized struggles of marginalized people would loosen the region's de facto segregation, especially after the Second World War. Time softened fears of modernity and a rapidly changing society. By the 1930s, movies had become commonplace entertainment for people of all classes and were no longer regarded as the moral threat that they were when first popularized. Several Northwest writers found their ideas and words projected onto the big screen—Montanans Dorothy Johnson (*The Man Who Shot Liberty Valance*, filmed in 1962, and *A Man Called Horse*, published in 1950 and made into a film in 1970) and A. B. Guthrie (*The Way West*, published in 1949 and filmed in 1967), to name two. On the other hand, the popular culture and literary magazines that published many Northwest authors declined in number over the course of the century. And the events of the 1930s would raise new fears, many of them tied to the depressed economy and reflected in the art and cultural institutions of the region.

5
Descent into Despair and War

At one time, Roy Olmstead was the boy wonder of the Seattle police force, joining the department in 1906 and rising to the level of lieutenant before he was dismissed in 1920 for running booze on Puget Sound. The end of his career as a cop, however, was fortuitous, giving Olmstead more freedom to pursue full time the more lucrative side of his life, his fast boats delivering liquor around the sound, especially to Seattle. Over the years he became wealthy, well connected with the Queen City's elites, entertaining in grand fashion, the dapper citizen who moved easily about the city. But Roy Olmstead's lavish lifestyle caught up with him; federal authorities arrested and indicted him in early 1925 for violating the National Prohibition Act. Several months later, a jury found him guilty and sentenced him to four years of hard labor at Washington's McNeil Island federal prison. Because the charges against him involved wire-tapped conversations, Olmstead remained out on bail while his lawyers appealed the case all the way to the U.S. Supreme Court. When the justices upheld the legality of wiretapping, Olmstead returned to McNeil Island to serve out his term.[1]

When the notorious bootlegger walked free from McNeil Island in May 1931 and crossed Puget Sound to Seattle, he entered a dramatically different world, one of shuttered mills and banks, moored fishing boats, and the city's notorious skid-road district filled with drifting men. "The parties, the adventure, the big money, the great humor, these were all gone," Norman Clark writes. The Seattle Olmstead returned to was in the midst of a downward spiral into social and economic turmoil. "Hoover-villes" were rising around the city, the most prominent at the waterfront site of abandoned shipyards, where homeless people scrounged through construction debris and packing boxes to piece together makeshift shanties—"a city within the city." With unemployment in the extractive industries rising daily, consumer purchasing power declined, rippling across the city and putting more people out of work. By the close of Roy Olmstead's first year out of prison, it was becoming increasingly apparent that unemployment would not go away.[2]

The city of Portland's self-proclaimed reputation for conservative and tradition-bound politics was put to the test with the onset of the Great Depression. Unemployment, on the increase since 1927 in the construction industries and building trades, worsened the lumber industry's perennial difficulties with overproduction and contributed to an increasing number of mill closures. During the depths of the Depression in the summer of 1932, with 25 percent unemployed nationally, an estimated thirty thousand people were out of work in Multnomah County, approximately one-third of the state's workforce. Elected as an independent to the Oregon governor's office in 1930, Julius Meier wrote to President Hoover asking for assistance: "We must have help from the federal government if we are to avert suffering and possible uprisings."[3]

The collapsing economy quickly overwhelmed Portland's private relief efforts, job placement services, donations of food and clothing, and meal tickets for destitute families. When Franklin Roosevelt was inaugurated in March 1933, forty thousand Portland residents were on various kinds of relief, and twenty-four thousand heads of households were registered with the local employment office. Like the city of Seattle, Portland also witnessed the emergence of progressive, even radical, unemployed councils. When the city's Unemployed Citizens' League requested a meeting with highway commissioner Leslie Scott (one-third owner of the *Portland Oregonian*) to discuss the potential for public works projects, Scott told the group: "What you people don't seem to realize is that there is no demand for your labor anymore. . . . The taxpayer has no use for your labor." The crusty patrician was apparently unaware that he was speaking to a doctor, teacher, lawyer, merchant, real estate salesman, and retired army officer.[4]

The stock market crash of 1929 confirmed a well-known reality for people in the Northwest—that they lived in a globalized economy that harbored special consequences for communities dependent on natural resources. Although Wall Street was distant from British Columbia, Canada's fastest-growing province fell to the same downward-spiraling economic chaos, with the stock market collapse reverberating through Vancouver, the province's principal metropolis, with devastating consequences. As the principal West Coast shipping port for Canadian resources, Vancouver was always vulnerable to cyclical shifts in the demand for lumber, processed fish, and agricultural products and minerals from the interior. Although Vancouver and the provincial economy prospered through most of the 1920s, the sharp decline in construction, collapsing markets, and shrinking tax base reversed British Columbia's fortunes. As conditions worsened through 1930 and 1931, a Vancouver council member telegraphed federal officials about the city's desperate circumstances: "More than 15,000 registered [for relief]. Twenty-five hundred relief families now requiring clothing and rent. Two thousand homeless single men increasing by seventy floaters daily."[5]

With hope fading that the failing economy would right itself, provincial officials argued that the crisis was a federal responsibility. Vancouver property values plummeted, with lots once valued at more than $1,000 selling for $50 or less.[6] With hungry and unemployed men wandering the countryside, the depression was especially hard on women, because provincial and Vancouver officials did not consider them to be part of the workforce. Left to fend for themselves, many women found it difficult to obtain relief, despite being homeless and without a job. Contemporary social activist Dorothy Livesay was alarmed by the condition of

Vancouver, British Columbia, May Day demonstration (May 1, 1936). During the Great Depression, unemployed workers gathered in front of the YMCA building on Dunsmuir Street, protesting for public relief and jobs. Vancouver witnessed periodic public demonstrations of this kind; they lasted throughout the 1930s.

many women, especially those who were "caught in the trap of having illegitimate children, begging on the streets, prostituting themselves, of women who had no training for anything but hard jobs cleaning offices."[7]

Even more desperate conditions existed in Montana and Idaho, states already witnessing an exodus of impoverished immigrants to the West Coast. Montana lost more than eleven thousand people during the 1920s, while Idaho's population remained flat. During the 1930s many migrants moving to Idaho from the Dust Bowl disaster on the southern Great Plains settled—and then failed—on inexpensive cutover timberlands in the northern counties. Drastically falling wheat and potato prices—two Idaho staples—helped push down average farm income from $686 in 1929 to a low of $250 in 1932. During the same period, average incomes in the state dropped by nearly 50 percent, creating fertile ground for political unrest.[8]

Sharply falling prices for wheat and beef devastated the state, and Montana's condition worsened when the state entered successive years of high winds, roiling dust clouds, and parched landscapes. The droughts that began in 1929 worsened in 1930 and 1931 and then reoccurred intermittently for a decade. The parched landscape left in its wake hunger, stark poverty, and desperate people. Twenty-eight of Montana's fifty-six counties applied for Red Cross relief in 1931, and by middecade one-quarter of the state's population was on relief.[9]

Added to these troubles were contracting markets and declining prices that flattened the domestic copper industry, forcing thousands of industrial workers in Butte, Anaconda, and Great Falls to lose their jobs. With worldwide copper prices at their lowest level since the depression of the 1890s, the Anaconda Copper Mining Company reduced wages and laid off one-third of its workforce. In the smelter town of Anaconda, eight hundred families were on some form of public relief by April 1934. While Anacondans appreciated public relief and New Deal programs such as the Works Progress Administration, historian Laurie Mercier contends that deeply ingrained values associated with the work ethic made public relief difficult for people.[10]

Suffering and hardship were equally apparent among Indian/First Nations groups. Some tribal people argue—with considerable truth—that federal, state, and provincial programs simply made Native struggles visible, that the onset of the Depression had not appreciably worsened their condition. Because the Umatilla still lived a partly subsistence lifestyle and possessed a "remarkable set of living skills," tribal elders remember that most reservation people usually had enough to eat. On Montana's hardscrabble Blackfeet reservation, however, 65 percent of Indian families were on relief. Although the Depression pushed thousands of Indians into the most difficult of circumstances in the early 1930s, there is little evidence to suggest that such dire conditions existed around Puget Sound.[11]

Western Washington Indians unquestionably suffered the loss of wage-earning jobs when the region's fish canneries, logging camps, and sawmills curtailed operations. During the early Depression years, Tulalip people fished for themselves, cut wood for fuel, and bartered game animals, berries, and garden produce for other necessities. When they appeared before a U.S. Senate committee hearing in Tacoma in 1931, however, their principal concerns were lack of health care, polluted shellfish grounds, inadequate education, and the erosion of their sovereignty. For the poet Richard Hugo, who lived in Seattle's Duwamish neighborhood in the 1930s, Indian people were neighbors, markers of the city's lower classes, and representatives of urban distress during the depths of the Depression. It is evident that Puget Sound Indians experienced the economic collapse in different ways, with reservation Indians in a better position to grub for food and the bare necessities for survival. Seattle's Natives, however, "were most likely to be found in places inhabited by the city's poorest people," according to Coll Thrush.[12]

The ordeal of the Lummi, who lived on the outer limits of western Washington's Bellingham Bay, provides a window to the experiences of other fisher tribes inhabiting the Puget Sound area. By the depths of the Depression, white commercial fishers had banished the Lummi from their once lucrative fishery and reduced them to the margins of the local economy. Washington Fish and Game officials arrested the Lummi for violating state law whether they were fishing on or off the reservation. To make matters worse for Native fishers, a successful statewide referendum in 1934 banned the use of fixed gear. Although the "antitrap legislation" exempted Indian fishing equipment, white commercial fishers convinced the state to prosecute Indians for violating the law. Prohibited from fishing on their reservation for subsistence purposes, the Lummi were reduced to destitution.[13]

Despite arrests and harassment and other infringements on their treaty-guaranteed rights, the Lummi continued to fish. Although they were excluded from the commercial fishery by the mid-1930s, families continued to fish for diminished runs of sockeye salmon at the mouth of the Nooksack River. With state fishery officials rigorously enforcing the antitrap measure, the total Indian catch of salmon on Puget Sound plummeted. Washington's legal officials used spurious arguments to deny Indian treaty rights, with the state's attorney general arguing in 1937 that the Indian Citizenship Act of 1924 effectively terminated all of the Lummi's treaty rights. State authorities continued to deny Indians the right to fish, even after the *Tulee v. State of Washington* case (1942), in which the U.S. Supreme Court upheld the treaty right to fish both off and on the reservation.[14]

The experiences of First Nations people on British Columbia's lower mainland and lower Vancouver Island were little different, with Native day laborers in urban Vancouver and Victoria suffering more than those living in fishing villages or isolated settings in the outback. Seasonal labor—such as cutting ties for the railroad—became increasingly scarce for both Indians and whites as the Depression deepened. Mary John, from the Stoney Creek Reserve in the interior, remembers that the Depression meant little to her neighbors: "Hard times in Stoney Creek were as natural and normal as the changing of the seasons. . . . We were always poor. . . . Our hard life became harder—that was all." The Stoney Creek band and others in outlying settlements turned to timeworn gathering practices, resumed traditional customs such as trapping, and otherwise reverted to older subsistence activities to survive.[15]

In the midst of the collapsing economy, British Columbia's aboriginal peoples were also making organizational moves that would ultimately reconfigure the legal standing of all First Nations. A group of Tsimshian chiefs met in Port Simpson in December 1931 and formed the Native Brotherhood of British Columbia, an organization consciously modeled after the Alaska Native Brotherhood of 1912. At its founding meeting, the British Columbia group requested a meeting with officials in Ottawa, asking for improvements in education and recognition of their right to fish, hunt, and gather in traditional, off-reservation places. In the next several years, the Brotherhood asked federal and provincial authorities to acknowledge aboriginal rights, to legalize the potlatch, and to provide day schools in Native villages. By the early 1940s, the Brotherhood was gaining greater credibility among Indian Bureau officials.[16]

It was a special moment in time, a gathering place on the arid northern rim of the Columbia Plain northwest of Spokane, Washington, where more than twenty thousand people came to hear President Franklin D. Roosevelt speak on August 24, 1934, during the early construction stages of Grand Coulee Dam. When it was completed, the president predicted, the gigantic project would help develop the region and provide opportunity for people suffering from want and hardship. But Grand Coulee, the lower Columbia Bonneville project, and the big earth-filled Fort Peck Dam on the Missouri River were much more; they were visible symbols of the New Deal's propensity for social innovation and experimentation—the administration's hasty and sometimes disorderly planning strategies to seek a way out of the nation's economic and social crisis. Despite the helter-skelter approach, Franklin Roosevelt's New Deal marked the emergence of a vastly expanded federal presence in the American Northwest.[17]

A series of river basin surveys and planning blueprints drafted in the late 1920s laid the groundwork for the huge federal investments in western water development projects that took shape under the New Deal. While Herbert Hoover allowed the Boulder Dam project on the Colorado River to proceed during his presidency, he opposed efforts to commence work on the Army Corps of Engineers' recommendations to build ten multipurpose dams on the Columbia River. Franklin Roosevelt's administration, however, gave immediate life to the corps' 308 Report (the title refers to House Document 308 of 1926), with the president releasing funds through the Federal Emergency Relief Administration to begin construction of Bonneville and Grand Coulee dams. The administration assigned the Bonneville project to the Corps of Engineers and the much larger Grand Coulee undertaking to the expanding operations of the Bureau of Reclamation. Completed in 1937, Bonneville Dam produced cheap hydropower for the Portland market and provided lock facilities that enhanced navigation on the Columbia River immediately above tidewater. Coming on line in 1941, the huge Grand Coulee project generated an enormous amount of electricity, surpassing the generating capacity of the entire Tennessee Valley Authority, and provided cheap power to run the region's important aluminum plants.[18]

The two big Columbia River projects employed thousands of workers who came from near and far to toil at the construction sites. Reflecting the work at Bonneville and Grand Coulee, federal investment in Washington between 1933 and 1939 exceeded that for all other states. Ultimately, the dams and their successors would bring dramatic changes to the farthest reaches of the Pacific Northwest, furnishing the cheapest electrical rates in the nation, providing an infrastructure attractive to industries, and enabling the region to broaden its economic base. There were long-term costs associated with the celebrated dam building, especially the alterations of the Great River into a series of slack-water lakes. "The Columbia no longer ran mightily to the sea," Richard White writes; "instead, the river ran between its dams like a circus lion jumping through hoops." As for Grand Coulee, the big dam was the end of the road for migrating salmon, a massive concrete wall preventing fish from access to some 1,100 miles of spawning habitat.[19]

Beyond the big public works projects, there were other dimensions to the New Deal's influence in the region, many of them linked to the government's willingness to help regenerate local economies, to use federal largesse to serve the needs of citizens. Roosevelt's overwhelming electoral successes in the West—he carried every western state in 1932 *and* 1936—provides some indication of the enormous popularity of New Deal projects. It also attests to the skills of a powerful political personality, a man whose rhetoric bridged social classes. In his four successful campaigns for president, Roosevelt garnered an average of 20 percent more votes than other Democrats on the same ticket.[20]

The beleaguered states of Montana and Idaho provide striking examples of the influence of New Deal largesse in reshaping western landscapes. Because of their small populations and vast public estates, Montana ranked second and Idaho fifth in the nation in per-capita federal expenditures between 1933 and 1939. The Civilian Conservation Corps (CCC) was the first of the New Deal agencies to set up shop in the two states, operating camps in national and state forests and national and state parks throughout the 1930s. The CCC operated 163 camps across Idaho and averaged 24 camps a year during the same period on Montana's federal and state lands. Although a few citizens in the two states opposed the agency as a boondoggle for lazy and incompetent youth, CCC crews did important work, planting trees, fighting white pine blister rust and forest fires, building mountain roads, trails, ranger stations, and lookouts, and doing valuable infrastructure work in Glacier and Yellowstone national parks.[21]

Even more visible, and the New Deal's largest local work-relief program, the Works Progress Administration (WPA) employed more than three million people nationwide during its first year and 8.5 million before it was disbanded in 1942. The WPA initiated rehabilitative projects in every Northwest state, constructing parks, schools, and community facilities; installing sewage systems; building highways, bridges, and small airports; and—most controversial of all—supporting the Federal Art, Theatre, and Writers projects. These programs funded musical performances, artwork, murals in post offices, and the research and writing of state guides (narratives of the state's history, physical landscape, and cultural heritage). The first to be published in the nation, Vardis Fisher's *Idaho: A Guide in Word and Picture* provided a model for other states. Both CCC and WPA workers were also involved in building Timberline Lodge on Oregon's picturesque Mount Hood and the artfully designed McCullough bridges along the Oregon coast.[22]

State histories generally praise Franklin D. Roosevelt's New Deal, with the authors of *Montana: A History of Two Centuries* praising the administration for fostering "the greatest reform movement—and the most revolutionary period in federal-state relations—that the United States has ever seen." Despite the cantankerous opposition of Idaho's irascible governor, Ben Ross, historian Ross Peterson applauds the New Deal for "balancing the human budget and propounding the philosophy that money is expendable and humanity is not."[23] Federal initiatives provided jobs, offered hope to the destitute, and contributed mightily to building an infrastructure of local and state parks for future generations.

This was especially so in Washington, where both the WPA and the CCC played significant roles in providing work relief for hard-pressed citizens. During the nine years of its existence, the CCC built roads, trails, and fire lookouts and erected more than 2,800 miles of telephone wires to provide communication for fighting forest fires. CCC "boys" also fought forest fires in Washington and planted more than seventeen million trees where natural reforestation appeared to be failing. In Mount Rainier National Park, crews rebuilt and developed campgrounds and picnic areas, work that is still visible to the present day. Washington's CCC camps also upgraded and constructed tables, bathhouses, shelters, and drinking facilities at Millersylvania and Deception Pass state parks and other recreation sites.[24]

The WPA was even more active in Washington, providing funds for the labor-intensive construction of thirty-one airports, airplane hangars, and terminal buildings. In addition to building urban sewage systems, city parks, and playgrounds, Washington counties used WPA funds for property surveys and similar projects. Financed with WPA support, the *King County Land Use Survey* (covering the city of Seattle) employed between three hundred and four hundred people who gathered data on buildings and private property. When the project concluded in 1940, the survey added hitherto missing buildings to tax rolls, contributed to an increase in real estate valuations, and left a photographic record of nearly every building in the county.[25]

New Deal programs provided little relief for independent and single women. At the insistence of First Lady Eleanor Roosevelt, however, the president's advisors included a women's division in the Federal Emergency Relief Administration. Following a November 1933 White House conference, the Civil Works Administration (CWA) put three hundred thousand women to work nationwide during the winter of 1933–34. The much larger WPA program employed about half a million women in a variety of "socially useful" jobs. Although the Oregon WPA hired women for service jobs, females comprised only a small percentage of agency employment nationwide. While Eleanor Roosevelt and a few others lobbied to employ more women, institutional sexism permeated the WPA guidelines, making it difficult for women to qualify for work relief.[26]

Male notions of what constituted useful labor guided most New Deal hiring practices, with the largest and most prominent projects the province of males. Men built dams and bridges, installed sewer lines, and worked on Oregon's Wilson River Highway west of Portland. Because WPA regulations limited work-relief jobs to one family member, married women were ineligible if their husbands were already employed. Women with work-relief employment, therefore, were usually single, widowed, or divorced, hiring on for jobs that required sewing, housekeeping, and serving school lunches to needy children. In Portland the WPA also placed women in jobs through a household service–training program, a carefully administered, class-based arrangement that provided domestic labor for elite families.[27]

New Deal reform programs introduced dramatic new directions in U.S. Indian policy, terminating the disastrous allotment program, initiating efforts to foster Indian arts and crafts, and ending the prosecution of Indians for exercising Native religious beliefs. New policy initiatives— most coming from the desk of John Collier, Roosevelt's reform commissioner of Indian affairs—reflected an effort to reverse decades of mismanagement and corruption in the nation's Indian programs. In the end, Congress modified and weakened Collier's primary vehicle for reform, the Indian Reorganization Act (IRA) of 1934. The IRA invited tribes to organize under the act, draft written constitutions, and form business corporations. In the midst of confusion and misunderstandings that exacerbated existing tribal factions, 172 tribes chose to organize under the IRA, and 73 refused. Despite the sometimes contentious politics, John Collier and the IRA marked a progressive shift in federal-tribal relations.[28]

Oregon tribes were sharply divided over the IRA, with the Grand Ronde and Warm Springs people choosing to come under the provisions of the act. The Klamath, riven by factions, each suspicious of the other, was the most conspicuous of the Oregon groups to reject the IRA. Enrollees on the Umatilla Reservation also rejected the Indian Reorganization Act, with 299 opposed and 155 in favor. Those voting against coming under the IRA feared that drafting a constitution would mean that Bureau of Indian Affairs officials would have veto power over tribal decisions. In Montana, home to IRA coauthor Senator Burton Wheeler, all of the state's federally recognized Indian groups voted to organize under the IRA with the exception of the Fort Peck and Crow tribes. Among Idaho tribes, the Shoshone-Bannock on the Fort Hall Reservation chose to incorporate under the IRA in 1936, and in western Washington several small tribes chose to come under the act. The Lummi, however, rejected the IRA, as did the large Yakama tribe.[29]

Although the province of British Columbia established work-relief camps in the interior early in the Depression, skyrocketing unemployment in Vancouver eventually fostered hunger marches and prompted the Conservative government to sponsor the Kidd Report, a study published in 1932. In what proved to be a reactionary document, the report recommended reducing expenditures, cutting social services, and restricting school attendance to children between ages six and thirteen. An outraged public treated the elitist report with dispatch, deposing the Conservatives and Premier Simon Fraser Tolmie and electing the Liberals and Duff Pattullo to cope with the Depression crisis. Flamboyant and confident, Pattullo campaigned on the catchphrase "socialized capitalism," promoting policies that mirrored some of Roosevelt's New Deal programs.[30]

The early Depression also witnessed the emergence of a new nationwide political party, the Cooperative Commonwealth Federation (CCF). Advocating a democratic-socialist platform, the CCF put the Conservatives and Liberals on notice of a new, more progressive voice in Canadian politics. The CCF emerged as "a child of the times," suggesting that there would have been no Canadian socialist party without the Depression.

The CCF became British Columbia's official opposition party in 1933, and with the passing years the party laid the foundation for shaping the nation's welfare state following the Second World War.[31]

Although the CCF pushed a "visionary socialism," Pattullo's practical-minded approach appealed to voters, who returned thirty-four Liberals to the legislature in 1933. The presence of the CCF, however, spurred Pattullo to initiate public works projects. In quick order, legislators reformed the tax system, extended aid to critical economic sectors, and initiated big construction projects. The enormous nature of the economic collapse also prompted Pattullo to pressure a reluctant federal government to become more active in helping to revive the national economy. Facing reelection in 1935, Conservative prime minister Richard Bedford Bennett prodded the federal Parliament to pass mildly reformist legislation, including a limited unemployment insurance measure. These tepid reforms apparently insulted Canadian voters, who returned McKenzie King and the Liberals to power on the premise that the federal government should provide a safety net for the unemployed. As for British Columbia, its economy continued to struggle until the German invasion of Poland in September 1939.[32]

Freshly graduated from high school and traveling by water along the British Columbia coast in the early morning hours of September 1, 1939, Ian MacSwan remembered the moment when the ship's radio broke the news that German armies had invaded Poland.[33] As Canadians and Americans alike were aware, Hitler's Germany had already marched through Vienna and Prague, annexing first Austria and then Czechoslovakia to the expanding German Empire. But when Hitler sent German panzer divisions and dive-bombers into Poland, Great Britain and France drew the proverbial line in the sand, with British prime minister Neville Chamberlain announcing to his fellow citizens on September 3: "This country is at war with Germany." A few hours later, French prime minister Edouard Daladier declared that France had joined the cause.[34]

Because Canada was still nominally part of the British Empire, the German invasion of Poland affected Canadians from Newfoundland to British Columbia. It can be said with considerable truth that the Second World War was the principal convulsion of the twentieth century. For the Greater Pacific Northwest, it altered careers and changed the course of people's lives. It was a time of endings and beginnings; it signaled an end to the Great Depression, first in British Columbia and then in the

American Northwest. And for the thousands of people who joined the armed forces or moved to urban settings for defense-related work, it brought closure to the seasonal rhythms of summer and winter, the steady pace of life, and the intimate associations with known worlds. Great Britain's declaration of war reminded British Columbians of their lingering ties to a fading empire, one that would survive the war but with only the symbolic trappings of its former grandeur. Both north and south of the forty-ninth parallel, the war brought full employment, deferred consumer purchasing, and inspired great personal savings that would unleash unprecedented prosperity and burgeoning economic growth following the conflicts in Europe and Asia.

In Canadian and American stories about the 1930s and 1940s, the Great Depression is always preface to the transforming events of the Second World War. The onset of the wars in Europe and Asia brought an abrupt end to years of unemployment and economic stagnation. Workers, accustomed to long periods without a job, suddenly found themselves in a seller's market. Despite long workdays, food rationing, and military conscription, the war years meant improved conditions, heady experiences for families who had suffered through a decade and more of want and hardship. When the United States declared war on Japan and then the Axis Powers, the region's newspapers began printing extra pages of help-wanted ads—a sharp reversal from Depression practices.[35]

After years of drought, devastated crops, weak copper markets, and a population exodus, Montana was left with a citizenry that had survived largely through the assistance of federal relief programs. The war economy dramatically transformed Montana's fortunes. The rains even returned, with farmers producing bumper crops in 1941, 1942, and 1943. Reaping the benefits of strong wartime demand, farmers and ranchers expanded their operations, adding acreage and investing in new mechanized equipment. The rising demand for copper and lumber revitalized Butte's fortunes and western Montana's lumber industry. However, people continued to leave the state, despite its booming economy, for the armed services or defense plants in Spokane, Seattle, Tacoma, and Portland. Even though the demand for labor in mining, lumbering, and agriculture attracted a sizable in-migration, the exodus to the military and defense plants had a negative effect, with Montana's population dropping from 559,456 in the 1940 census to about 470,000 in 1943.[36]

On the late Sunday afternoon of December 7, 1941, seventeen-year-old Horace Axtell was playing marbles and listening to the radio with friends in the Nez Perce reservation town of Ferdinand, Idaho. "All of a sudden," he recalled years later, "they had a news break and they announced that Pearl Harbor was bombed." Although he did not enlist in the army until 1943, he remembers that one of his relatives was in the Bataan Death March and eventually died in a Japanese prison. Before his discharge in 1946, Axtell was with the first troops to visit the horrible destruction at Hiroshima and Nagasaki.[37] Statewide, 11 percent of Idaho's population—greater than the national average—served in the military. The state's other principal contributions to the war were its large exports of food, lumber, and metals.[38]

Although Idaho's agriculture, mining, and lumber industries were recovering by 1939, it took the war economy to reach full employment. The federal government established two major military installations in the state: Mountain Home Air Force Base east of Boise and Farragut Naval Training Station on Lake Pend Oreille. While Mountain Home still functions as a Strategic Air Command base, the navy's Farragut facility was dismantled after 1945. During the war, however, some seven hundred buildings on Farragut's four thousand acres accommodated approximately three hundred thousand navy recruits, who trained at the southern end of Lake Pend Oreille. The hurried construction at Farragut in early 1942 provided an immediate economic fix for small communities such as Sandpoint.[39]

The effects of the Second World War were even more dramatic for the coastal states of Oregon and Washington, with sharp increases in the demand for lumber, market conditions that continued to accelerate with the return to peacetime. Seattle's celebrated aircraft industry and metropolitan Portland's acclaimed shipbuilding facilities attracted new and more ethnically diverse people, the beginnings of a demographic transformation that in time would broaden the region's cultural matrix. The war years scrambled communities, reshaping the far corners of Oregon and Washington, with people moving from rural sectors to defense jobs in Portland and Seattle. The Pacific Northwest was also the recipient of a nationwide movement of people from east to west. As numerous writers have indicated, the shift of federal investment westward between 1941 and 1945 tilted the country toward the Pacific, and people, money, and military personnel "all spilled west."[40]

Unlike the First World War, the Second World War involved the United States in a two-ocean conflict, with Japan posing an immediate danger to the West Coast. As a consequence, for the first time the federal government provided huge expenditures to build an industrial infrastructure in the region. The Second World War contributed mightily to turning the Far West into a major producer of manufactured goods. By the end of the war, the government had put up 90 percent of the investment in the region's defense-related manufacturing. The war in the Pacific and military concerns about the concentration of the nation's vital manufacturing facilities in the Northeast forced these decisions.[41] In that respect, the Second World War initiated systemic change to the economies of Oregon and Washington with an infusion of new people, new ideas, and new demands on natural resources.

Although wartime conditions severely disrupted rural communities and created acute labor shortages, the most visible signs of change in the American Northwest were in the region's two principal centers of war production, the Portland-Vancouver and Seattle-Tacoma areas. During its peak year of production—1944—Seattle's Boeing Company employed 50,000 workers, and along the Columbia River the three big Kaiser shipyards in Portland and Vancouver employed approximately 120,000 men and women during peak production months. The two urban centers were alive with daily train arrivals and departures, immigrant workers looking for jobs, and an outgoing population heading for basic training camps.[42]

A Seattle newspaper's characterization of "the narcotic effect of war contracts" accurately described what took place in the Greater Seattle and Portland areas between 1941 and 1945. Puget Sound's population nearly doubled during the war, with Seattle growing from 368,000 in 1940 to 530,000 in 1944. The inrush of new people created a critical housing shortage, forcing Seattle to loosen building restrictions to stimulate remodeling and converting vacant buildings to residential apartments. Huge federal expenditures in Pacific Coast cities and cheap hydropower from the recently completed Bonneville and Grand Coulee dams stoked the fires of the Washington and Oregon economies.[43]

Portland and its suburbs (including Vancouver across the Columbia River) increased by more than 250,000 people during the war, with Oregon's population growth reaching nearly 40 percent for the decade. At the peak of wartime production, some 140,000 defense workers lived in metropolitan Portland, numbers that would accelerate with the passing decades. With the opening of Henry J. Kaiser's shipbuilding facilities on the Willamette and Columbia rivers, Portland confronted an urgent housing crisis. To alleviate the problem, Kaiser's company constructed a federally subsidized housing development for thirty-five thousand residents just north of Portland near the Columbia River. Built with fiberboard walls and standing on wooden blocks, Vanport was the nation's largest wartime housing project, providing schools, nurseries, and child care for working families.[44]

Vanport was also home to a mix of people, including a sizable percentage of African Americans, most of them making the move west to work in the shipyards. By the fall of 1944 Portland's shipyards employed approximately seven thousand blacks, with thousands more working in support industries around the metropolitan area. Estimates of the number of African Americans in Portland suggest a high figure of twenty-two thousand, with some eleven thousand remaining when the shipyards closed after the war. Vanport underscores another reality that linked race and class to place of residence, with African Americans comprising 35 percent of the community's population at the end of the war. With real estate covenants prohibiting blacks from living in much of Portland, African Americans would remain—along with their working-class white neighbors—in temporary living quarters on a floodplain abutting the volatile waters of the Columbia River.[45]

Seattle's black population experienced similar trials with racial discrimination. With the city's African American population tripling by 1944, blacks increasingly encountered difficulty applying for certain jobs, and Whites Only signs appeared in restaurants, taverns, housing, and public recreational facilities. Seattle's largest employer, Boeing, had no black workers prior to the war, and even in the face of dire labor shortages, the company employed only 1,600 African Americans at the height of its payroll in 1943. Despite opposition from Boeing and one of the big shipyards, Seattle's public housing projects provided some relief for the city's seven to eight thousand blacks who were seeking decent places to live. With the private market providing only substandard and overcrowded dwellings, African American applications for public housing more than doubled by the end of 1943. Elsewhere, the Seattle Parks Department limited black access to a public swimming pool in west Seattle to one day each week, and Harborview Hospital rejected black applicants to its nursing program.[46]

For Native American/First Nations people, the Second World War provided opportunities to escape the grinding poverty of reservation life, and for some, the war was a point of departure in modern Indian history. Although New Deal programs like the Civilian Conservation Corps brought many Indians into the wage-labor force, the outbreak of war in 1941 encouraged Native people to look beyond the reservation for defense industry jobs or enlistment in the military. With the Depression now a fading memory, Indians flocked to lumber and fishing jobs, while others sought work in the shipyards or with the Boeing Company. These were heady experiences for people making increased connections with life beyond the reservation.[47]

The Second World War recast the gender mix of the American and Canadian workforces, with thousands of women taking wage-earning jobs for the first time. In the United States, women taking jobs in defense industries numbered between 2.7 and 3.5 million. Seattle-Portland area statistics show very large percentages of women in industrial employment, especially in shipyards and aircraft plants. Women entered the Canadian workforce in equal or even higher percentages, especially in British Columbia. Females worked in plywood and pulp and paper mills, jobs traditionally closed to them. Women also made up a sizable percentage of the workers in aircraft and shipbuilding manufacturing in Victoria and Vancouver.[48]

At the peak of Boeing's wartime production in late 1943, women made up 46 percent of the company's fifty thousand employees. Comparable figures for Portland's shipyards indicate that women made up about 30 percent of the workforce. When Kaiser's Oregon Shipbuilding Company hired two women welders in April 1942, the event marked the first time that a U.S. Maritime Commission yard employed females for production work. Welding schools began training more women when news circulated about the shipyard's readiness to hire females. Eventually, the shipyards offered free welding instructional programs to help alleviate the labor shortage. The Portland shipyards also hired women earlier and in greater numbers than elsewhere in the nation.[49]

The employment of women in Portland and in Boeing's sprawling facility in Seattle was uneven, with most working as welders but making little headway in more skilled positions held by male workers. The mere fact that shipyards hired women, however, challenged conventional notions about appropriate work spheres for females and ideals about feminine identity. But these dramatic changes in the employment of women shifted to more traditional notions of gender when females were first to receive "quit-slips" at the end of the workday as the war was winding down.[50] Real and lasting gains and full equality between men and women in the workplace lay somewhere in the future.

Following the Japanese attack on Pearl Harbor, racial politics played itself out along the Pacific Coast in one of the more notable violations of civil rights in Canadian and American history. The removal of more than one hundred thousand Japanese Americans from the Pacific Coast states and twenty-two thousand from British Columbia to interior internment camps marked a gross violation of American and Canadian civil law. More than two-thirds of the Japanese were native-born citizens of their respective nations. Racial animosities against the Japanese date to the early twentieth century, when immigrants began to succeed as truck gardeners and orchardists. Japan's invasion of Manchuria in 1937 further heightened discrimination against the Japanese, but that was only a pretext for the firestorm unleashed with the bombing of Pearl Harbor.[51]

Although most of America's mainland Japanese lived in California at the outset of the Second World War, some fourteen thousand resided in Washington, approximately four thousand in Oregon, and another one thousand in Idaho. Most of Washington's Japanese lived in the Seattle-Tacoma area, 8,900 of them native-born U.S. citizens. Within hours of the attack on Pearl Harbor, the FBI arrested 122 people of Japanese descent in Seattle on various charges of colluding with the enemy. When Japanese forces accomplished a stunning series of military victories in the Pacific, reason took flight along the Pacific Coast as rumors spread that the resident Japanese presented a military danger to coastal districts. Responding to these pressures, Gen. John L. DeWitt, chief of the Western Defense Command, requested permission in early February 1942 to move all Japanese people away from coastal areas. In his letter to the president's cabinet, DeWitt wrote: "A Jap's a Jap. . . . It makes no difference whether he is an American citizen or not."[52]

DeWitt's request caused considerable discussion among Roosevelt's advisors, but the president subsequently agreed and signed Executive Order 9066 on February 19, 1942, authorizing the removal of all persons of Japanese ancestry from the strategic military zone along the Pacific Coast. DeWitt moved quickly, ordering the Japanese to report to assembly centers in preparation for transportation to interior internment camps. What took place in Oregon was similar to the experiences of Japanese elsewhere. Ordered to assemble at Portland's Livestock Exposition Center in March 1942, families had only a brief period to gather up personal belongings and leave their homes. For the next several months, the Livestock Exposition Center was home to approximately 4,500 Japanese, with families crowded into whitewashed, two-hundred-square-foot livestock stalls. Amid the straw mattresses, single light bulbs, and uninsulated walls and floors, George Azumano remembered that the stench of animal dung hung heavy in the air.[53]

America's Japanese population spent most of the duration of the war in one of ten internment camps, most of them scattered across the arid western interior. Three U.S. Supreme Court cases tested the constitutionality of removal and incarceration, all of them upholding the executive order. As the conflict in Asia was winding down, Attorney General Francis Biddle wrote President Roosevelt in late 1943 that the internment camps were "dangerous and repugnant to the principles of our government." In mid-1944 Interior Secretary Harold Ickes warned the president that the continued incarceration of innocent Japanese "would be a blot upon the history of this country."[54] Only after the president's reelection to an unprecedented fourth term were most Japanese Americans allowed to leave the camps. With good reason, historian James Patterson has called the treatment of Japanese Americans "the most systematic abuse of constitutional rights in twentieth-century United States history."[55]

An oft-remembered footnote to the experiences of Japanese Americans during the Second World War was the large number of Nisei males who enlisted in the army and served in mostly segregated units in the European theater of war. The most famous, the 442nd Regimental Combat Team, fought with great distinction through North Africa, Italy, France, and Germany, becoming the most highly decorated military unit in U.S. history. Among the twenty-one members of the regiment awarded the Congressional Medal of Honor was George Oiye, who grew up near Three Forks, Montana. Although his family was not subject to Executive Order 9066, Oiye, a student at Montana State College, joined the U.S. Army when the Roosevelt administration lifted the ban against Nisei serving in the armed forces. Thirty-five hundred Nisei, most of them from Hawaii, trained near Hattiesburg, Mississippi, before sailing for Europe in May 1944. Shortly before his death in 2006, George Oiye told an interviewer that serving in the 442nd Regimental Combat Team made him proud to be a Japanese American: "If I hadn't been in an all-Japanese-American unit, nobody would have known me but Montanans."[56]

Historic prejudice against Japanese in British Columbia paralleled that in the United States. When Japan invaded China in 1937, the federal Parliament directed the Royal Canadian Mounted Police to investigate whether British Columbia's Japanese-owned fishing vessels might be providing cover for Japanese military officers. But it was Japan's military advances in Asia, culminating in the attack on Pearl Harbor, that unleashed the full weight of federal and provincial authorities against British Columbia's Japanese. The Canadian government's first action following Pearl Harbor was to order the immediate confiscation of 1,200 Japanese-owned fishing boats in British Columbia. A few days after President Roosevelt signed Executive Order 9066, the Canadian government followed with its own directive, ordering the removal of all people of Japanese ancestry at least 160 kilometers from the Pacific Coast.[57]

British Columbia's Japanese first reported to processing centers such as Vancouver's Hastings Park, where horse stables and cattle stalls were temporarily converted to family living quarters. From there, some single males were sent to Alberta and Manitoba to work on sugar-beet farms. Most families lived in camps such as abandoned mining towns in the West Kootenay district, with a detachment of Royal Canadian Mounted Police on hand to monitor movement into and away from the camps. Federal authorities quickly sold the confiscated Japanese fishing boats "at fire sale prices," thereby creating opportunities for whites to enter the fisheries.[58] At war's end, the government continued to ban Japanese from the coastal area, an order that remained in effect until 1949. Ken Adachi, a British Columbia native who spent part of his childhood in a wartime relocation camp, termed the Japanese evacuation a crisis in Canadian democracy, "without precedent in the past and with disturbing implications for the future." Rationalized for protecting national security, the excuse became shallow when the wartime restrictions continued for nearly four years after Japan's surrender.[59]

The war in the Pacific ended abruptly in mid-August 1945 with the dropping of atomic bombs on the Japanese cities of Hiroshima and Nagasaki. When the battleship *Missouri* steamed into Tokyo Bay on September 2, 1945, Gen. Douglas MacArthur and Japanese officials signed surrender documents under the shadow of the ship's big guns. The United States was officially at peace, and so was Canada, which had remained in the war to the end. The Japanese surrender marked the end of "the good war" for both nations. The joyous celebrations that took place from New York City to San Francisco, from Portland to Seattle, were repeated in Vancouver and Victoria when radio stations and newspapers announced the surrender.[60]

Beyond the celebratory ending of war, it is obvious that the atomic destruction unleashed on Japan signaled that the world had crossed a threshold into an era in which human ingenuity had appropriated the ability to end life itself. Because the plutonium used in the second bomb had been produced at the Hanford complex on the Columbia River, the region would be at the center of future weapons production and cold war defense strategies. The war's end also ushered in an extended period of feverish economic growth that would be remembered as the greatest boom in Canadian and American history, a surging tide of development that brought popular conveniences to the farthest reaches of the north-western outback.

III
Toward a Postindustrial Society

6
The Great Boom

The end of the Second World War ushered in a new world of expectations for a generation of rural families accustomed to outhouses and kerosene lamps. Plumbed and wired homes, telephones, and the conveniences of modern electrical appliances were the new order of the day. As the leading economic and military power, the United States was positioned to realize Henry Luce's dream of an "American century," in which the nation's institutions and values would spread around the globe. If the twentieth-century world was to be vigorous and healthy, *Time* magazine publisher Luce wrote in 1940, it "must be to a significant degree an American century."[1] Popular newspaper columnist Walter Lippmann was equally euphoric after the Japanese defeat in 1945: "What Rome was to the ancient world, what Great Britain has been to the modern world, America is to be to the world of tomorrow."[2] When Communists assumed power in China in 1949 and the Soviet Union exploded its own atomic bomb the same year, some of America's bluster and brag began to fade.

Beneath the hoopla, swagger, and bravado of the immediate postwar era, there were widespread concerns about the transition from war to peacetime production. With the social and economic crisis of the Great Depression an ever-present memory, policy makers, journalists, and the business community worried about "reconversion" to a peacetime economy. With expected cutbacks in the shipbuilding and aircraft industries, Oregon journalist Richard Neuberger thought the region would face difficult times. To what end, Neuberger asked, "will the shipbuilding yards be converted?" Seattle leaders worried that slowing wartime production would lead to increases in unemployment and a return to the conditions of the Great Depression. Neuberger was especially alarmed because the region's civilian population had increased 17 percent during the war. In British Columbia, those with longer memories feared the reoccurrence of the deep recession that followed the Armistice of November 1918.[3]

Federal, state, and provincial governments all took steps to ameliorate the conversion to peacetime production. In the United States, the

V-J Day, Portland, August 14, 1945. The announcement of Japan's surrender on August 14, 1945, set off riotous celebrations across the United States and Canada. Because of its proximity to the Pacific theater of operations, the surrender held special meaning for citizens of the Greater Northwest, who celebrated the end to "their" war.

Office of Mobilization and Reconversion began issuing quarterly reports in January 1945. At the state level, California governor Earl Warren led the way, establishing the California State Reconstruction and Reemployment Commission in 1944 to inventory the state's future industrial potential. Oregon followed suit, appointing its own Postwar Readjustment and Development Commission in the same year. Although its monthly reports heralded the virtues of private enterprise, there was an occasional echo of the old New Deal passion for planning. The Boeing Company was the centerpiece to Washington's postwar planning, with the expectation that the aircraft industry, unlike shipbuilding, held bright prospects for the future.[4] Although large-scale civilian aircraft production was not an immediate reality, the future would prove that the close cooperation between Boeing officials and Washington's political leadership would be the key to Seattle's burgeoning postwar economy.

For defense industry workers and returning service personnel, uncertainty, apprehension, and anxiety would be daily points of reckoning following Japan's surrender. Scholars too often focus on the great economic boom that took off in 1946, passing lightly over the summer, fall, and winter of 1945, seasons of high unemployment and worries about the future. Employment in Portland's shipyards had already dropped by half in August 1945, especially among women, and would soon fall even further. The transition to a peacetime economy revealed that most women provided temporary relief for men in a dire labor shortage. Although a few unskilled females held onto their jobs after the war, the Oregon Shipyard Corporation laid off its last three women welders in October 1945.[5]

As the U.S. and Canadian governments canceled or reduced military orders, fears about an economic collapse were very real. In British Columbia, construction in Victoria and Vancouver shipyards slowed with Germany's surrender in the spring of 1945 and then stalled completely when Japan surrendered in the autumn. As troops returned home and shipyards shut down, unemployment rolls in Seattle and Portland increased, with Boeing reducing its labor force from more than forty thousand to eleven thousand workers. In mid-August the navy canceled orders for eight aircraft carriers and twenty-seven ships, all of them to be built in Portland-area shipyards. With more than half of the nearly one hundred thousand shipyard workers expressing an interest in staying in Portland after the war, the local economy faced an immediate crisis. In eastern Washington's Tri-Cities area, reductions in the number of employees at the Hanford nuclear works directly affected the company town of Richland, where construction of new housing ceased and the area's population plummeted from a wartime high of fifty thousand to some fifteen thousand residents.[6]

Lumber industry and longshore workers in western Washington and Oregon added to these difficulties when they went on strike for higher wages and benefits, setting in motion a series of labor conflicts that lasted well into 1946. Jurisdictional struggles between American Federation of Labor (AFL) and Congress of Industrial Organizations (CIO) unions complicated the maritime workers' walkout on October 1, 1945. Although the strikes ended in late November, the International Longshoremen's and Warehousemen's Union (ILWU), a CIO affiliate, demanded safety considerations that were not resolved until a major dock strike in 1948. Another lengthy western Washington strike involving three Seattle daily newspapers forced the companies to cease publication until printers gained wage increases in early 1946.[7] The nationwide postwar strikes also prompted congressional moves to introduce antilabor legislation.

Unemployment in the Pacific slope states increased sharply, peaking in March 1946 well above the national level but then dropping precipitously. The transition to peacetime production in the Northwest built upon traditional extractive industries but also added a dynamic new component to the region's increasingly industrialized economy. An important element in the rapid turnabout along the entire Pacific slope was the fact that the war economy never fully demobilized. In San Diego, Los Angeles, and Seattle, aircraft production was still the largest single industry in 1947, with military orders the principal mainstay. Washington employed 8.9 percent of the nation's aircraft workforce in 1950, compared with 3 percent in 1944, and statewide, workers building military and civilian airplanes outnumbered those in logging and lumbering by 1956.[8] Although Washington had added an important industrial component to its economy, the aerospace industry was inextricably linked to hot and cold war ventures, reflecting the twists and turns of what President Dwight Eisenhower called the "military-industrial complex."

The two inland states of Idaho and Montana faced different problems in the months following the Japanese surrender. Men and women returning from the armed forces or coastal defense plants reversed Montana's population losses, diminished by depression and war. While the Second World War spurred copper production in Butte, restored coal mining in

Red Lodge, and pushed crude oil output to new highs in eastern Montana, the state's wartime gains paled in comparison with its neighbors. One significant military installation, the Army Air Corps base built near Great Falls in 1942, lived on into the cold war era as Malmstrom Air Force Base, an important Strategic Air Command post. Malmstrom later served as the nerve center for some two hundred intercontinental ballistic missile silos in central Montana. And in a sharp reversal of Depression-era experiences, federal price supports, growing West Coast markets, and booming sales for agricultural goods brought prosperity to Montana farmers.[9]

Montana's postwar economy continued along traditional lines, with a greater dependence on natural resources than perhaps any other state. With its small, dispersed population and distance from major markets, Montana struggled with problems common to the northern Rocky Mountain region. While agriculture remained the state's leading industry, western Montana's lumber industry benefited from lively Pacific Coast and Midwest markets. Although copper production dominated Butte's industrial world, technological advances continued to diminish labor as a factor in production. With its huge smelter facilities at Anaconda, the company still provided direct employment for some 1,600 smelter workers. The firm's earnings in the state, however, were in slow decline as the Anaconda Copper Mining Company increased its operations in Chile.[10]

For Idaho, the end of the war meant closing the Farragut Naval Training Station on Lake Pend Oreille and the small Mountain Home Air Force Base east of Boise. For a brief period, the vacated naval training center was home to a vocational and technical college, but when the institute folded, nature reclaimed much of the area. The federal government eventually deeded the Farragut site to the state, and the Idaho legislature created the four-thousand-acre Farragut State Park in 1965. Although Mountain Home was placed on inactive status in 1945, it was reactivated as Mountain Home Air Force Base under the newly christened United States Air Force in 1949. Functioning as a cold war base for supersonic aircraft, military officials transferred Mountain Home to the Strategic Air Command in 1953. At the height of the cold war during the 1950s and early 1960s, Mountain Home's bomber squadrons stood ready at a moment's notice to carry nuclear weapons to the distant Soviet Union.[11]

Idaho's most lasting cold war legacy is the Idaho National Engineering Laboratory (INEL), a large defense installation occupying 890 square miles in southeastern Idaho. Initially established as the National Reactor Testing Station under the Atomic Energy Commission in 1949, the area eventually hosted fifty-two nuclear reactors, more than any other place in the world. The huge reservation was also an economic boon to the sparsely populated area west of Idaho Falls, attracting scientists and a large supporting cast of engineers. The federal government increased INEL's military and civilian payroll to approximately ten thousand people by the early 1990s, nearly 5 percent of the state's workforce. The nearby company town of Arco gained worldwide attention in 1955 when it became the first community powered with atomic energy.[12] The future would also show the INEL reservation to be one of the most polluted sites in the United States and the subject of periodic antinuclear protests.

Major segments of Idaho's postwar economy remained at one with the state's past, especially agriculture, which provided the mainstay for most citizens through the 1960s. Because good crop prices continued after the war, Idaho farmers expanded their irrigation systems, producing large-scale crops—alfalfa, grains, and potatoes—for export to expanding coastal markets. To augment their supplies of water, farmers tapped underground aquifers, and the Bureau of Reclamation completed Anderson Ranch Dam on the South Fork of the Boise River and Palisades Dam on the upper Snake River. The large earthen Palisades project produced hydroelectric power and provided water for newly cultivated lands near American Falls and Rupert.[13]

California's booming population growth was the proverbial elephant in the room, propelling the extractive economies of British Columbia, Washington, Oregon, Idaho, and western Montana. Despite the appearance of "new" industries such as aircraft construction and aluminum smelting, the old staples/resource economy continued to provide support for the majority of citizens. Through good times and bad, even in the darkest of winter months, people were optimistic that the slackening rains would bring improved job prospects in logging camps and mill towns. That sense of optimism extended from logging towns at ocean's edge to Butte at the literal top of the continent. From Idaho's small agricultural communities to tiny mining and lumbering towns in interior British Columbia, people were confident that the future promised better times.

For Japanese Americans, the immediate postwar period continued to be traumatic. When the U.S. government permitted internees to return home in January 1945, few of them left the camps because of widespread anti-Japanese sentiment. A few regional politicians made matters worse, with Washington's senator Warren Magnuson demanding tough restrictions on the Japanese when they left relocation centers. The aged former Oregon congressman Walter Pierce toured rural corners of his state protesting the return of Japanese to Hood River and Malheur counties. Speaking to a large audience of the Oregon Property Owners' Association in February 1945, Pierce urged state legislators to rescind what he called the illegal land titles held by native-born children of Japanese immigrants. The Oregon legislature promptly amended the 1923 Alien Property Act, making it illegal for Japanese aliens to hold land purchased in a relative's name. Although Governor Earl Snell signed the bill into law, the Oregon Supreme Court declared the measure unconstitutional.[14]

Ethnic hatred was not confined solely to the legislative halls in Salem. When Japanese farmer Ray Yasui returned to the Hood River Valley, local shopkeepers put up signs such as No Jap Trade Wanted, sentiments that forced him to drive twenty-five miles to The Dalles for supplies. The Hood River Valley's newspapers also published a "citizens' petition" under the heading "No Japs Wanted." In the most notorious instance of ethnic hostility, an incident that garnered national attention, the Hood River American Legion removed the names of sixteen Japanese servicemen from the local honor roll for veterans. Elsewhere, Japanese Americans returned to hostile communities and loss of property, especially in metropolitan Portland, where the former internees lost homes and small businesses.[15]

Japanese evacuees returning to Puget Sound encountered similar experiences. At first the *Seattle Post-Intelligencer* led the anti-Japanese accusations, spreading rumors and feeding the white community's sense of paranoia. But the newspaper soon reversed direction, asking for calm and tolerance in the face of public vindictiveness. As the Japanese returned in larger numbers to the Seattle-Tacoma area, the *Seattle Post-Intelligencer* and the *Seattle Times* urged citizens to receive the internees "on Their Merits," quoting a War Department memo that "mass exclusion . . . [was] no longer a matter of military necessity." Washington's political leadership, however, was divided, with Governor Monrad Wallgren emphatically opposing the return of the Japanese, while Seattle mayor William Devin worked with the Civic Unity League and Council of Churches to mitigate the potential for trouble. Mayor Devin and the Unity League ultimately played an important role in reducing opposition to returning

Japanese. The most important determinant in defusing the hatred of local Japanese was the heroic fighting of the 442nd Regimental Combat Team.[16]

The experiences of Shiro Kashino, who fought with the 442nd Regimental Combat Team in Italy, earning six Purple Hearts, a Silver Star, and a Bronze Star, underscores the problems of Japanese veterans. When Kashino returned to Seattle, he was banned from a place to live because homes were set aside only for returning "veterans." Kashino eventually hired on with an automobile dealership, where he succeeded as a salesman. Except for the building-services union, Seattle-area unions continued their long-standing opposition to Japanese employment. When the Teamsters Union refused to deliver Japanese-grown produce, the U.S. Justice Department intervened with an antitrust suit. Elsewhere, Japanese were finding jobs in first-rate hotels and hospitals, especially Catholic institutions. Still others worked as store clerks or typists or hired on with civil service agencies.[17]

Postwar anti-Japanese policies were even more persistent in British Columbia, with Japanese Canadians prohibited until April 1949 from traveling within one hundred miles of the Pacific Coast without a permit. Aside from their forceful removal from the coastal area, the most grievous injustice done to British Columbia's Japanese was the compulsory sale of their property at very low valuations. Postwar discussions about the rights of British Columbia's Japanese population were also linked to the national debate over the Canadian Citizenship Act. Canada's federal leaders heeded the directives of provincial members of Parliament elected in 1945 on a mandate to oppose the return of the Japanese to the coast. The issue for most British Columbians was "dispersal," the notion that Japanese residents should seek job opportunities elsewhere and not return to the coast. After a lengthy fight that included the Japanese Canadians Citizens Association, federal authorities finally lifted the ban on April 1, 1949.[18]

The global symbol of the American Northwest's new postwar reality was centered in activities taking place at the U.S. government's Hanford nuclear facility along an isolated stretch of the Columbia River. Officials repeatedly assured the public that Hanford's operations, which took place under a veil of secrecy and without independent review, were prudent and safe. Nearby communities were unaware that in the race to produce plutonium for the first atomic and hydrogen bombs Hanford had released more than 685,000 curies of iodine 131 (units of radioactivity) during its first three years of operation. This early pattern of granting primacy to plutonium production above human health and misleading the public about reactor discharges, according to journalist Daniel Grossman, would continue into the future. Perhaps the most flagrant of these harmful releases was the so-called Green Run of December 1949, when Hanford conducted a cold war "experiment," emitting a highly radioactive, uncooled plume that dispersed over hundreds of miles from Spokane to Klamath Falls.[19] For better or worse, Hanford's location on the southernmost bend of the Columbia River would serve to remind future generations of the lethal power of modern science.

The increased cold war funding that poured into Hanford benefited the company town of Richland. Under federal ownership for fifteen years, Richland prospered and increased in population to twenty-two thousand residents in 1950, presenting a picture of community stability with neat homes, carefully manicured lawns, and numerous churches. White, middle class, highly educated, and well paid, residents proffered the image of a pleasant, disciplined, and orderly community. Although the federal government moved slowly, land and buildings passed into individual ownership in 1958, and the town of Richland was incorporated. But the community was still known far and wide as "Atomic City," with the local high school adopting "Bombers" for its club and sports teams and a logo that pictured a mushroom cloud.[20] The waxing and waning of cold and hot wars and eventually a huge Superfund cleanup project would continue to influence the economies of Hanford and its dependent Tri-Cities communities.

The Boeing Company, one of three leading aircraft manufacturers to come out of the war, was another important component to the region's industrializing economy. When the simmering cold war intensified in the late 1940s, the newly fledged U.S. Air Force began directing procurement orders to Boeing, acknowledging the Seattle company's ability to produce military aircraft. The emergence of this "military-metropolitan-industrial complex" involved company executive William Allen, local union leaders, the Seattle Chamber of Commerce, air force officials, Washington senator Warren Magnuson, and, with his ascendancy to the Senate in 1952, Henry Jackson. In their support for Boeing, Seattle's leaders joined in President Dwight Eisenhower's military-industrial complex.[21] By the 1960s and 1970s, the ties between Henry Jackson and Boeing were so intimate that his detractors referred to him as "the Senator from Boeing."

Seattle and Boeing's fortunes were closely linked to national and international events: the Soviet Union's blockade of West Berlin, the Korean War, tensions between Communist China and the United States over the Formosa Strait, and a growing American commitment to suppress a colonial rebellion in Southeast Asia. The development of two impressive aircraft, the B-47 and the B-52, clearly illustrates the alliance between defense industry needs and Boeing's genius in transforming military requirements into assembly line production. Fearful that Boeing's health would perpetually be linked to war and the threat of war, company head William Allen pushed the firm's engineers to begin developing a serviceable passenger aircraft in 1952. Although the B-707 did not become operational until 1959, Boeing's gamble placed the company alone among all competitors in aircraft technology. The production of successors, the B-727, B-737, and B-747, sharply reduced Boeing's dependence on the war economy.[22]

The ebb and flow of cold war anxieties contributed to cycles of boom and bust in Greater Seattle's economy. The most notable of these occurred between 1969 and 1970, the "Boeing depression," when the company's employment rolls dropped from 105,000 to 38,000 workers. Boeing's major period of growth between 1947 and 1958 and the explanation for its long-range success stemmed from its ability to capture a major share of the national and international market for commercial airline production. Korean War orders, cold war–related production contracts, and the development of the lucrative B-707 passenger aircraft brought thousands of engineers and other manufacturing personnel to the Puget Sound region. The "Boeing effect" reverberated through the University of Washington, where enrollment exploded, increasing from 13,675 students in 1956 to nearly 30,000 by 1968. University president Charles Odegaard encouraged faculty to aggressively pursue lucrative federal research grants in the sciences.[23] The contractual ties involving universities, the defense industry, and the military explain in part the rise of the counterculture and antiwar movements on the West Coast during the late 1960s.

The economies of Seattle and King County remained almost exclusively dependent on the health of the Boeing Company until the 1970s. King County had become more dependent on Boeing by the mid-1950s because the company provided employment for about half of all manufacturing workers. The company imported most of what it needed and shipped most of its production elsewhere, giving emphasis to the colonial nature of the city's economy. The lack of economic diversity had a self-fulfilling prophecy—pursuing a traditional line of production tended to reinforce the notion that the economy should continue doing the same thing. Because Boeing's facilities housed a workplace for engineers and a spacious assembly plant, Seattle developed few spin-off businesses during those years.[24]

Washington's Inland Empire metropolis, Spokane, emerged from the Second World War with a considerably larger population, much of it related to the construction and expansion of military bases. Because of its historic location as a strategic crossroads for transcontinental rail transport (the Northern Pacific, Great Northern, and Milwaukee railroads all passed through Spokane), military officials designed a strategy to protect the city from enemy attack. In quick order, Spokane became home to the Velox Naval Supply Depot and the large Galena Army Air Corps Supply and Repair Depot ten miles west of the city. Officially renamed Fairchild Air Force Base in 1948, the facility became an integral part of the Strategic Air Command and an operating base for the nation's nuclear deterrent program. Although Spokane emerged from the war with two sizable aluminum plants, Fairchild became the most important factor in the city's economy, providing significant payrolls, especially when the cold war turned hot during the Korean and Vietnam conflicts, and sustaining Spokane's economy and its population (161,721 in 1950 and 181,608 in 1960).[25]

Native American/First Nations people emerged from the Second World War with a strengthened sense of self-identity and a renewed interest in self-government. They were committed to improvements in education, living conditions, and the administration of reservation operations. Locked out of employment during the Depression, Puget Sound Indians found jobs in sawmills, logging operations, and the fishing industry during the war. Still others worked in the shipyards or at one of the sprawling Boeing plants, and a large number served in the armed services. With the end of hostilities in 1945, however, tribes across the West faced a new threat, the federal government's concerted effort to reverse the successes of the Indian Reorganization Act, to abolish the Indian New Deal.[26] The buzzword for this policy reversal? *Termination.*

The House Subcommittee on Indian Affairs conducted hearings around Puget Sound in 1944 to assess the wardship status of American Indians and to investigate potential revisions to federal policy. With findings that were already predetermined, the committee reported that federal policy functioned to perpetuate the Indians' special status rather than to prepare them for full citizenship. Conservative lawmakers like Utah's Republican senator Arthur Watkins eventually coalesced around a new policy, termination, a directive that would end the federal government's special responsibility for Indians. Despite the fact that many Indians rejected the termination legislation, Congress and presidential administrations pushed ahead with the proposals.[27]

Congressional pursuit of termination fit nicely with federal cold war policy, emphasizing ethnic integration and narrowly construed conceptions of freedom and liberty. Conservative politicians pushed termination as the antithesis to "concentrations camps" or "socialistic" environments. Termination discourse fit with cold war objectives to "liberate" people enslaved behind the Iron Curtain. Utah's Arthur Watkins referred to termination as an "Indian freedom program," with an emphasis on liberating Indians from reservation life. In the longer course of events, Indians reacted to cold war conformities with a heightened sense of their own identity.[28]

Termination legislation gained momentum in the postwar years, becoming formal policy with the passage in 1953 of House Concurrent Resolution (HCR) 108, which announced the intent of Congress to end its trusteeship relationship with Indians "at the earliest possible time." The resolution also directed the secretary of the interior to select tribes ready for termination and to submit legislation to terminate "certain named tribes." The largest and most controversial of all the groups selected for termination in the Pacific Northwest were the Klamath Tribes of Oregon, whose reservation embraced huge stands of ponderosa pine. Congress passed the Klamath termination bill in 1954 and a subsequent measure for several smaller western Oregon tribes. The legislation, which included loss of reservation timberland, ultimately proved an abysmal failure, with rising unemployment in Indian communities, rampant alcoholism, increases in welfare rolls, downward-spiraling personal health, and lower life expectancies.[29]

Before the end of the 1950s it was clear that termination was disastrous policy. It was not until 1968, however, that President Lyndon Johnson proposed a new Indian policy that emphasized self-determination and a modest move toward autonomy. But the wreckage of termination was strewn across south-central Oregon's Klamath country and among the small tribes in the western parts of the state. Although the Klamath Tribes regained federal recognition in the 1980s, termination remained an indelible collective memory among the Klamath people. "While the policy of termination has since been repudiated," the tribal narrative observes, "those tribes and Indian people subjected to its horrors still suffer significant and irreparable scars from the experience."[30]

The small tribes of western Washington initially expressed mixed reactions to termination. Although most Indians now view termination policy as an enormous federal error, at first western Washington tribes were uncertain about the initiative. After three trips to Puget Sound and countless meetings with Indians, Glenn Emmons, commissioner of the Bureau of Indian Affairs, proposed that a variety of termination approaches should be used for the Puget Sound area. By the mid-1950s, however, the small tribes had coalesced around two demands: guarantees to certain treaty stipulations and federal payments for rights that had been denied. The bill to terminate the Puget Sound groups eventually stalled in Congress, victim to greater resistance from the tribes and growing congressional disillusionment with the policy. In the end, the effort to terminate western Washington tribes had the ironic effect of strengthening tribal identity.[31]

Washington's Colville Indian Reservation, with its eastern and southern boundaries bordering the Columbia River, covers nearly 1.5 million acres of forest and grazing land and valuable mineral deposits. The Colville encounter with termination involved the tribe's long struggle to gain back the large "North Half" of their old reservation, land the federal government seized in the early twentieth century. With this objective in mind and with the assistance of Washington congressman Walt Horan, the Colville agreed to a bill that would return the North Half to the tribe if they adopted a termination plan. Laurie Arnold points out that the tribal business council opposed termination but wanted to regain the North Half, considering termination a necessary concession to recover their land.[32]

The tribe's internal deliberations were hotly contested and dragged on for nearly two decades. During that time several federal polls showed tribal members conflicted over termination, although no government questionnaire explicitly asked directly whether the Colville wanted to terminate. Tribal infighting persisted until Lucy Covington was elected to the tribal council in the late 1960s and successfully moved the tribe away from the termination debate. As the most widely recognized tribal spokesperson beyond the reservation, Covington (and the Colville) learned to effectively make the tribe's case to the non-Indian world. In a speech at

Washington State University in 1970, tribal councilman Mel Tonasket remarked that if termination had come to the reservation, the Colville "would lose those things that cannot be paid for with money: culture, heritage, identity and ... something very dear to an Indian's heart, hunting and fishing rights." Lucy Covington, Mel Tonasket, and other Indian spokespersons were among an emerging group of Native leaders who were asserting that reservations were sacred grounds.[33]

When British Columbia's Indian veterans returned from military service, they still were not considered citizens in the land of their birth. Hubert Evans, who published a description of cultural conflicts in a Native village in 1954, pointed to the hypocrisy of treating military personnel returning from Normandy, Holland, and other battlefields as second-class citizens. Although Indians had long participated in the wage-labor force as fishers and loggers, race continued to be the one constant that determined their everyday relationships with the larger society. Many Native children still attended residential boarding schools, and, along with all their other shortcomings, these institutions were powerful reminders to students of their inequality with respect to other Canadians.

Change for British Columbia's First Nations, however, was on the horizon, with legal challenges reflecting a growing restiveness among Native people. A Canadian House of Commons Select Joint Committee inquiry in 1946 urged members of Parliament to pave the way for Native integration into the larger society and to repeal the most coercive aspects of the Indian Act. Although the joint committee recommended that Indian children be admitted to provincial schools, field reports in British Columbia indicated that Native students still sat apart from others in the same classroom. The federal Parliament shifted gears in 1951, repealing prohibitions against the potlatch, removing the ban on alcoholic sales to Indians, and permitting Natives to engage in political fund-raising with other citizens. After repeated protests, British Columbia officials returned many Kwakiutl ceremonial pieces seized early in the century. These were still minimalist improvements in the Native condition. A mid-1950s study indicated that Indians remained marginal players in the regional economy, that they lacked security in their property, and that their ambiguous legal status made Indian land titles equivocal.[34]

Before the Second World War, Seattle's small black community lived in a relatively "benign racial environment," according to Quintard Taylor. Although racial prejudice and discrimination were evident on every hand, "the harsh, caustic edge of race relations" in the South and in many eastern cities was mostly absent from Puget Sound. Because of the thousands of African American defense workers who flocked to Seattle and other West Coast cities during the war, however, older norms of racial etiquette quickly eroded. Seattle's African American population increased from 3,789 to 15,666 during the 1940s, with many of the new arrivals coming from rural Louisiana, Texas, and Arkansas. Although unemployment in the black community during the postwar years was higher than in white and Asian communities, federal-contracting guidelines enabled blacks to hire on with Boeing and to obtain civil service appointments. But liabilities accompanied these modest successes because of growing segregation in housing and the exclusion of blacks from professional work in banking and finance. Some labor unions also continued to discriminate against blacks.[35]

African Americans also found it difficult to find employment in the professions, including as teachers in the public schools. When some parents approached the Seattle School Board about hiring teachers irrespective of race or ethnicity, board member James Duncan (an International Association of Machinists member who opposed membership for blacks) reminded the superintendent of schools that district policy required hiring the best candidate. With a new school superintendent in 1947, the Seattle district proceeded under new hiring guidelines, and two African American women began teaching in the fall of that year, an indication that the school board was slowly adjusting to new demographic realities.[36]

During the Second World War, the Portland Housing Authority directed black defense workers to the city's Guild's Lake project or the community of Vanport. With the close of hostilities in 1945, there were five thousand blacks at Guild's Lake and another six thousand in Vanport, prompting one Housing Authority staffer to observe that city commissioners always wanted to provide separate housing for blacks. When conditions worsened for Portland's African American population by the winter of 1947, with more than one-third of them unemployed, a National Urban League official remarked that Portland was "just like any Southern town ... the most prejudiced [city] in the west."[37]

Between 1945 and 1949, federal and local housing officials discussed razing the Vanport buildings to clear space for industrial development. If the Columbia River flood of May 1948 had not demolished Vanport, there is evidence to suggest that federal officials would have transferred Vanport to the jurisdiction of Portland, and the city would have evicted the remaining residents. Housing Authority officials were fearful of mixed-race occupancy of blacks and whites. With seventeen thousand people homeless (35 percent of them black) in the aftermath of the Vanport disaster, Portland officials continued to push ahead, demolishing the Portland Housing Authority's Guild's Lake units to make way for industrial development. As blacks relocated to crowded conditions in Portland's mostly segregated Albina district, the city muddled through the next few months, including voter rejection of a plan to build two thousand low-rent housing units. When reformer Dorothy McCullough Lee became mayor in 1950, however, Portland moved affirmatively, using federal funds to purchase 4,300 housing units and prohibiting discrimination in its public rentals.[38] In many respects, however, open discrimination remained a fact of life in renting to minorities.

Racial segregation, job discrimination, and other indignities were also daily points of reckoning for Spokane's African Americans. Carl Maxey, who was born in 1924 and became one of the city's most prominent lawyers (and first black attorney), remembered returning home from the war and being refused service in local bars—while he was still in uniform. Maxey recalled the "unwritten" rules at Spokane's popular Natatorium Park, where blacks could attend dances but were forbidden to enter the swimming pool. "The deal was this," Maxey told an interviewer. "If you were black and a black band was playing, you could go," but when a white band played, park officials evicted blacks. Beginning in the 1950s, Maxey led successful efforts to desegregate Spokane's public and private institutions, facilities, and clubs. He accomplished much of his work through litigation or the threat of litigation. Later in life, Maxey remembered the Second World War as a turning point in the fight against segregation and discrimination: "Change was never explosive in Spokane. It happened with the war more than anything else."[39]

Although a few Hispanics had been in the Pacific Northwest since the days of the fur trade and the interior gold rushes, an increasing number of Mexicans and Mexican Americans began making the trek northward to work in southern Idaho's sugar-beet fields in the early twentieth century. Still others found better wages building and maintaining railroads. But Idaho's and the American Northwest's agricultural fields remained the key attraction until well beyond the Second World War.[40] While the influx of Mexicans ceased—even reversed—during the Great Depression, the Second World War created intense labor shortages in western American agriculture. One scholar estimates that nearly five hundred

Carl Maxey (1924–97), who grew up as an orphan in Spokane, became a talented attorney and an outspoken proponent of civil rights in the state of Washington. An unwavering, in-your-face opponent of racial discrimination, Maxey was both loved and despised in his home state.

thousand Mexican-heritage American citizens served in the military services during the war. Still others, including large numbers of Mexican American women from the Southwest, worked in war industries in southern California.[41]

As white workers enlisted in the armed services or trekked to defense plants on the Pacific Coast, agricultural recruiters launched an aggressive campaign in the Southwest and northern Mexico to seek replacement labor. Corporate agricultural groups also put pressure on Congress, prompting lawmakers to pass Public Law 45, establishing the bracero policy, a federal program that brought thousands of Mexican workers into the United States to sustain the agricultural industry. Growers benefited from low-cost Mexican labor and their ability to sustain high levels of production during the war. With the end of hostilities in 1945, Mexicans and Mexican Americans continued to migrate north to Oregon, Washington, and Idaho to seek work.[42]

In the next two decades, a few Hispanics began to "settle out" in small family enclaves near the region's highly productive fields and orchards. Small Mexican and Mexican American communities developed in far eastern Oregon's Ontario, Vale, and Nyssa districts, in the Rogue and

Farmworkers at their camp, ca. 1942–47. Mexican farmworkers posing in their camp in Hood River, Oregon.

Willamette valleys, and in the lush pear- and apple-producing Hood River Valley. Washington's rich Yakima Valley attracted large numbers of Hispanic immigrants, while still others headed for Wenatchee Valley orchards or the fields and processing plants around Pasco and Walla Walla. Southern Idaho's fertile Snake River Plain continued to attract Mexican and Mexican American families to cultivate and harvest crops or to work in vegetable processing. But the genesis of much of the American Northwest's present Hispanic population can be traced to the Second World War and the federally sponsored bracero program.[43]

The Second World War and the cold war years embedded a "garrison state" mentality in national politics and turned the American West into an important spatial arena for national power, projecting the region's influence on the global stage. The region served as the launching base for "hot" wars in Korea and Vietnam and a point of transshipment for military hardware and troops heading for bases in Alaska and the Pacific. West Coast cities, including Seattle and Tacoma, thrived as manufacturing centers, supply depots, training bases, and air force stations. Largely dependent on military budgets during the 1950s, the booming economies of cities such as Seattle, San Francisco, Los Angeles, and San Diego accelerated the extraction of natural resources and boosted agricultural production. With the exception of Washington, timber districts in the Greater Pacific Northwest increased harvesting rates, with production in Oregon reaching a postwar high of 9.1 billion board feet in 1955.[44]

Weyerhaeuser, Simpson, Georgia-Pacific, and MacMillan-Bloedel in British Columbia set the pace during those halcyon years of lumber production, but smaller logging and sawmill outfits—"gyppo" contractors both north and south of the border—contributed mightily to that record output. Operating on marginal capital through subcontracts and with secondhand equipment, the hundreds of small operators who logged second-growth stands or less desirable old-growth timber paid good family wages across the region. Although there were many small operators in the interior, most gyppo outfits logged and milled timber in the Douglas fir region. Their numbers dropped sharply in northern California, Oregon, and Washington in the early 1960s, when timber prices increased and environmental requirements became too expensive. In British Columbia, the licensing system that favored large firms thinned the ranks of independent loggers and sawmill operators.[45]

The story of the region's modern lumber industry is also a tale of merger, consolidation, corporate takeovers, and the concentration of landownership in ever-larger units. The 1951 merger between the H. R. MacMillan Export Company and Bloedel, Stewart and Welch in British Columbia was the largest corporate consolidation in provincial history. Although not all consolidations were significant, a few—especially the expansion of Georgia-Pacific into an industrial giant—have been truly impressive. Beginning from a small base in Georgia, the company purchased mills and timberlands along the rich forested belt in northern California and Oregon between 1956 and 1959. The corporation's policy of selling its newly purchased timber to create a "cash flow" to pay for its acquisitions revolutionized the Pacific Northwest lumber industry, sustaining for several years smaller sawmills without access to timber. Through all the postwar production frenzy, however, the huge Weyerhaeuser Company dominated every wood-fiber sales category. The firm also ramped up its harvests in the early 1960s and began an aggressive log-export program to East Asia.[46]

For the region's diversified agricultural industries, the development of rubber-tired tractors, mechanical harvesters, and other automated equipment meant fewer field hands during planting and harvesting seasons. The wholesale mechanization of most agricultural work processes during the war meant fewer jobs with the return to peacetime. The Agriculture Extension Service and state and provincial educational institutions distributed circulars to farmers about the latest research, the newest miracle chemicals and fertilizers, and other information important to increasing production.

Farmers on British Columbia's southern mainland and southern Vancouver Island took advantage of improved transportation to advance their economic ties to provincial cities. A small, highly productive, and diversified agriculture in the lower Fraser River Valley and in the Okanagan district produced fruits and vegetables for coastal markets. British Columbia's agricultural production differed from the output of mines and sawmills because crops were processed and consumed in the province. In an effort to strengthen British Columbia agriculture, the provincial legislature passed an agricultural land reserve act in 1973 to preserve valuable acreage for exclusive farm use.[47] With high capital and operating costs and the persisting threat of reduced trade barriers with the United States, British Columbia's farmers could expect increased competition in the future.

On the American side of the border, mechanization and rapid increases in agricultural production triggered a vast demographic shift from farm and ranch to seemingly more promising opportunities in urban environments. That movement was especially apparent along the great metropolitan corridor from Seattle to Eugene. The human flood tide moving to urban settings represented one of the most striking population movements in modern history. The Greater Northwest—like the Canadian and American nation-states—was literally a region in motion following the Second World War. Federally subsidized highway systems linked town and country in mutual symbiosis, providing farmers with access to markets and other amenities and urbanites with easy travel to the countryside. In British Columbia, the completion of the Trans-Canada Highway in 1962 provided an alternative to the Canadian Pacific Railroad, linking the province with prairies and points farther east.[48]

Federal, state, provincial, and private initiatives created the infrastructure that propelled the great boom that took place following the Second World War. The advances in industrial activity that occurred between 1940 and 1970 would have been impossible without a vastly expanded hydropower capacity, improvements in water and land transportation, and intensification of mechanized processes in agricultural production. The great multipurpose dams constructed on the Columbia, Snake, upper Missouri, and Peace rivers as well as numerous other waterways provided the primary source of energy to power those industrial advances. The great dams served several other purposes: to improve navigation, to protect against flooding, to store water for irrigation, and to expand recreational opportunities. In the end, the engineering works transformed Northwest streams into utilitarian, efficient waterways, known through their storage capacity and controlled flow in cubic feet per second.

7

Remaking Northwest Landscapes

Big things begin in small ways! From the time the first European American boats began plying the waters of the Columbia, Fraser, and other rivers of the Northwest, dreamers with grandiose imaginations envisioned transforming the region's streams into utilitarian, efficient waterways, linking the interior with oceanic highways to the west. Beginning with the canal and locks at Willamette Falls in 1873, public and private engineers have built jetties, revetments, and dams on rivers, dramatically transforming the regional landscape. The most important of those "improvements" were the multipurpose dams constructed after the Second World War. On the American side of the border, cold war fears about the need for greater electrical-generating capacity propelled many of the projects.

During the 1880s and 1890s, Tacoma City Light, Seattle City Light, Portland General Electric, and the Washington Water Power Company (Spokane) constructed small dams to generate and deliver electrical power over short distances to urban markets. With two great waterways—the Columbia and Fraser rivers—draining much of the interior, early-twentieth-century visionaries developed an enthusiasm for even more impressive projects. By the close of the twentieth century, that collective vision had turned the majestic Columbia into a series of dams and slack-water reservoirs to generate huge amounts of electricity and to provide ship passage far into the interior. The eleven major dams on the mainstem Columbia in the United States and Canada—and hundreds of smaller dams on tributaries—have transformed the Great River into the most productive hydroelectric system in the world.[1]

With its headwaters at Columbia Lake near the literal roof of the continent in the Canadian Rockies, the Columbia is the fourth largest river in North America, discharging more water into the Pacific Ocean than any other stream in the Western Hemisphere. Described in the 1940s and 1950s as the world's "greatest power stream," the 1,243-mile-long waterway drains approximately 259,000 square miles. British Columbia's Fraser

River originates in Mount Robson Provincial Park high in the Canadian Rockies, with its 850-mile winding course to the Pacific draining 84,000 square miles. Together the Columbia and Fraser drain approximately 343,000 square miles in seven states and two provinces. The tidewater areas of the two rivers have been dredged and channelized to accommodate oceangoing ships, and the stepladder dams and locks on the Columbia enable barge traffic to navigate 460 miles inland to Lewiston, Idaho, on the Snake River. It is widely acknowledged that the aggressive river projects have come at a cost, contributing to cataclysmic declines in salmon runs, severe injury to Indian fishers, and the disappearance of iconic landmarks such as Celilo and Kettle falls.[2]

Although the makeover of the Columbia River and its tributaries dates to the nineteenth century and the construction of the canal and locks at Willamette Falls in 1873, the difficult feat of building the south jetty at the mouth of the river between 1884 and 1895 marks the initial alteration to the great waterway itself. Improvements to the south jetty, the completion of the north jetty in 1917, and continued dredging of the Columbia River bar eventually provided a depth of forty feet. Shipping interests then turned their attention to two major upriver obstacles to navigation—the Cascades Rapids in the Columbia Gorge and the rough, rock-strewn stretch of river between The Dalles and Celilo Falls. With heavy lobbying pressure from Portland developers and upriver shipping interests, army engineers completed the Cascade Locks and Canal in 1896 and the more difficult The Dalles–Celilo Canal in 1915. More ambitious projects—those requiring huge infusions of federal money—would await advances in engineering technology and the crisis of the Great Depression.[3]

The collapsing economy and massive unemployment of the early 1930s were critical events in the transformation of the Columbia River. The onset of the Great Depression and the election of a president willing to take risks putting people to work on large public projects provide the background to the great multipurpose dams on the Columbia system. Developing Northwest rivers, federal officials reasoned, would help resolve the nation's economic crisis. Building expensive giant dams and turbines required huge infusions of capital, revenue requirements far beyond the means of state budgets. The shattered economy provided the incentive for President Franklin D. Roosevelt's New Deal administration to implement the findings of the Army Corps of Engineers' famous 308 Report, *The Columbia River and Minor Tributaries*. Referring to the River of the

West as "the greatest system for water power to be found anywhere in the United States," the report was confident that there was "nothing . . . to cause a belief that the engineering difficulties cannot be surmounted."[4]

The 308 Report recommended ten dams for the main stem of the Columbia, with Bonneville just above tidewater, the most downriver on the engineers' blueprints, and Grand Coulee the principal upriver undertaking. The release of the 308 Report in the early stages of Roosevelt's administration was timely, attracting the attention of New Deal planners. Shortly after his inauguration, the president released emergency relief funds to begin work on Bonneville and Grand Coulee dams. The Bonneville project, completed in 1938, was a run-of-the-river dam, that is, a relatively low dam with the ability to produce hydropower and with a canal and locks to aid navigation. Grand Coulee, completed in 1941 ("the biggest thing on earth," Richard Neuberger called it), was a magnificent hydropower structure with a huge storage capacity. Rising 350 feet above the Columbia and nearly a mile long, Grand Coulee Dam was the end of the road for migrating salmon, eliminating more than 1,100 miles of spawning habitat.[5]

Franklin Roosevelt and the New Deal "Brains Trust" were idealists, visionaries who thought the Pacific Northwest would provide an alternative to economic, social, and environmental chaos elsewhere.[6] Speaking at the Grand Coulee construction site before twenty thousand people in 1934, the charismatic president told the gathering that the project would provide opportunity for families in the "settled parts of the nation to come out here" and make a better life for themselves. In later addresses, Roosevelt praised the public benefits Columbia River projects would bring to common people: cheap electrical rates, reduced flooding, and abundant supplies of water to reclaim unproductive lands.[7]

The military conflicts that took place in Europe and the western Pacific in the late 1930s forced the federal government to postpone additional projects for the Columbia system. But with the wars winding down in 1944, shipping interests, construction companies, and local chambers of commerce once again turned their attention to the region's waterways. Dams on the Columbia River and its tributaries, proponents contended, would improve navigation, control flooding, provide irrigation water for the arid Columbia Plain, and—equally important—produce abundant electricity for the region's aluminum and aerospace industries. Completing the army engineers' design would provide the infrastructure necessary to power regionwide economic development. Promoted with great enthusiasm immediately following the Second World War, the dam-building frenzy eventually attracted opposition from sports and commercial fishers, Indian tribes, and citizens who wanted to protect scenic streams such as Oregon's McKenzie and Deschutes rivers and Washington's Cowlitz River.

Two significant events pushed the dam-building juggernaut—the Columbia River flood of 1948 and heightened cold war tensions. Columbia Basin water development projects appeared to reach a stalemate in the fall of 1946, when the U.S. Fish and Wildlife Service recommended a ten-year moratorium on the construction of additional dams. Suspending the projects, Wildlife Service biologists argued, would enable engineers to design efficient fish ladders for upstream-migrating salmon and to provide safe passage through the dams for downstream-migrating smolts. Those issues were the centerpiece to hearings held in Walla Walla, Washington, in June 1947. Following the hearings, the Federal Inter-Agency River Basins Committee denied the moratorium, declaring that "facts and evidence . . . do not substantiate the fear that additional dams on the main stem of the Columbia and Snake Rivers will result in major loss or extinction of fish life."[8]

Within a year of the Walla Walla hearings, nature placed powerful propaganda tools in the hands of Columbia River developers. During the winter of 1947–48 heavy snows fell in the interior Northwest and northern Rocky Mountains. Cool early-spring weather followed, and then above-normal temperatures in April and May. Higher temperatures and heavy rainfall after mid-May combined to send a torrent of water cascading down the Kootenay, Clark Fort, Clearwater, and Snake rivers to the Columbia. For three weeks the Columbia flowed at approximately 900,000 cubic feet per second (cfs) at The Dalles in comparison to an annual peak flow of about 583,000 cfs.[9]

The downstream-rushing waters crested in late May, but far below the level of the great flood of 1894. There was a marked difference with the high waters of 1948, however, because broad areas of the downriver floodplain had been developed, much of it during the Second World War. When the flooding river breached a railroad embankment (which served as a dike) and surged through Vanport, the jerry-built wartime housing project north of Portland, the roiling waters destroyed the development. Because the destruction took place on the bright, sunny afternoon of Memorial Day, with many residents away because of the threatening waters, only fifteen people lost their lives. When the news reached Woody Guthrie, the Columbia River's songmeister, he pointed to the need for more flood control and power dams, which "will give us plenty to make up songs and to sing about for the rest of our native lives."[10]

When President Harry S. Truman flew to Portland to see firsthand the flood-ravaged lower Columbia, Vanport became an instant symbol of the need for flood control. Within three days of Vanport's destruction, the *Portland Oregonian* called for the federal government to accelerate appropriations for river development. The Army Corps of Engineers joined the chorus, citing data to show how flood damage would have been reduced with the construction of specific dams. Congress moved quickly, appropriating funding for additional dams.[11] If there was a defining moment in the postwar history of the Columbia River, it should be attributed to the finicky forces of nature and the great flood of 1948.

Writing for *Holiday* magazine in June 1949, Richard Neuberger argued that Americans should use their technical and engineering talents to control flooding, to generate cheap electricity, and, for the arid Columbia Plain, to create "a new civilization out of the dead desert." The architects of Bonneville Dam, Neuberger assured readers, had provided conclusive proof that salmon could successfully climb fish ladders and make their way to upstream spawning areas. There were technical solutions, he believed, to managing any problems that might arise. Mirroring the developers' cry ("We can have fish and dams too!"), Neuberger praised the heroic work of fishery biologists who trapped salmon below Grand Coulee Dam, milked the females and males of eggs and sperm, and hatched millions of fingerlings on tributary waterways. When the first generation of hatchery-produced salmon returned to their natal streams, Neuberger was ecstatic: "Man had masterminded the salmon's breeding habits."[12]

At the time of the Columbia River flood, the Army Corps of Engineers was in the midst of updating the old 308 Report on the Columbia system. Published in 1950 as House Document 531, the eight-volume report provided a panoramic blueprint to control flooding and expand hydropower development on the Columbia and its tributaries. With the updated report in hand, Congress quickly authorized the army engineers to begin several new projects: Albeni Falls, Libby, Priest Rapids, John Day, The Dalles, and smaller dams in the Willamette River Basin. The die was cast. Between 1952 and 1958, engineers completed one to three dams every year, and then in the late 1950s, Congress authorized a second burst of dam projects.[13]

As many writers have suggested, the genius in the corps' plan was its grand design to regulate and rationalize the flow of the entire Columbia River system and to achieve a uniform seasonal runoff. Doing so would protect against floods, and then releasing water during the low-flow summer and fall months would generate additional power. There were no caveats to House Document 531 recommendations. Releasing stored water during the low-flow summer months would augment power production, improve navigation, and dilute pollutants in streams.[14]

Ultimately, the corps' design created a river stilled and obedient to producing cheap hydropower and providing deep water for ship and barge traffic on the Columbia and lower Snake rivers. Completing the dam projects also served a grand patriotic purpose: it would strengthen national security, protect human life, improve standards of living, and bring stable employment. The benefits of moving forward with construction, the corps argued, would far outweigh "conflicts with resources of lesser significance that cannot be avoided."[15] Among those "resources of lesser significance" were Columbia River salmon.

More than twenty years of superheated cold war rhetoric provided a self-perpetuating catalyst, driving the work of the Army Corps of Engineers and the Bureau of Reclamation. During most of this period, river developers enjoyed the support of influential members of Congress, including Oregon senator Wayne Morse and Washington senators Warren Magnuson and Henry "Scoop" Jackson. Between them, the two agencies deployed multitudes of construction companies to complete main-stem and tributary dams. In a few instances, Congress refused funding or downsized specific projects. In others (most notably, the Snake River's Hells Canyon), the Idaho Power Company put up three hydroelectric dams. For the most part, the river developers had their way, carrying out congressional authorizations that dramatically remade landscapes throughout the Columbia system.[16] The Columbia Basin dams turned the river into the greatest hydropower complex in the United States, the system's turbines producing surpluses of electricity marketed as far distant as southern California.

The reservoirs that inundated long stretches of arable land in the Columbia Basin had a dramatic and negative effect on the lives and cultural practices of Indian people. The Dalles Dam, in particular, flooded Indian fishing, burial, and ceremonial sites and shifted the river's bounty to favor the river developers. The staircaselike dams flooded some of the most significant Indian fisheries in North America, mocking federal pay-offs to tribes for lost resources. The destruction of the Indian fishery and the denial of access to other resources are underrepresented stories in the region's dominant narrative. While Indian and non-Indian alike looked upon salmon as an iconic animal, only the former treated the fish as a being of great cultural importance, a significance dating back at least ten thousand years. To the modern world of industrial capitalism, how-ever, fish and places sacred to Native people took on a far different mean-ing in the immediate postwar years.

Building The Dalles Dam and flooding the magnificent stretch of water from the small town of The Dalles upriver beyond spectacular Celilo Falls should rank as one of the most notable and destructive acts committed against an Indian cultural and resource space. The ten thou-sand non-Native people who turned out on the shores of the Columbia to watch the water pool behind the giant dam on March 10, 1957, were certain they were celebrating greatly improved navigation on the Colum-bia and the promise of an abundance of electricity that would transform The Dalles into a thriving industrial center. For the Yakama, Warm Springs, Umatilla, Nez Perce, and Indians who lived permanently on the river, the narrative flows in a different direction. The Dalles project obliterated the most significant Native fishery on the Columbia River, and it annihilated an economic and cultural place of several millennia. Rosita Wolsey, a small Indian child when she watched the waters rise behind the dam, remembers her grandmother trembling uncontrollably as if "something was hitting her."[17]

Ancient Indian fishing sites at Cascades Rapids were lost to the waters behind Bonneville Dam in 1938. The loss of fishing places—or salmon—was seemingly no worry to some federal officials, with one Bureau of Reclamation staffer confiding in a 1947 Interior Department memo, "The overall benefits to the Pacific Northwest from a thoroughgoing develop-ment of the Snake and Columbia are such that the present salmon runs must be sacrificed."[18] Other than the tribes, commercial and recreational fishers, and a few conservationists, most citizens either watched passively or cheered the construction of more dams. In a keynote address to the Celilo Stories Conference in The Dalles in March 2007, Charles Wilkin-son expressed "great sadness" about the "passivity" of the larger society that stood by and watched the developers have their way. America was in a hurry, he observed, and wanted immediate results.[19]

Another little-known consequence of the disruption of the Indian fishery on the Columbia involved the government's promise to provide "in-lieu" fishing sites to replace traditional fishing places inundated behind dams. With the construction of Bonneville Dam, which displaced some thirty-five strategic fishing places through the Cascade Rapids, army engineers promised six in-lieu sites along other sections of the Columbia. When journalist Roberta Ulrich first investigated the issue forty years later, she found that the corps had set aside five small sites with limited acreage. In later travels through the Columbia Gorge, she observed new federal and state parks, boat-launching sites, and, later, small inlets retrofitted for wind surfers. "The unfairness of a promise unfulfilled while the land went to other uses," she writes, "is on display every day."[20]

The litany of promises and simple federal delays regarding the in-lieu question escalated with the passing years. The corps and the Bonneville Power Administration (BPA) would request funding for additional in-lieu sites, and Congress would authorize spending a certain amount of money. But when the authorizations went to the appropriation committees, the requests would disappear. The construction of The Dalles and John Day dams further complicated the in-lieu sites issue, because displaced Bonneville fishers had simply moved up to the Long Narrows and Celilo after the flooding behind Bonneville. When the corps and BPA developed a plan in the early 1970s to raise the water level in the Bonneville pool to increase its generating capacity, the Confederated Tribes of the Umatilla Reservation sued. At issue was the effect of rising water levels on existing in-lieu sites. In an out-of-court settlement, the federal government agreed to ask Congress to request funding to acquire additional sites for those lost with the construction of Bonneville, The Dalles, and John Day. The corps submitted the proposal to Congress in 1974, but lawmakers never acted on the request, an example of federal foot-dragging that would carry into the twenty-first century.[21]

A lesser-known displacement of Indian fishers took place when the gates were closed at Grand Coulee Dam, creating 151-mile-long Roosevelt Lake and flooding Kettle Falls. To clear the vast reservoir site, the Bureau of Reclamation relocated some 1,200 Colville graves, but when officials discovered another 2,000 graves, the bureau called off the effort. Even more traumatic for the Colville was their last gathering at Kettle Falls before rising waters submerged one of the great Native fishing sites on the Columbia River. In mid-June 1940, the Colville and Indians from around the Northwest (estimates range to nearly ten thousand) gathered for the three-day Ceremony of Tears at Kettle Falls to mourn the drowning of their traditional fishing stations. Within a year of the ceremony, Kettle Falls lay beneath ninety feet of water.[22]

The Bureau of Reclamation treated the loss of tribal lands with the same disregard it treated fisheries issues, disbursing predetermined payments to Colville who held land in individual ownership and then presenting tribal members with $174,000 for inundated reservation land. During the ensuing years, the Colville sought redress through the courts. Cases involving lost fishing sites at Kettle Falls and flooded home sites, root-digging areas, and traditional burial grounds dragged on until 1994, when the federal government agreed to pay the Colville Confederated Tribes a lump sum of $53 million and minimum prorated annual payments as a share of hydropower revenue. Colville activist Lucy Covington summarized federal commitments in 1977: "The promises made by the government were written in sand and then covered with water, like everything else."[23]

Lucy Covington (1910–82). Lucy Friedlander Covington (center at age four) became one of the most prominent spokespersons for the Colville Confederated Tribes. She led the tribal effort in the 1950s and 1960s to save the reservation from termination.

Embracing an impressive span of British Columbia's ecological diversity, the Fraser River Basin is home to 63 percent of the provincial population. The river passes through widely different ecosystems and traverses much of the lower British Columbia mainland, with the lower Fraser delta supporting some of the most productive agricultural enterprises in the province. From time immemorial, however, it was the river's aquatic habitat that attracted humans, especially the enormous salmon runs, which provided valuable sources of protein, first for Indian groups that dipnetted salmon from the river and later for the industrial canneries that took fish in huge quantities. Unlike the Columbia, the Fraser watershed has many large interior lakes that provide breeding habitat for sockeye salmon, but like the Columbia, environmental deterioration and heavy commercial fishing have contributed to sharply diminished salmon runs.[24]

The Fraser River was also a gleaming symbol of hope and opportunity to Canadian engineers, who saw in the river's severe descent the potential for unlimited hydropower development. Journalist Bruce Hutchinson argued for developing the Fraser to provide abundant and cheap electricity for rapidly growing coastal communities. Inexpensive electrical power and industrial development, he contended, were more valuable than salmon. If it was impossible to build salmon-friendly dams, the province should pursue artificial propagation, a well-established precedent on the Columbia River. During the immediate postwar years, engineering plans for the Fraser included dams on four major tributaries and a high dam on the main stem, some twenty miles upriver from Lillooet. The proposed 720-foot-high Moran Dam would be the end of the road for the upstream movement of salmon and steelhead.[25]

Because Moran Dam threatened to alter the river's ecology and sharply reduce the number of salmon, federal and provincial officials directed the International Pacific Salmon Fisheries Commission to review salmon mitigation strategies. Published in 1960, the commission's report was blunt: "At the present time, artificial propagation is not a proven method of maintaining even small localized stocks of Fraser River sockeye and pink salmon." The naturalist and conservationist Roderick Haig-Brown—a member of the commission—observed that the value of salmon involved much more than economics. To objectively discuss salmon and dams, he commented, would be "a betrayal of the salmon and their meaning." The commission's report effectively killed Moran Dam.[26]

Today British Columbians celebrate the Fraser, still free-flowing to the Pacific, as the world's foremost salmon-producing stream. Dams on the Fraser system are confined to upper tributaries beyond the reach of migrating salmon. To explain the difference between the series of dams on the main-stem Columbia and their absence on the Fraser, fisheries scientist Jim Lichatowich contends that American biologists were more willing to compromise and accept mitigating technofixes such as artificial propagation. In contrast, Canadian policy makers placed their faith in the work of fishery biologists who advised against building hatcheries as a technological trade-off for developing the Fraser River. Although Canadian water projects elsewhere destroyed salmon-bearing streams, during the critical dam-building era following the Second World War, biologists used the best science to argue against putting up dams on the Fraser River proper. The British Columbia government formally put the coup de grâce on the issue in 1997, when it enacted a law banning dam construction on the main-stem Fraser.[27]

During the twenty-year premiership of W. A. C. Bennett, British Columbia truly became modern—with all modernity's attendant social costs, especially to Native people. When William Andrew Cecil Bennett switched from the Conservative to the new Social Credit Party in 1951, his confederates won a narrow plurality of seats in the provincial legislature, enabling Bennett to begin two decades as premier of British Columbia. Critics and friends alike point to his ambitious record of building highways and railroads, expanding ferry service along the coast and interior waterways, and constructing bridges and hydropower facilities. Bennett and Social Credit expropriated British Columbia's leading private utility and coupled it with the provincial Power Commission to create a new Crown corporation, BC Hydro and Power Authority. BC Hydro quickly took the lead in promoting aggressive economic development projects, especially in British Columbia's interior.[28]

Although the premier and Social Credit were both firm believers in the free-enterprise system, Bennett's policies greatly expanded the government's role in the economy. Bennett's well-known "Two Rivers Policy"—fulfilling British Columbia's commitment to the Columbia River Treaty (1961) with the United States and developing the Peace River—tripled the province's electrical output. The Columbia River Treaty funded Mica, Keenleyside, and Duncan dams in British Columbia and Libby dam in northwestern Montana. The transnational agreement further rationalized and "evened out" the Columbia's seasonal flow. In 1984 BC Hydro

W. A. C. Bennett (1900–1979). Premier of British Columbia and head of the provincial Social Credit Party from 1952 to 1972, Bennett remains the longest-serving premier in British Columbia history.

completed the huge Revelstoke Dam (separate from the treaty agreement), which produces hydropower and operates in concert with Mica Dam. Bennett's projects entailed social costs, inundating productive farmland, valley-bottom forests, and scenic canyons. In some instances, entire towns had to be moved above the high-water line of reservoirs.[29]

Bennett's greatest monument, the W. A. C. Bennett Dam on northern British Columbia's Peace River, created one of the world's largest hydro-electric facilities and the world's largest human-made lake at that time. During Bennett's tenure in office, there was a transcendent assumption that increased energy production would lead to higher standards of living. First proposed in the mid-1950s, the mammoth Peace River project was completed in 1967, flooding a long section of the Peace River Valley, including the homeland of the Tsay Keh Dene (the Ingenika band of Indians), many of whom did not speak English. Because he was anxious to push the project to conclusion, Bennett excused the government of all responsibility for the aboriginal population whose homeland would be flooded. As the reservoir filled with water, the government moved about 125 Tsay Keh Dene hunting and trapping families to a reserve some 120 miles to the south and paid the band a total of $35,000.[30]

The Tsay Keh Dene, however, did not go quietly into the night. With the passing years, band members drifted away from the reserve, many of them returning to Ingenika Point, a bluff above the reservoir covering their old homeland. In the late 1980s, provincial officials "discovered" the sordid circumstances of the Natives, with one cabinet member describing conditions as "the most primitive I have ever seen." The government continued to procrastinate until 2006, when it presented the Tsay Keh Dene with a more equitable compensation package. Armed with Supreme Court of Canada decisions in behalf of First Nations people, the Tsay Keh Dene now have a heightened sense of government perfidy. When British Columbia authorities, especially BC Hydro, announced plans to build another hydropower project in the Peace River Valley, band members cited U.S. Supreme Court rulings that require government consultations with First Nations people when resource activities affect their traditional lands.[31] With these new and powerful legal prerogatives, the Tsay Keh Dene are in a much stronger bargaining position in the twenty-first century.

The most contentious of all water-related developments in the American Northwest is the Klamath Reclamation Project astride the Oregon-California border. By the close of the twentieth century, the extensive series of canals, siphons, pumping plants, tunnels, laterals, and drainage ditches watered approximately 240,000 acres of agricultural land. The reclamation blueprint for the upper basin drained marshes and shallow lakes for crop production and redirected water from three lakes and two rivers to irrigate the former lake beds. Two sources of water serve the project: (1) Upper Klamath Lake and the Klamath River and (2) streams and a small reservoir in an internally drained basin to the east. Before damming and water diversions remade the landscape, the upper Klamath Basin's 185,000-acre marshland provided one of the most prolific waterfowl breeding areas in North America. Today, the once extensive natural wetlands of Lower Klamath Lake depend on water available after agricultural withdrawals have been satisfied.[32]

Two national wildlife refuges further complicate jurisdictional dilemmas in the upper Klamath region—Lower Klamath Lake Wildlife Refuge, established in 1908, and Tule Lake National Wildlife Refuge, set aside in

1928. The Lower Klamath Refuge was unique because it was the first of its kind established inside the boundaries of a federal reclamation project. Against the advice of federal botanists who argued that Lower Klamath Lake soils would prove too alkaline to grow crops, Reclamation Service officials directed the draining of the lake bed in 1917. Within two years, waterfowl were dying in large numbers, and the eighty-five-thousand-acre marshland was drying up. "By 1922," William Kittredge writes, "all that remained was a 365-acre pond." And, as federal biologists had warned, the alkaline soils in the old lake bed proved ill-suited for farming.[33]

The Lower Klamath Refuge was devoid both of agriculture and wild-life through the 1930s, "a wasteland and a monument, symbolic and actual, to heedlessness and greed," Kittredge argues. A series of technical adjustments beginning in 1942—pumping excess water from the expanding Tule Lake irrigation district into the refuge and the development of deep drains to leach alkali from the soil—restored waterfowl marshes and enabled farmers to profitably grow crops such as barley, oats, and wheat. But how to manage the thousands of acres of refuge land within the reclamation project remained the larger question for the U.S. Fish and Wildlife Service and the Bureau of Reclamation.

At the close of the Second World War, Reclamation worked out an agreement with Fish and Wildlife to develop and lease refuge lands to farmers for growing crops. That arrangement continued into the early 1960s, when Congress enacted legislation to settle the jurisdictional struggle over the management of refuge lands. Authored by California senator Thomas Kuchel, the measure directed that upper Klamath refuges "shall be administered by the Secretary of the Interior for the major purpose of waterfowl management, but with full consideration to optimum agricultural use that is consistent therewith." Fish and Wildlife and Reclamation entered into a cooperative agreement in 1977, with Reclamation granted jurisdiction for managing the leased refuge lands. This proved to be a Catch-22, because farmers expected Reclamation to serve their interests, while critics contended that Reclamation decisions have skewed refuge management practices.[34]

In the end, the problem of water, its allocation, and federal environmental legislation would keep the Klamath Basin in the nation's news. Prolonged periods of drought, cutover timberlands, overgrazed riparian vegetation, and non–point source pollutants flowing into the Klamath system worsened conditions for the troubled waterscape. Domestic and industrial sewage was causing high coliform levels in the Klamath River below the city of Klamath Falls by the 1960s. Passage of the federal Clean Water Act in 1972 and local efforts to improve sewage treatment facilities eventually brought coliform counts within legal requirements. But the Klamath River's troubles have persisted, especially during the summer and early fall months, when large volumes of water are diverted to irrigate crops in the upper basin, with catastrophic consequences for endangered salmon. Even in years of average precipitation, the Klamath system does not generate enough water to satisfy the needs of upper-basin farmers and the requirements of the Endangered Species Act.[35]

Legal bombshells of a different order descended on the Klamath Basin in 1974, when Judge Gus Solomon of the United States District Court for Oregon determined that at the time of termination (1961), enrolled members of the Klamath Indian Tribes still retained the right to fish, hunt, and trap on the old reservation lands free of state regulations. Ten years later another blockbuster decision determined that tribal members also held superior "rights to as much water on Reservation lands as they need to protect their hunting and fishing rights." By virtue of the "first-in-time, first-in-rights" legal doctrine, Indians had prior claims to Klamath Basin waters before all others.[36]

The Klamath Indian Tribes subsequently used their senior water rights and the Endangered Species Act to press home a matter of great cultural importance—maintaining sufficient water levels in Upper Klamath Lake to protect endangered Lost River and shortnose suckers. Federal District Judge Michael Hogan (Eugene, Oregon) determined in 1998 that the tribes' senior water rights held precedence over more than two thousand basin farmers who used project water to grow crops. The Klamath Tribes water rights proved volatile and stirred undercurrents of racism in the larger community. Environmental organizations added to the heated exchanges in the basin, accusing the U.S. Fish and Wildlife Service and the Bureau of Reclamation of shortchanging water allocations for the refuges and dumping pesticide-laced water on the land.[37] In the face of persisting drought, all of these issues—endangered fish, troubled wildlife refuges, fights over water allocations, and aboriginal treaty rights—would escalate in the new century.

During the last 150 years farmers have transformed southern Idaho's arid Snake River Valley into one of America's most productive agricultural landscapes. From the time the first whites settled in the Bruneau, Boise, Payette, Owyhee, and Weiser river valleys in the 1860s, people have been taking advantage of the Snake River Valley's excellent soils, abundant sunshine, and plentiful flows of water to turn the windswept sagebrush plains into a greenscape of alfalfa, wheat, barley, and more lucrative specialized crops. Beginning with the construction of the Minidoka Project in 1904 and 1905 and continuing through the 1970s, engineers have extended the reach of the sophisticated system of canals and laterals to water, increasing acreages of land.[38]

The huge Minidoka Project extends intermittently from far eastern Idaho for three hundred miles west along the Snake River to the appropriately named town of Bliss in south-central Idaho. The project included Minidoka Dam, completed in 1906, and five additional dams, with the large Palisades Project and Palisades Dam providing important supplemental and mitigation waters for the Minidoka Project by 1970. Through its elaborate system of canals, pumping plants, and laterals, the project initially watered 120,000 acres in the vicinity of Rupert, Burley, and Declo. Minidoka and four additional dams provided storage for some 1,111,178 acres by 1992.[39]

As many people recognize, reclamation projects are not fail-safe systems. Problems arose early at Minidoka and other Snake River projects with seepage, or "bogging"—areas where irrigation water did not drain properly. A major problem on all reclamation projects, bogging occurred when farmers flooded land with too much water. Seepage also happened when canals, laterals, and ditches leaked and added to the groundwater. On the Minidoka Project, approximately ten thousand acres became so saturated from rising groundwater that farming became difficult as early as 1909.[40]

In the process of making the desert bloom, therefore, engineers were forced to drain waterlogged land, a tactic that had the unintended consequence of charging the Snake River aquifer far beyond preirrigation levels. Because seepage was a community problem, farmers organized districts to design and build drainage systems. But the most fascinating part of this story was the supercharged Snake River aquifer. Filled with irrigation seepage, the Snake River aquifer subsequently provided a source of water for additional acres of irrigated agriculture. High crop prices and the development of efficient electrical pumps immediately following the Second World War prompted farmers to tap the swollen aquifer for additional sources of water. During the next three decades, the aquifer provided enough water for farmers and a growing number of agribusiness corporations to grow crops on another one million acres. The aquifer-fed fields, however, have a different look, sporting a variety of giant mechanical sprinklers that dominate the newly irrigated landscapes.[41]

Troubles emerged again when irrigators, believing that underground water supplies were limitless, failed to treat the aquifer like a dinosaur with a limited food supply. In the eastern Snake River Plain, irrigation water pumped from the river supplied about 60 percent of the aquifer's recharge. The increase in sprinkler irrigation in the 1950s and 1960s reduced the farmers' need to use river diversions to supply their irrigation needs. Those circumstances have slowed the aquifer's ability to recharge, thereby reducing underground water levels to the point that restrictions have been placed on further withdrawals in some places. The future productivity of Snake River agriculture will depend on constant readjustments to maintain the appropriate balance for the orderly distribution of water.[42]

The most cataclysmic event in southern Idaho's reclamation story took place on the morning of June 5, 1976, when Teton Dam collapsed. The Teton River's downstream-rampaging wall of water obliterated the towns of Wilford and Sugar City and caused millions of dollars of damage to Rexburg. The consequences were eleven deaths and damage estimates of $2 billion, with the federal government eventually settling $300 million in claims. Fingers of blame were pointed in every direction, with an overly aggressive Fremont-Madison Irrigation District and the Bureau of Reclamation faulted for inflating the benefits of the dam and deflating its real costs. Cecil Andrus, Idaho's governor when Congress authorized the dam, later reflected that his staff was split, with several younger advisors opposed to the project.[43]

The state's leading newspaper, the *Idaho Statesman*, sharply criticized the undertaking from the beginning. Even more damaging were Geological Survey reports that questioned the construction of a dam in an area with an elevated seismic risk and with fragile ash flows and rhyolitic rock. But the geologists' report had been thoroughly vetted along the way, with Andrus remembering that the Geological Survey timidly "questioned site stability and the ash flows and volcanic rock to which the earthen dam was anchored." In retrospect, he admits that he should have used better judgment and listened to those who voiced caution. When voters returned Andrus to the Idaho governor's office in the late 1980s, a few irrigators and the Bureau of Reclamation approached the incredulous governor about rebuilding the dam. When Andrus erected stringent environmental conditions, the proposal was abandoned.[44]

Oregon's Umatilla River Basin provides another example of a contested landscape involving irrigators, whose water diversions dried up the lower river during the summer months, and the Confederated Tribes of the Umatilla Indian Reservation, who held superior water rights. Beginning in the 1880s and gathering momentum with the passing decades, non-Indian agriculturalists drew ever-greater quantities of water from the Umatilla River. One of the first Reclamation Service undertakings in the United States, the initial project funded a small upriver diversion dam and the Feed Canal to carry water several miles to Cold Springs Reservoir, completed in 1908. Reclamation added McKay Reservoir to the system in 1927. Although seepage was a perennial problem with the Feed Canal, by 1950 the Umatilla Project irrigated more than twenty-two thousand acres, with the water diversions drying up the lower portions of the Umatilla River during the summer.[45]

The most damaging legacy of the water withdrawals has been the elimination of salmon and steelhead from the Umatilla River. Over the years, the Reclamation Service (renamed the Bureau of Reclamation in 1923) deliberately favored a growing agricultural economy and made decisions that drove salmon to extinction. When the river became a slow-moving, ugly mix of farm runoff and wastewater in the late summer months, the Umatilla Tribes served notice (under an 1855 treaty) that they held superior water rights under prior-appropriation doctrine. Tribal chair Antone Minthorn told Harvard University's "Honoring Nations" program in 2004 that the federal government ignored its treaty responsibilities when it granted irrigators large allocations of water in the early twentieth century: "When the irrigation water was taken from the river without any consideration for salmon populations, the river dried up and salmon were extinguished from the Umatilla."[46]

Secure in their belief that the tribe held treaty-guaranteed rights to both water and fish, the Umatilla engaged in hundreds of hours of discussions to broker a deal that would avoid putting farmers out of business. The Umatilla wanted to work cooperatively, Minthorn noted, and gain federal support for a solution that would return water to the river and restore salmon runs. Facing the threat of tribal and environmental organization lawsuits, Congress passed the Umatilla Basin Act in 1992, a measure that funded a pump-and-canal scheme to provide Columbia River water to irrigation districts in exchange for leaving sufficient water in the Umatilla to sustain viable fish populations. In effect, the federal government subsidized a technical solution to a problem of its own making—the overappropriation of Umatilla River water. The hard work of the Umatilla Tribes paid off when hatchery-introduced salmon and steelhead began returning to the Umatilla River to spawn early in the twenty-first century.[47]

Montana's Rocky Mountain river basins were also subject to significant makeovers in the years following the Second World War. Western Montana became an arena for several flood-control and hydropower projects, oftentimes for places far removed from the dam sites themselves. Northwestern Montana's Libby and Hungry Horse dams, both constructed on upper tributaries of the Columbia River, were designed to regulate downstream flows to the Great River itself. Located on the South Fork of the Flathead River and completed in 1953, Hungry Horse controls seasonal runoff to the Flathead and Columbia rivers.[48]

Farther west on the Kootenay River, the much larger Libby project has a similar function—flood control and electrical-power generation. One of the projects designated in the Columbia River Treaty of 1961, Libby is part of an integrated system of dams on the upper Columbia system designed to control the river's flow to maximize power generation during periods of peak demand. The treaty stipulated that the United States would pay Canada $64.4 million to build three dams to store water during the spring melt, benefits that would help the United States in its flood-control efforts. Releasing water later in the season would also augment the hydropower capacity of downriver dams. More than eighty miles long, the Libby Reservoir extended some forty miles into British Columbia. The treaty agreement also stipulated that Canada was guaranteed half the downstream power benefits.[49] Located in some of western Montana's most remote country, neither Hungry Horse nor Libby displaced significant populations nor flooded valuable farmland.

The same cannot be said for Pick-Sloan, the coordinated development plan for the Missouri River Basin whose main-stem dams and tributary reservoirs transformed the Missouri's landscape. The principal Pick-Sloan beneficiaries were flood-prone communities in the lower basin, consumers of electricity, farmers, and barge traffickers. The biggest losers were the Mandan, Hidatsa, Arikara, and four other tribes whose reservations bordered the Missouri River or its tributaries. In that sense, the Missouri and Columbia rivers are intertwined in significant ways, especially those involving the numerous Indian tribes who protested the destruction of traditional resources and cultural space.[50]

Pick-Sloan projects in western Montana included Canyon Ferry Dam on the Missouri River in the Helena Valley, Tiber Dam on the Marias River near Chester, and Clark Canyon Dam on the Beaverhead River. Of those projects, Canyon Ferry, a Bureau of Reclamation dam, was the largest and most problematic because it flooded valuable farm and ranch land. The powerful Montana Power Company, operator of the original Canyon Ferry Dam dating to the early twentieth century, also opposed the project. Although purchasing land delayed construction, the Bureau of Reclamation completed the project in late 1954.[51]

Located approximately fifteen miles northeast of Helena, Canyon Ferry reconfigured Helena Valley's landscape, flooding significant bottomlands but augmenting water available for the city of Helena and for farmers through a pumping, tunnel, and canal system. Designed to generate electricity and store water for irrigation, Canyon Ferry became an important upstream component in the Pick-Sloan flood-control program. Canyon Ferry Lake also provided expanded recreational opportunities—fishing, boating, a variety of water sports, and picnicking and camping. Always anxious to celebrate the multipurpose functions of its projects, the Bureau of Reclamation praised Canyon Ferry for occupying an important niche "in an ambitious, cooperative undertaking of the Bureau of Reclamation and the Army Corps of Engineers."[52]

Growing environmental concerns over what many considered excesses in the development of western waterways eventually slowed the construction of new water projects in the American and Canadian Wests. Designed for the Columbia River between Priest Rapids and McNary dams, the proposed Ben Franklin Dam would create a huge reservoir through the last free-flowing stretch of the Columbia between Bonneville Dam and the Canadian border. Hanford scientists raised early questions about the effects of rising water tables on the adjacent nuclear reservation's subsurface storage facilities. Still others valued the so-called Hanford Reach as a nature preserve for migratory waterfowl, game animals, and a wealth of Native archaeological sites. Those collective, grassroots environmental pressures eventually became the major stumbling block to building Ben Franklin.[53]

Although Washington's powerful senators, Warren Magnuson and Henry Jackson, enthusiastically supported Ben Franklin, the federal Office of Management and Budget eventually recommended against the project in September 1971.[54] Environmental apprehensions and greater awareness of the social costs of dams during the 1970s also convinced British

Columbians to oppose building new dams. Those changing social views convinced the provincial legislature to protect salmon-producing rivers from further dam-building projects. Two important programs—the BC Heritage Rivers System and the Canadian Heritage Rivers System—signified the effort to protect national and provincial waterways of outstanding significance.[55]

The public's questions about major water development projects in the Greater Northwest were not isolated to the region itself. Beginning in the late 1960s, and with gathering momentum, a series of studies criticized the social and environmental effects of large-scale water projects. Edward Goldsmith and Nicholas Hildyard argued in a 1984 book that the disruptive effect of large dams was unavoidable and intrinsic to the technology. Large "superdams" were not benign and cost-free. Canadian scientists found that reservoir waters produced fish with elevated levels of mercury contamination, and by altering free-flowing water, dams destroyed the natural rhythms of rivers and the unique habitats and species that depended on those rhythms.[56]

Nowhere were the deleterious effects of dams more obvious than on the Columbia, a river once abundant in prodigious runs of anadromous fishes. Despite the expenditure of billions of dollars in the last half of the twentieth century, the annual runs of salmon continued to decline. While both terrestrial and ocean conditions were contributing factors, the stair-step series of Columbia River dams were the most critical element in the diminishing number of salmonids. Progress and human comfort were seemingly inimical to the river's indigenous species.[57]

8
The Conflicted Politics of Environmentalism

At nearly six and a half feet tall, charismatic and ambitious, Oregon's Tom McCall was a striking and formidable figure. "His massive frame," writes biographer Brent Walth, "dwarfed everyone around him, and the sweeping cornice of his jaw was always poised to talk." His voice was as unusual as his appearance, a unique "barnyard-Harvard" accent that reflected his Boston birthplace and eastern Oregon upbringing. But there was more to McCall than his physical size and singular rhetoric. He also articulated forthright and candid positions that resonated with a generation of people who saw government as a positive force, capable of maintaining clean water and air, protecting open spaces and ocean beaches from private development, and providing a good education for its citizens.[1]

McCall began his professional career in print journalism, moving first to radio and then migrating to television news broadcasting in the mid-1950s. Joining Portland's newest television station, KGW-TV, in 1957, McCall quickly became an on-air celebrity, and with the passing months he turned his investigative talents to water pollution issues, especially the Willamette River. With the encouragement of his boss, Tom Dargan, who saw television as a vehicle to social change, McCall worked nearly a year on a documentary that would set the tone for his future political career. Aired on November 21, 1962, and expensively produced, *Pollution in Paradise* staked out a moral position on pollution that placed livability and quality of life at the forefront of public discourse. McCall narrated the script off-camera in his distinctive voice, pointing his sharpest criticisms at the pulp and paper industry, whose effluent produced "foul-smelling masses of filth."[2]

Pollution in Paradise was a tour de force, pressing home the powerful argument that quality of life, a clean environment, and a healthy economy were one. In advance of national events, the documentary signaled a new spirit in Oregon that placed environmental issues at the forefront of politics and vaulted Tom McCall to the pinnacle of statewide elective office in 1966.[3] The events taking place in Oregon, however, should be framed in larger regional and national geographies that reflected increasing attention to the degraded nature of air, land, and water across North America. The publication of Rachel Carson's *Silent Spring* the same year set in motion a nationwide debate over the use of chemicals and pesticides and offered a strident critique of the ecological and health risks associated with the indiscriminate use of chemicals.[4]

Rachel Carson's signal accomplishment was to push ecological science into the mainstream of environmental discussion and to question a host of issues beyond DDT. With the creation of the U.S. Environmental Protection Agency (EPA) in 1970, ecologists had an increasingly public voice and authority to conduct surveys and research and to analyze environmental risks. The emergence of the ecosystem sciences was especially critical in the Pacific Northwest, where natural resource production was wreaking havoc with water, air, and terrestrial landscapes. When the EPA prohibited the use of DDT in 1972, the timber and agricultural industries raised a storm of protest. Timber companies, agricultural interests, and their powerful allies in state and federal agencies continued to protest prohibitions against banned herbicides and pesticides, complaining that they were necessary to profitably grow trees, grain products, and fruits and vegetables.[5]

There was more to the stories about North America's troubled environment. *Time* magazine dubbed Lake Erie—one of the boundary lakes between the United States and Canada—a "North American Dead Sea" when foamlike soapsuds and untreated sewage washed up along its shores. Two signal events that captured headlines in 1969 added to the sense that the heedless pursuit of affluence and materialism had contributed to the problem. First was the Santa Barbara oil spill, the blowout of a Union Oil drilling platform six miles off the coast that spread two hundred thousand gallons of crude along thirty-five miles of shoreline and took an enormous toll on seabird and mammal populations. Six months later, fires broke out on Cleveland's oil-soaked Cuyahoga River, an event that became the poster child for environmental awareness and prompted musician Randy Newman to write and perform the song "Burn On, Big River."[6]

Decades of resource dependency in the Greater Northwest—and frenetic infrastructure building during the postwar years—carried negative environmental rewards in loss of species diversity, silted streams, overgrazed riparian zones, toxic minerals leaching into waterways, and other environmental stresses. Differing federal, provincial, and state authorities in Canada and the United States complicated and fuzzed jurisdictions and the ability to deal with air and water pollution. Because the Canadian Constitution delegates to provinces strong legislative and proprietary powers over natural resources such as timber, minerals, and waterways, provincial governments have been reluctant to enact regulations that would jeopardize local economies. Because British Columbia controls virtually all Crown resources within the province, when the Canadian parliament has intervened, the consequences have often been a series of counterproductive federal-provincial standoffs.[7]

British Columbia's politics between 1950 and 1980 provide striking examples of the tensions between federal policies and realities at the provincial level. During W. A. C. Bennett's two-decade tenure as premier, the province embarked on a massive public works program, building highways, bridges, tunnels, railroads, and huge dams. Believing that postwar British Columbia was North America's last frontier, Bennett promised citizens "the good life" through a commitment to free enterprise and a willingness to use provincial authority to direct economic development. The journalist Bruce Hutchison referred to Bennett as "the high priest of the new British Columbia," a man with a "bustling salesman's assurance" who would lead the province to the promised land. Because he was convinced that energy development was the wave of the future, Bennett persuaded the legislature to fund hydropower projects on the Peace and Columbia rivers—and to disregard the rights of First Nations who might be in the way.[8]

During Bennett's tenure as premier, British-born Vancouver Island naturalist Roderick Haig-Brown articulated an alternative vision of British Columbia, one that was broadly critical of Bennett's ideology of progress. Haig-Brown criticized Bennett's witless modernizing project, the heedless exploitation of British Columbia's forests, rich mineral deposits, and fisheries. He faulted British Columbians for measuring everything in "dollars and cents" and the premier for being ignorant of how to properly conserve and develop resources. In several letters, Haig-Brown warned Bennett that his ineptitude on conservation issues would have consequences. "Has industry," he wrote in the mid-1960s, "some inalienable right to invade public lands wherever found and destroy them?" Haig-Brown's "counternarrative" challenged the government's narrative of progress and forward movement.[9]

The persistent challenges of critics like Roderick Haig-Brown and the stirrings of environmentalism in the late 1960s began to erode support for Bennett and the Social Credit Party. The left-leaning Cooperative Commonwealth Federation (CCF) used grassroots discontent with inflation and rising unemployment to challenge the premier's long tenure in office. Opposition to Bennett's free-market approach became the critical factor in provincial politics. The public became less enamored with Bennett's propensity to reduce complex issues to simple answers. There were other problems: inadequate reforestation on Crown lands and the absence of regulations for strip-mining and air and water pollution further muddied British Columbia politics. Despite Bennett's warnings about its socialist tendencies, the New Democratic Party (NDP, successor to the CCF) out-polled Social Credit in the provincial election of 1972.[10]

With Bennett's departure, British Columbia had lost its "confidence man," a person who believed his task was to give people confidence in the future of the province. The rise of the NDP to the pinnacle of provincial politics established the polar opposites for political discourse in British Columbia for several decades. The presence of a viable leftist party also distinguished British Columbia's politics from the adjacent American states. Essentially, the NDP functioned as a leftist/socialist party in expanding the state's role for delivering social services.[11]

There were undercurrents of change everywhere across British Columbia during the early 1970s, especially with the emergence of environmental organizations and the increasing assertiveness of First Nations people. Greenpeace, with its initial objective to stop nuclear testing in the Pacific, had its beginnings in Vancouver's Kitsilano district in 1970. Student environmental activism at Simon Fraser University was part of a broader counterculture movement that addressed environmental issues and opposed U.S. intervention in Vietnam. Those protests and countercultural groups would eventually provide important support for promoting quality of life issues in British Columbia.[12]

The dawn of British Columbia's environmental age began with fits and starts. Budget reductions hampered the province's capacity to deal with water pollution, and the British Columbia Forest Practices Code had limited regulatory authority to provide biodiversity and endangered species protections. Pollution in the lower Fraser River became the subject of a raging controversy in the late 1960s, when the Vancouver Pollution Control Board mandated that sewage be treated before being emptied into waterways. Although grassroots fishery and recreational groups led the protests, municipal leaders argued that the river's assimilative capacity would adequately protect human health. An equally egregious pollution debate simmered across the water in the capital city, Victoria, where authorities insisted into the twenty-first century that raw sewage piped one kilometer into Juan de Fuca Strait was harmless. British Columbia's minister of land and air protection approved Victoria's 2005 plan to continue dumping raw sewage into waters near the city's main harbor until its sewage-treatment plants came on line.[13]

With its strong federal presence in environmental issues, the United States provides a significant contrast to British Columbia. Several environmental initiatives in the United States have mandated standards for state-level activities: the National Environmental Policy Act (1970), the Clean Air Act (1970), the Water Pollution Control Act (1972), the Coastal Zone Management Act (1972), the Marine Mammals Protection Act (1972), and the Endangered Species Act (1973). The Environmental Protection Agency has developed into one of the nation's largest and most controversial bureaucracies, with the agency suspending the use of the pesticide DDT (dichlorodiphenyltrichloroethane) in 1972. Other legislation, such as the Comprehensive Environmental Response, Compensation, and Liability Act (1980), provided federal money for Superfund cleanup sites.[14]

While U.S. environmental laws were imperfect, and while politics often played havoc with enforcement, federal legislation has provided a body of statutory requirements to address a broad array of environmental issues. In the American Northwest, well in advance of federal legislation, Oregon set the tone for environmental achievement, especially in the effort to purge its waterways of pollution. Under Governor Tom McCall (1967–75), the new Department of Environmental Quality required all municipalities to have primary and secondary sewage treatment facilities, and the agency mandated sharp restrictions on industrial discharges into waterways. Differing sharply from preceding governors, McCall directed state agencies to actively enforce environmental regulations, especially those dealing with water pollution.

Although a few industries, especially pulp and paper mills, were slow in complying with state mandates, when Congress passed the Clean Water Act in 1970, Oregon's waterways were remarkably free of conventional pollutants. In the heavily populated Willamette Valley, several dams constructed by the Army Corps of Engineers between 1940 and the 1960s enabled the corps to store seasonal precipitation behind tributary dams.

The release of water in late summer and early fall maintained a relatively even flow in the main river, flushing contaminants downriver and out of sight. A *National Geographic* article in 1972 praising McCall for his "cleanup" of the river is deserving, but an oft-neglected part of that story has been the regulated flow of the river.[15]

Time has not diminished the significance of Tom McCall's election to the Oregon governorship. While he shares credit with other policy makers for several wide-ranging environmental achievements during the late 1960s and early 1970s, it was the Willamette River that gave McCall a national platform. He was named Oregon's "Livability Governor" by Associated Oregon Industries in 1969, and his two administrations moved on several fronts to enhance Oregon's quality of life. Oregon's 1971 Bottle Bill requiring minimum deposits on glass and aluminum beverage containers was another measure that brought national recognition to the state. With the broad support of legislators, McCall also signed into law the Beach Bill, which reasserted public ownership of Oregon's coastal shoreline. In all of those initiatives, the Republican McCall enjoyed significant legislative support across party lines.[16]

The capstone to Oregon's environmental reforms during McCall's governorship was Senate Bill 100, signed into law in 1973 as the nation's most progressive land-use legislation. Two state senators, liberal Democrat Ted Hallock and Republican dairy farmer Hector Macpherson, joined the governor in the legislative battle to pass Oregon's pioneering land-use law. Historians agree that Senate Bill 100, designed to curb urban sprawl and to protect valuable agricultural and forest land and open spaces, was Tom McCall's most lasting legacy. The effects of Senate Bill 100 are visually scripted across Oregon's landscape. The measure survived largely intact into the twenty-first century, when it was overturned by an initiative in 2004 and then reinstated with modifications in 2007. Acclaimed Indian historian Charles Wilkinson argues that Oregon's pioneering environmental laws give a different "feel" to Oregon's politics and landscapes, separating the state from other western states.[17]

The state of Montana also underwent a significant transformation in the early 1970s, with the resurgence of a progressive political temperament that for a time broke the conservative hold on state-level politics. Following several U.S. Supreme Court decisions in the early 1960s, Montana was directed to reapportion its legislative seats to meet "one-man, one-vote" constitutional requirements. Because the Montana Constitution of

1889 mandated one senator for each county, rural areas of the state held significantly more legislative power than their voting population justified (Petroleum County, population 894, had one senator, as did Yellowstone County, population 79,016). When the Montana legislature failed to implement a reapportionment plan, federal courts interceded in 1965 and did the job. The newly redistricted legislature brought a sea change in representation, with urban areas making significant gains and rural areas losing legislative seats. Redistricting led directly to voter approval of Referendum 67 in November 1970 to convene a constitutional convention.[18]

The early 1970s marked the emergence of a new generation of Montana political activists interested in quality of life issues and preserving the integrity of communities. In its 1971 session, the legislature enacted strong environmental laws, passed the state's first minimum-wage law, and set the stage for the constitutional convention.[19] To implement Referendum 67, voters elected one hundred delegates to meet in early 1972 to draft a new constitution. Because a clause in the Montana Constitution of 1889 prohibited current legislators from holding two offices at the same time, the delegates who assembled in Helena in January were all fresh faces and mostly liberal-minded. After raucous debate, in a remarkable fifty-four days the assembly produced a new constitution, a document that would go before voters on June 6, 1972. Barred by the Montana Supreme Court from using convention funds for voter education, delegates conducted town meetings and promoted the constitution through newspaper articles. The June ballot favored the constitution by a popular vote of 116,415 to 113,883, with *Time* magazine calling it a "model document."[20]

Although Montana's more conservative politics would constrain state-level environmental advances from the mid-1980s into the early twenty-first century, the new constitution strengthened the legislature, provided single-member districts, and assessed statewide property taxes. The Montana Environmental Policy Act, enacted in 1971, also contributed to the strong environmental sections in the new constitution. Article 2, section 3 of the constitution states that among citizens' inalienable rights are "the right to a clean and healthful environment." Article 9, section 1, "Protection and Improvement," is equally direct: "The state and each person shall maintain and improve a clean and healthful environment in Montana for present and future generations."[21]

Montana's progressive spirit continued through the 1970s, with voters returning Democrat Lee Metcalf to a third term in the U.S. Senate in 1972 and electing liberal Democrat Thomas Judge to the first of two terms in the governor's office. The liberal flood tide reached its peak in the midterm elections of 1974, when Montana Democrats won control of both legislative branches in 1974, with Max Baucus winning the state's western congressional seat. During Thomas Judge's tenure in the governor's office, the legislature enacted a tough strip-mining law and a coal severance tax, the highest in the nation at 30 percent. The severance tax was to be paid into a permanent endowment fund, with the state drawing on the interest, leaving the principal untouched except in cases of dire hardship. When a coalition of midwestern utilities and mining companies challenged the severance tax, the U.S. Supreme Court upheld the measure in a landmark decision in 1981.

Beginning in 1980, Montana voters began to mirror national trends, electing increasingly conservative individuals to state and national offices and rolling back progressive measures of the previous decade. Conservative Democrat Ted Schwinden succeeded Thomas Judge in the governor's office, and antitax sentiment, a spin-off of California's Proposition 13, led to a successful initiative to freeze property tax rates. These steps included indexing the income tax, eliminating the business inventory tax, accelerating the depreciation of business property, cutting taxes for oil companies, and rolling back the severance tax on coal. A sharp downturn in the state's economy in the mid-1980s turned revenue surpluses to deficits and prompted the legislature to make steep reductions in state funding for education and other services.[22]

In truth, Montana's experiences were similar to those of other western states largely dependent on natural resources. With the loss of good-paying jobs in the mines, smelters, and sawmills, Montana faced an uncertain future. As the twentieth century came to a close, there were fewer than two thousand metal-mining jobs in the state, and the Montana Mining Association closed its Helena lobbying office. Butte, which once employed fifteen thousand underground miners, had none at the outset of the new century. "In a sense," historian Harry Fritz argues, "Montana is Butte, writ large," and like much of the rural West has turned into a "sales-and-service economy." Montana's mining past, however, lives on, especially as Butte's huge Berkeley Pit slowly fills with toxic, metal-laden water.[23]

With its traditional dependence on mining and timber extraction, northern Idaho faced similar difficulties in the last two decades of the twentieth century. During its long history, the famed Coeur d'Alene mining district turned out more than one billion ounces of silver, the largest and richest mineral-producing site in the world. But it was also a place where mining companies treated streams and airsheds as a giant commons for dumping and spewing waste from industrial practices. At a very early time companies dumped tailings next to mills, in gullies, or directly into the South Fork of the Coeur d'Alene River. With increases in production, disposing of tailings became a greater problem. Floods destroyed holding ponds and sent toxic debris cascading downstream. Residents of Coeur d'Alene complained in the early 1930s about mining detritus in Coeur d'Alene Lake, with the local newspaper reporting the enormity of the pollution problem.[24]

Although mine owners denied the Coeur d'Alene district posed a health risk, the dangers that lead and related compounds posed to human health were well known as early as 1930. Following the Second World War, mineral production in the Coeur d'Alene mines increased dramatically, attaining an all-time high in the mid-1960s. The largest producer, the Bunker Hill Mining Company, was recovering six different metals by 1972, a production rate that continued even when the pollution-control "bag house" burned the following year. Gulf Resources, Inc., then purchased the facilities and continued operations without the pollution-control device. The huge volume of lead spewed into the air triggered an Idaho Department of Health and Welfare investigation, which revealed that children in Smelterville had some of the highest lead levels ever recorded. The public outcry prompted the company to upgrade its technology to reduce pollutants. With the worldwide collapse of metal prices in 1981, however, Gulf Resources closed the plant, putting 2,100 people out of work in Kellogg and surrounding communities.[25]

A century of mineral production left the Coeur d'Alene district highly polluted. Two years after Bunker Hill closed, the Environmental Protection Agency placed a seven-mile section of the newly christened "Silver Valley" on its priority list for cleaning up toxic residue. The state of Idaho and the Coeur d'Alene Indian Tribe sued the mining companies, with the state settling out of court for a fund to help finance the cleanup. Responding to pressures from the tribe, the state of Washington, and other complainants, the EPA designated the 1,500-square-mile Coeur d'Alene Basin a Superfund site. A National Research Council study published in 2005 concluded that mining's toxic legacy would "take longer to overcome than it did to create."[26]

In addition to its polluted mining districts, Idaho became a battle-ground over federal and state lands in the 1960s, with arguments center-ing on time-worn themes of use versus preservation. With more than twenty-one million acres in national forests, the state was at the epicenter of debates over the Wilderness Act of 1964, mining claims, and the mul-tiple use of resources. The central political figure in those struggles was Democrat Frank Church, first elected to the U.S. Senate in 1956 at the age of thirty-two. Despite his liberal politics, Idaho's conservative voters reelected Church in 1962, 1968, and 1974. He fell victim to an increasingly conservative regional and national mood in 1980, when Republican Ste-ven Symms narrowly defeated him during the "Reagan Revolution."[27]

Frank Church emerged from political obscurity to become Idaho's most acclaimed politician since William E. Borah. An excellent public speaker with no political experience, Church and his wife, Bethine, toured the state in the winter of 1955–56 to narrowly defeat maverick Glen Taylor in the Democratic primary. Church easily prevailed against the vicious Red-baiting of Republican incumbent senator Herman Welker in the November election. Welker, who had defeated Taylor in 1950 by telling audiences that he would "throw out the Commies, pinks, and socialists," made similar charges against Church. Because Church supported the 1954 Supreme Court desegregation decision, Welker accused his challenger of being Communist inspired. Despite Church's later opposition to the Viet-nam War, conservative Idaho voters twice returned him to the Senate.[28]

A leading proponent of the Wilderness Act, Frank Church also sup-ported civil rights legislation during the 1960s, and as chair of the Sen-ate Foreign Relations Committee, he led an investigation of the Central Intelligence Agency. As a latter-day New Dealer when he first entered the Senate, Church joined with Oregon's Richard Neuberger in supporting a big federal dam in the Snake River's Hells Canyon. When Republican president Dwight Eisenhower backed the Idaho Power Company's appli-cation to build three low-head dams immediately upstream from the deep canyon, Church began to lose enthusiasm for developing spectacular land-scapes. He eventually championed creation of 662,000-acre Hells Canyon National Recreation Area, a measure President Gerald Ford signed into law in 1975.[29]

Church's conversion to preserving significant landscapes was a difficult one. Representing a state with powerful constituencies in natural resource development required delicate maneuvering and compromise. Despite Idaho's conservative politics, Church led the floor fight as a freshman senator and voted for the legislation that eventually became the Wilderness Act in 1964. He also cosponsored the Wild and Scenic Rivers Act and the creation of Redwood National Park in 1968, warned about the dangers of radioactive pollution, and negotiated compromises that led to the creation of the Sawtooth National Recreation Area in 1972. But Church was no mere political opportunist, because he often moved in directions that were politically treacherous, especially on environmental issues. When Republican Steven Symms used "simplified nastiness" to defeat Church in 1980, Cecil Andrus observed that Idaho had lost "a politician of conscience who took unpopular stands."[30]

Two legendary and powerful political figures—Warren Magnuson and Henry Jackson—dominated Washington State's politics from the 1960s through the early 1980s. Unlike Frank Church and Oregon senators Wayne Morse and Mark Hatfield, who were outspoken in their opposition to the Vietnam War, neither Magnuson nor Jackson stepped beyond the political mainstream on most issues. Like their colleagues in the region, Washington's senators wholeheartedly supported the Bonneville Power Administration, the federal agency responsible for planning and promoting regional growth. Both in the House of Representatives and then in the U.S. Senate, Henry Jackson was firmly wedded to public power, believing that cheap electric power would contribute to the common good—and that it was smart politics.[31]

While Jackson supported significant conservation and preservation measures (the Wilderness Act, Redwood National Park, the Wild and Scenic Rivers Act), his signal achievement for his home state was creating North Cascades National Park in 1968. As chair of the Senate Interior Committee, Jackson commissioned a study of the park's feasibility, negotiated compromises over boundaries and agency jurisdictions, and responded to the concerns of mining, timber, and environmental interests. Stuart Udall, then secretary of interior, pointed out that North Cascades National Park was "a monument to Henry Jackson, which never would have been done unless he wanted it done." At the national level, Jackson's consummate achievement was passage of the National Environmental Policy Act in 1970.[32] It is important to acknowledge that one of America's foremost cold war hawks was the architect of, arguably, the nation's most significant piece of environmental legislation.

Warren "Maggie" Magnuson, who served in the U.S. Senate from 1944 to 1980, worked closely with Henry Jackson to "bring home the bacon" for the state of Washington. In an amusing commentary on Maggie's influence, Vice President Walter Mondale once remarked: "He is scrupulously fair with federal funds; one half for Washington state, one half for the rest of the country." But Magnuson's contributions were much greater: he supported consumer-protection legislation and funding for health care research and promoted normalizing relations with China. He authored two popular environmental protection measures important to western Washington: the Marine Mammals Protection Act in 1972 and an amendment that prohibited "super" oil tankers from passing beyond Port Angeles in the Strait of Juan de Fuca in 1977.[33]

Both Washington senators, but especially Henry Jackson, supported the work carried out at the Hanford nuclear facility. The Hanford complex was important to Jackson's ambitions to expand the nation's nuclear program and to use atomic energy for peaceful purposes. He gained federal funding for two new reactors in the 1950s, both of them capable of producing plutonium for peacetime and military purposes. When one of the reactors later proved hazardous, environmental activists, including Ralph Nader, cited the damaged facility and its radioactive waste as a strong argument to oppose nuclear power plants. But the real problems with radioactive pollution at the Hanford site unfolded only gradually, with opposition to nuclear facilities slowly building through the late 1960s and 1970s. The coup de grâce, revelations that Hanford was much more a toxic dump than expected, took place in 1987, when the government released nineteen thousand pages of classified documents that removed the wall of secrecy surrounding the reservation. The declassified material revealed that between 1944 and 1951 Hanford operators deliberately released into the atmosphere experimental emissions of iodine 131, releases several times above what was considered the safe limit.[34]

Two years after the release of the documents, the EPA declared the northern section of the nuclear reservation—the Hanford 100-Area—a Superfund site. In a *Federal Register* notice of October 4, 1989, the EPA announced that it had found more than 110 waste disposal locations in the 100-Area, with the contaminated surface and groundwater area covering approximately eleven square miles. The *Register* also reported that contaminated groundwater was seeping toward the Columbia River.[35]

The Washington State Department of Health reported that the first eight plutonium-production reactors had used enormous amounts of Columbia River water to cool pipes in the reactor cores before returning the water to the river. With the passage of time, workers eventually cooled the water in retention basins before pumping it back into the Columbia.

That technique, however, fell short when the reactors were working full time to produce plutonium. Tests disclosed that radioactive contaminants entering the Columbia River were at their highest levels between 1957 and 1964. Problems continued to plague the cleanup into the twenty-first century, most of them linked to inadequate funding, failure to follow proper procedures, quality-control issues, and delayed work schedules.[36]

In Washington's more densely populated Puget Sound region, pollution of a different kind was placing increasing stress on waterborne environments. Since the arrival of the first commercial sailing ships, water has been at the center of the sound's economic geography—for transportation, for the salmon-canning industry, for the disposal of toxic wastes from pulp mills, and as a repository for diluting untreated sewage from cities and towns. Although people had always dumped wastes into the sound, there was a major difference with pulp liquors, which spelled death even to barnacles. By the 1950s pulp mills were the most visible symbols of pollution, from Anacortes in the north to Shelton in the south.[37]

The pulp and paper industry, as it did elsewhere, wielded considerable power in Washington's legislature, especially in fighting regulatory enforcement. Although pulp mills had installed modest pollution-control devices, the vastly enhanced productive capacity of the plants negated such improvements. Eventually, federal enforcement of the Clean Water Act of 1972, shifting market demand, and the antiquated character of many of the pulp mills spelled their demise. Newly emerging threats to Puget Sound's waters, including new oil refineries on the upper sound and the increased volume of non–point source pollutants (runoff from farmland and urban landscapes), continued to exacerbate the problem. A booming regional economy, a growing environmental consciousness, and a public that increasingly valued the amenities of forests and clean water continued to spur efforts to clean up the sound.[38]

Until the mid-1950s there was little public pressure to do anything about urban sewage pouring into Puget Sound or Seattle's heavily populated Lake Washington district. These mounting problems finally prompted officials to form an urban-planning district, the Municipality of Metropolitan Seattle (METRO), to coordinate sewage disposal and related issues. Although the measure garnered a majority in Greater Seattle, voters in smaller communities defeated METRO amid charges that it was socialistic. In November 1958 citizens approved a pared-down version of METRO that focused only on the sewage problem. The measure contributed mightily to cleaning up Lake Washington.[39]

Clear, clean water and healthy aquatic ecosystems became increasingly important to the economies around Puget Sound after the 1970s. Sports and commercial groups and treaty Indians harvested oysters, clams, salmon, trout, herring, yellow perch, and sole from its waterways. Sailing and motorized watercraft use on the sound's intricate inlets also became increasingly popular. Despite herculean efforts to keep pollutants from the sound, however, a burgeoning population threatened to overwhelm preventative measures. From 1970 to 2000 Kitsap, Pierce, Snohomish, and King counties increased by 1.3 million people, a population explosion that contributed to dramatic modifications to the Puget Sound shoreline, further degrading near-shore habitats. The sound's increasing ship traffic has also introduced an ever-increasing number of invasive species, especially from Asia.[40]

American Indian/First Nations people have been at the forefront of hotly contested environmental politics in the Greater Northwest. The most contentious issues pertained to Indian treaty fishing rights on the Columbia River and Puget Sound and land claims for British Columbia's First Nations. The settlement of aboriginal land claims and other equity-related matters increasingly captured news headlines in British Columbia, with provincial officials refusing to recognize aboriginal claims until the 1990s, arguing that the federal government was responsible for land issues. Ultimately, Native land questions threatened to disrupt the basis of the provincial economy. The environmental and cultural politics of Native groups in the United States were equally complex, including radioactive contamination from the Hanford nuclear reservation and its effect on the Yakama, Umatilla, and Nez Perce tribes. Hanford's contaminated underground plumes, according to the Umatilla tribes' history, "are a direct concern to the health of the rivers, to the salmon, and to people." In northern Idaho, the Coeur d'Alene Indians were among the downstream victims of a century of mining along the Coeur d'Alene River system.[41]

In Oregon and Washington, more than seventy years of litigation and court decisions burst forth anew during the 1960s when Columbia River and Puget Sound Indians became more aggressive in asserting treaty-reserved fishing rights. The controversy reflected the influence of non-Indian sports and commercial fishers, whose increasing numbers paralleled sharply declining salmon runs. When good-paying defense industry jobs disappeared after 1945, many Indians found themselves economically marginalized with dwindling opportunities. The civil rights movement

Hanford nuclear reservation, January 1960. Nuclear reactors line the
Columbia River at the federal government's Hanford site. The N Reactor
is in the foreground, with the KE and KW reactors in the immediate
background. The world's first plutonium-producing reactor, the historic
B Reactor, is visible at the top of the photo.

of the 1960s, a heightened sense of ethnic pride, and optimism that there
were legal precedents for enforcing the treaty right to fish convinced tribes
to seek redress in three fundamental areas: (1) the right to fish free of state
regulation; (2) the right to regulatory authority for on-reservation and off-
reservation fishing; and (3) the right to catch significant numbers of fish.[42]

Although claims to salmon were not new, none has proved more significant than the treaty rights of Northwest Indians. Except for the on-
reservation fishery, both Oregon and Washington insisted that states, not
the federal government, should regulate the catch, legal gear, and off-
reservation fishery. A Washington Supreme Court decision in 1963 further
emboldened state agencies to broadly interpret their regulatory authority. For their part, Columbia River and Puget Sound Indians increasingly
defied state regulators, insisting on their treaty right to fish. In Washington, arrests and seizures of fishing gear on the Nisqually and Puyallup

rivers prompted "fish-ins," with movie star Marlon Brando and civil rights activist Dick Gregory participating. Washington officials blamed Indians for declining salmon runs, despite evidence that the Indian catch was less than 5 percent.[43]

As violence and verbal bellicosity erupted across Puget Sound and the mid–Columbia River, the controversy shifted to federal courtrooms, where decisions began to favor the Indians' treaty rights. In *Sohappy v. Smith* (1969), U.S. District Judge Robert Belloni ruled that the state of Oregon had discriminated against David Sohappy, a decorated Yakima veteran of the Second World War, when it denied him the right to fish. Treaty tribes, the judge decreed, were legally entitled to a "fair and equitable share" of fish, and state officials should assure that Indians were able to take a "fair share" of fish from the Columbia River. Although Belloni's decision was more detailed than previous cases, he was less specific about the meaning of a "fair and equitable share."[44]

Within a year of Belloni's decision, and acting as trustee for seven western Washington tribes, U.S. Justice Department lawyers filed suit in the U.S. District Court in Tacoma in the fall of 1970 (*United States et al. v. Washington et al.*), charging that the state could not regulate treaty Indian fishers as it did non-Indians. Seattle Federal District Judge George Boldt presided over the case, which extended over three years. In the interim, Washington's attorney general, Slade Gorton, fought federal enforcement of treaty rights, arguing that such rights would turn Indians into "supercitizens." Pandering to anti-Indian sentiment, Gorton used the state's full legal mechanisms to prosecute tribal fishers.[45]

United States et al. v. Washington et al., the Boldt decision, was a stunner. After three years of background preparation and hearings, Boldt's complex decision, handed down in February 1974, declared that treaty Indians had superior rights to fish compared to non-Indians. He determined that the state of Washington could not regulate the Indian fishery except in dire emergencies. Boldt affirmed the Indians' right to fish in "their usual and accustomed places" both on and off the reservation. Boldt also added specificity to Belloni's reference to a "fair and equitable share" when he determined that the treaty stipulation "in common with citizens of the territory" meant the tribes could take up to 50 percent of the harvestable fish. The judge also clarified the extent of the tribal right: "The right secured by the treaties to the Plaintiff tribes is not limited as to species of fish, the origin of fish, the purpose or use, or the time or manner of taking, except to the extent necessary to achieve preservation

Federal District Judge George Boldt (1904–83). In *United States et al.
v. Washington et al.*, Judge George Boldt issued his historic ruling on February
12, 1974, affirming the treaty rights of western Washington tribes to fish in
their "usual and accustomed" places "in common" with other citizens. The
legal ruling, twice upheld by the U.S. Supreme Court, determined that tribes
could take up to 50 percent of all harvestable fish.

of the resource and to allow non-Indians to fish in common with treaty fishermen outside reservation boundaries."[46] The Indian treaty fishery in the American Northwest would never be the same.

For the next five years, however, non-Indian commercial fishers aggressively challenged the decision in court and defied orders to implement Boldt's legal directives. Slade Gorton and his attorneys pursued political and legal avenues to overturn the decision, including an appeal in 1976 to the U.S. Supreme Court, where the justices declined to review the case. But with the assistance of senators Warren Magnuson and Henry Jackson, the state persisted and placed the Boldt decision before the U.S. Supreme Court in 1979. This time the justices affirmed the Boldt decision six to three and concurred unanimously on the critical treaty rights issue. Although the violence and open warfare on Puget Sound abated, Attorney General Slade Gorton used his strident opposition to the treaty question to elevate himself to the U.S. Senate in 1980. From that position Gorton remained true to form, introducing various bills (unsuccessfully) to deprive Indians of their treaty rights.[47]

The Boldt decision and its affirmation in the U.S. Supreme Court energized a powerful regional and national Indian identity. Alexandra Harmon believes Boldt's opinion "lent coherence and an aura of purpose to Indians' history by summarizing the abundant evidence of Indians' ancient zeal to fish." In the larger effort to preserve fish runs, *United States et al. v. Washington et al.* led to peaceful and cooperative relations between treaty tribes and the state of Washington. Billy Frank Jr., the longtime Nisqually activist, told Indian scholar Charles Wilkinson that Boldt "gave us the opportunity to make our own regulations, our own management systems. We have to think about what he did for us; that's a responsibility we have. We can never forget that responsibility." For tribal fishers, the 1855 treaty right "of taking fish at usual and accustomed grounds and stations" was now a central component of Indian identity.[48]

But the most persistent problem for tribes and non-Indian fishers remained—the continued decline in the region's anadromous fish runs. Court-sanctioned treaties guaranteeing the right to catch 50 percent of harvestable fish had little meaning if there were none to catch. Matters drifted until 1983, when the Ninth Circuit Court urged the state and the tribes "to take reasonable steps . . . to preserve and enhance the fishery."[49] Nearly two decades later, the tribes again charged that the state of Washington was violating the 1855 treaties because it did not properly maintain culverts that blocked fish passage. The federal district court heard the suits and countersuits over the next several years, finally determining that the state had an obligation to properly manage culverts to allow fish passage.[50] These ongoing struggles occurred in the midst of a growing population around Puget Sound and the stepped-up consumption habits of Washington's citizens.

A collective Indian identity took a different path in British Columbia, where the most critical issues were unresolved land claims. The respected Kwakiutl fisherman and activist James Sewid remarked in his 1969 autobiography that the big issue for Native people was the land question. Although the Canadian government was moving forward with a new constitution and new initiatives to resolve Indian land claims in the early 1980s, British Columbia leaders refused to acknowledge that aboriginal people had *any* claims to land. To counter provincial intransigence, Native bands and groups formed the National Indian Brotherhood, an organization that reconstituted itself as the Assembly of First Nations in 1984. The name change was an assertion of Indian sovereignty and the right to negotiate as equals in land claims issues.[51]

Although Quebec, the Yukon, and the Northwest Territories had negotiated land claims settlements as early as the 1970s, British Columbia stood apart in refusing to acknowledge or even engage in arbitration. A growing Native activism and major court decisions would soon change this dynamic. Paul Tennant, an authority on Native land claims, contends that, beginning in 1963, the province has been at the forefront of all Indian land claims cases in Canada. A court case involving two Indians arrested for hunting deer on unoccupied land on Vancouver Island in 1963 made its way through the court system and finally to the Supreme Court of Canada, where the jurists dropped the charges against the two men. The issue of aboriginal title—linked to the case—lingered in the provincial and federal courts until 1973, when the Canadian high court in *Calder v. Attorney-General of B.C.* determined unanimously that aboriginal bands held title to land when the colony of British Columbia came into existence in 1858.[52]

The court's *Calder* declaration was the first of its kind to affirm the existence of aboriginal claims to land. Although another Supreme Court finding, *Guerin* (1984), firmly established preexisting Indian title in Canadian law, British Columbia officials continued to ignore Native land claims. Two weeks after the *Guerin* decision, the Clayoquot and Ahousaht bands blocked MacMillan-Bloedel's access to a logging operation on Meares

Island, arguing that timber harvesting should cease until aboriginal title was resolved. In 1985 the British Columbia Court of Appeals issued an injunction against further logging, determining that there was merit to the land claim question and urging the province to negotiate. Following the Meares judgment, the province's supreme court regularly issued decrees involving unresolved land claims.[53]

The new Canadian Constitution of 1982 opened up other opportunities for Indians to assert unextinguished rights. Section 35(1) recognized "the existing aboriginal and treaty rights of aboriginal peoples of Canada." (This section was deleted from a draft of the constitution at the request of British Columbia officials and then reinserted.) Section 35(1) came into play in a 1986 case involving Ronald Sparrow, a Musqueam Indian who was arrested and convicted of illegal fishing on the lower Fraser River. Although the fishing location was beyond the reach of any Native reserve, the British Columbia Court of Appeal ruled in 1986 that section 35(1) meant that the right "to fish for food in their traditional fishing grounds . . . has always been recognized." When British Columbia game management officials appealed the case to the Supreme Court of Canada, the high court overturned Sparrow's conviction in 1990.[54]

Premier William Bennett (1976–86) and British Columbia's Social Credit Party were the source of much of the hostility to aboriginal rights. The opposition New Democratic Party agreed to negotiate Native land claims during the 1980s, although it did not do so when it was in power between 1972 and 1975. During Social Credit's long tenure in power (1976–91), party leaders insisted that aboriginal land claims and related issues were federal matters. Three powerful Social Credit leaders—Allan Williams, Brian Smith, and Garde Gardom (all lawyers)—ignored land claims issues and pressed the interests of non-Indian citizens. Smith, the most vocal, believed that money was at the root of land claims: "All they want is dollars. They don't want to throw anybody off the land, they just want billions and billions of dollars." Political columnist Vaughn Palmer summed up Premier Bennett's Social Credit strategy in 1985: "Its first position is that aboriginal title never existed. The second holds that if it ever existed, it was extinguished."[55]

When Social Credit's influence weakened in the early 1990s, Premier William Vander Zalm (1986–91) established a task force and a five-member commission to guide treaty negotiations. Those deliberations eventually involved 70 percent of the province's registered Natives. By the close of the twentieth century, the ongoing negotiations had strengthened Native self-identity and contributed to numerous economic and cultural initiatives. Tribal groups and bands have also been active in efforts to repatriate cultural and human remains. Through all of this forward movement, however, conflicts between First Nations and non-Native citizens will likely continue into the future.[56]

At the onset of the twenty-first century, political environments across the Greater Northwest involved progressive and conservative partisans in debates over the region's new economy, especially the shift from extracting and processing natural resources to high-tech production, amenity services, and an expanding retail sector. Listing the spotted owl as threatened under the Endangered Species Act in the American Northwest precipitated more than a decade of litigation and troubled economies in rural communities dependent on federal timber. The curtailment of national forest timber sales during the 1990s followed a decade of record harvests across the national forest system, especially in Oregon, the nation's leading lumber producer. The emergence of high-tech manufacturing in Seattle, Portland, Boise, and other population centers largely offset declines in timber production. For participants in the new economy, nature's amenities in the mountainous outback, plunging whitewater streams, and spectacular coastal headlands provided spectacular places to recreate. For communities away from the Interstate 5 corridor, however, the new environmental restrictions were hurtful.[57] In that sense, the world that once provided a decent livelihood for resource-dependent communities had been transformed into a playground for those atop the new economy.

There were parallels in British Columbia, where dependence on natural resources continued to sustain the economy into the twenty-first century. A decline in natural resource production, however, pushed the Greater Vancouver and Victoria areas toward increasing investments in knowledge-based and service-oriented enterprises. While metropolitan areas enjoyed booming economies, excessive timber harvests in the coastal districts and continuing litigation over unresolved Indian land claims slowed the wood-products sector. Since the early 1980s, the closure of forest-products mills has been widespread across both sides of the border. Along the coastal districts of British Columbia, Washington, Oregon, and Alaska, fishing fleets have lost some five thousand boats, and elsewhere more than ten thousand small ranches and farms have gone out of business. The economic transformation ushering in the new century also favored upper-middle-class and upper-income groups, with declining take-home wages daily points of reckoning for people at the bottom.[58]

9
Culture Works, 1930–2000

When novelist Vardis Fisher opened the telegram from Washington, D.C., in the mid-1930s, its contents likely came as a great relief to the unemployed writer. The Works Progress Administration (WPA), part of President Franklin Roosevelt's New Deal plan to mitigate unemployment during the Great Depression, included a program to support artists and writers while they worked on creative projects beneficial to the nation. The telegram invited Fisher to become the director of Idaho's Writers Project and Historical Records Project, a position that paid $2,300 a year. Fisher readily accepted and held the position from 1935 to 1939. Fisher hired a staff of researchers and writers of varying quality to produce *Idaho: A Guide in Word and Picture*. Published in 1937, Fisher's guidebook was the first and became a model for guidebooks in other states. Despite his assistants, Fisher wrote "374 of the 405 pages of text" and "all but two of the fifteen essays on Idaho history and physical attributes." The guide was well received, with one critic describing it as "actually a bit of literature," thanks to Fisher's efforts.[1]

Martina Gangle Curl, a "muralist, painter, sketch artist, engraver, and block printer," applied for a position with the WPA to support herself, her son, and her aging mother. Gangle had been a student at the Portland Art Museum School, whose teachers facilitated her efforts to depict poor and rural workers. It took her some time to recognize the worsening state of the economy: "I had depression all my life so I didn't know there was one until about the middle of the thirties." Gangle produced several Portland-area murals as part of her employment with the federal government, which paid her $90 each month.[2]

Oregon artist Charles Heaney called the Depression era federal support of the arts "manna from heaven." Even under ideal economic circumstances, most Pacific Northwest artists did not expect to make a living from their work. Fisher worked as a writing instructor at Montana State University under Harold G. Merriam, who recommended Fisher for the WPA post. Although he was a prolific writer of award-winning books,

Idaho author Vardis Fisher. Vardis Fisher, pictured here with his wife, Opal Fisher, was one of Idaho's most prolific writers.

Fisher supported himself and his family by occasionally teaching and being frugal. Martina Gangle Curl picked fruit and worked in a boarding-house and as a domestic. Charles Heaney was a ditch digger and restaurant waiter. Federal funds to paint or write seemed like a gift to many artists. Leo Beaulaurier, who painted one of the six WPA post office murals in Montana, said that the program was "a real boon to us because it was a hard time for the arts. People could barely afford necessities, much less paintings."[3]

Public funding for the arts was controversial in some circles, including in Congress, which allocated the funds. Canada had no equivalent program. Nonetheless, the assistance led to a broader discussion of state support of the arts, eventually culminating in public funding such as the subsidy many American and Canadian cities now require be put aside for art in the construction of public buildings. The legacy of the WPA arts projects can be seen throughout the region in post office and elementary school murals, on the walls of art museums with Pacific Northwest collections, in the guidebooks that documented state and local history, and in Depression era buildings like the Boise Gallery of Art in Idaho and Mount Hood's Timberline Lodge in Oregon.

Despite common ties to agriculture and living as creative types in the same region, Martina Gangle Curl and Vardis Fisher did not share a common understanding of the historical events through which they lived. Although neither trusted the federal government, Vardis Fisher disseminated his often-conservative views through several of Idaho's newspapers in a regularly published column, Vardis Fisher Says. Curl's experiences radicalized her, and she joined the Communist Party in about 1936 and was a community activist throughout her life. Their beliefs and their work reflected the issues that many Pacific Northwest residents wrestled with in the mid- and late twentieth century—the legacies of American expansion in the West, tensions between the desires of individuals and the needs of the wider community, and a natural environment that both inspired creativity and was increasingly degraded. Art and literature in the Pacific Northwest during the latter half of the twentieth century grappled with those same issues, mirroring the transformations within the region at large.

The Great Depression shaped many of the cultural expressions of the region, as artists were paid to celebrate the wealth of the land and the resilient spirit of the nation's citizens. By the 1930s, radios and automobiles were becoming increasingly commonplace, technologies that made cultural endeavors more accessible to a general audience. While nineteenth-century technological changes also had a significant impact on the lives of Pacific Northwest residents, twentieth-century technologies dramatically and rapidly altered the way northwesterners lived and played. Historian Carlos Schwantes asserts that the 1920s "was the Pacific Northwest's first truly modern decade," transformed as it was by cars, radios, and new entertainments such as moving pictures.[4]

Automobiles reshaped the landscape by promoting the development of thousands of miles of roads and acres of parking lots and strip malls and by consolidating people in urban and suburban areas. Theaters, parks, and museums tens and even hundreds of miles away became easier to visit, shrinking distances between villages, towns, and cities even for rural residents. Automobile tourism led to British Columbia's adoption of the American-style right-hand drive in 1921 (previous to that residents drove on the left, as drivers did in Britain), and the Alaska Highway, completed in 1943, linked mainland Americans to their Alaskan counterparts and to western Canadians as well. Rural electrification, a Depression-spawned initiative, changed the pace and types of farm, ranch, and household work for residents in eastern Washington, western Montana, and central British Columbia. Electricity also powered radios and eventually televisions, which brought faraway news and entertainment to even the most remote households. Those same radios could broadcast local weather warnings, while increased use of telephones ensured that northwesterners could immediately locate emergency help or chat with friends. Automobiles and radios shortened distances and integrated rural dwellers into the social and economic fabric of the region, leading to increased urbanization.

The White Spot, Vancouver, British Columbia's first drive-in restaurant, epitomizes the changes cars brought to the Pacific Northwest. Opened in 1928, the restaurant catered to the booming numbers of middle-class families that registered their autos in British Columbia. In 1916 fewer than ten thousand cars were registered in the province; by 1925 the number had grown to fifty-six thousand, certainly enough to keep a new-fangled restaurant afloat. Drivers supported the development of roads as well as of novel destinations. Oregon was the first state to institute a tax on gasoline in 1919, with Washington (1921) and Idaho (1923) not far behind. The taxes funded road building across the region, which by 1940 could boast "a total of twelve thousand miles of all weather roads." Under the government of W. A. C. Bennett, British Columbia spent more to build roads between 1952 and 1958 "than in the entire history of the province." The rise of the automobile weakened nineteenth-century transportation modes such as railways and steamboats. It also led to the rise of ferry systems adapted to car traffic in Puget Sound and in southern British Columbia. Cars, of course, made travel to work, school, and shopping easier. As historian Leonard Arrington points out in his history of Idaho, they "also enabled those on farms and in small towns and villages to take advantage of cultural offerings in nearby cities—libraries, movies, musical performances, and Chautauquas."[5]

Northwesterners could entertain themselves without leaving their homes by the early 1920s because radio stations across the region began to broadcast music, news, and sporting events. A fur trapper in remote British Columbia recalled being able to "move a couple of knobs, and at the twitch of a squawfish's fins be in San Francisco, or Seattle. . . . The radio, an R. C. A. Victor, cost us four mink and a coyote pelt. . . . [I]t was often our only tie for months on end with the outside world." An Idaho schoolteacher and one of his students built the state's first radio transmitter and licensed its first station in the early 1920s. Montana's first radio station broadcast from Great Falls in 1922, and by the 1930s nearly all of Montana's larger communities had a station. As with automobiles, radio communication closed geographic distances in the region, bringing news and entertainment to its far corners.[6]

The region's artists and writers reflected the impact of new technologies in their work. Nard Jones's first novel, *Oregon Detour* (1930), was set in rural Oregon during the 1920s and examines the effects of modernization on the fictitious small town of Creston. A group of teenagers drive out of the confines of their community; their automobile means freedom, but it also presents a threat to their hometown. One character complains that "it won't be long now until there aren't any more small towns around here. . . . You'll see. These paved roads have spoiled the small town. People can get to Portland in a day. They can get to Walla Walla or Pendleton in an hour. . . . These bigger places will *absorb* the smaller ones." In her Montana novel *Winter Wheat* (1944), Mildred Walker's protagonist, Ellen Webb, learns the United States has entered the Second World War over a radio broadcast on the same set that brings her father daily wheat prices and weather reports. When she leaves her family's ranch to teach at a remote one-room school, her parents surprise her with a radio on their first visit. After they leave Ellen "turned my radio on. The static was like the sound of a machine gun, but the dance music filled the emptiness. If the sheepherder passed by now, he'd have to look this way, I thought. It must be funny to have so much music and noise suddenly bursting out in the snow. I ran outdoors to see how it sounded. In the dusk the snow hid the teacherage from sight and the clatter of the radio seemed to come from nowhere."[7]

New roads and automobiles made one-room schoolhouses like the one where Ellen Webb taught less necessary. Suddenly, rural students could travel speedily to bigger schools far from their homes. In the American Northwest and in British Columbia, school systems underwent a period of consolidation as a result. The growth of school districts continued in most parts of the Pacific Northwest until the mid-1940s, when the American states and British Columbia began to take advantage of modern road systems to consolidate their schools. British Columbia had more than seven hundred school districts in 1920, but between 1942 and 1947 the province closed more than two hundred schools. In Idaho the number of school districts "was reduced from 1,118 to 268 as a means of equalizing educational opportunity, achieving greater uniformity of school tax rates, and providing more effective use of state funds for the support of public schools."[8]

The number of students enrolled in elementary, middle, and high school grew steadily throughout the twentieth century, as did the number of teachers hired to teach them. School buildings were larger, with rural children bussed into town to attend classes and local control giving way to fewer and more professional school boards. Consolidation made educating students less expensive, but it also meant the demise of important local institutions. Historian Jean Barman compares the loss of small schools in British Columbia to the loss of rural post offices, noting that each civic institution was the lifeblood of rural communities. In his history of Long Creek Valley in eastern Oregon, William Willingham writes, "The completion of paved highway U.S. 395 in 1935 meant that trips to bigger shopping centers such as Pendleton, which used to take days, could now be accomplished in hours. The small, main-street businesses that once denoted a thriving community gradually disappeared over the course of the twentieth century, leaving at the end a crossroads supporting a consolidated school, post office, gas station, and mini market."[9]

"The demise of WPA funding in 1942 may not have been the worst prospect for Martina Gangle," claims David Horowitz, her biographer. "After returning to strawberry picking with her family that spring, she signed up as a welder for the Kaiser Shipyards in Vancouver [Washington]." Martina Gangle Curl used her short breaks to sketch what she saw around her at the shipyards, leaving behind a detailed documentation of work life during that hectic period. With the onset of war, many of the Depression era federally funded opportunities for artists evaporated. Nonetheless, the war and postwar prosperity made a significant impact on the cultural life of the region. Art historian Margaret Bullock points out that "art also functioned as part of the visual fabric of the shipyards in the form of posters, magazines, and other forms of graphic art."[10]

More than any single form of technology, the Second World War shattered the seeming isolation of the Pacific Northwest and its cultural workers. The war sent new populations into the western cities of the region, populations that brought musical, literary, and artistic tastes and talents to their new, if temporary, homes. Moreover, the war transformed regional communities as the federal government forcibly interned resident Japanese and Japanese Americans, West Coast populations braced for possible invasion, and some communities adapted to the appearance of conscientious objectors and prisoners of war. The war would leave nothing untouched. British Columbia artist Emily Carr wrote in her journal: "Nobody mentions the war clouds hanging so low and heavy over everything."[11]

African American soldiers and shipyard workers brought innovative styles of jazz and bebop with them when they relocated to Vancouver Barracks in Washington or to the Kaiser shipyards in Vancouver and Portland. Historian Robert Dietsche describes 1942 to 1957 as "the golden years of Portland jazz," with clubs such as the Dude Ranch, Lil' Sandy's, the Frat House, and the Chicken Coop, mostly located in Portland's inner north black neighborhood, attracting black and white musicians and music lovers. Bulee "Slim" Gaillard, "a six-foot-six lunatic" who became renowned for his lyrical humor and word play, came to the Pacific Northwest in 1943 as a soldier stationed at the Vancouver Barracks. On weekends Gaillard could be found pounding the ivories and singing at the Frat House on Portland's Williams Avenue. In Seattle clubs lined the African American–dominated Jackson Street, with the city's jazz history beginning in 1918, according to music critic and historian Paul de Barros. The scene expanded into the Central District as Seattle's black population grew during the war years. The clubs, which ranged from venues that included illegal gambling among their offerings to respectable multiracial establishments, hosted nationally known musicians as well as local talent. Even homogeneous Spokane, Washington, supported forty-two nightclubs that brought black and white jazz and bebop musicians to the city.[12]

Musicians enlivened the popular music scene in the region's cities by introducing new strains of blues and jazz to often mixed audiences. But the introduction was not without controversy in a region that was overwhelmingly white. Blues and jazz clubs clustered along Williams and Vancouver avenues in Portland and in the Central District and along Jackson Street in Seattle because redlining had relegated African Americans to the residences near those streets. Because white-owned radio stations refused to play "race" music, neighborhood businesses as varied as "soda fountains, churches, school, nightclubs, diners, dance halls, even gas stations and drycleaners" sported jukeboxes filled with the latest music. Moreover, Seattle's unionized music industry was racially segregated, with white musicians represented by Local 76. According to historian Cassandra Tate, "Black musicians, represented by 'Negro' Local 493, found work primarily in small nightclubs and dancehalls in racially mixed neighborhoods. The wages were lower on Jackson Street but, ironically, the tips were better."[13]

Wartime was full of unexpected mobility, opportunity, and convergence. For several years, a group of artists descended on the Oregon Coast, brought there by a common belief in pacifism and an appreciation for creative endeavor. Glenn Evans, a native of Fort Worth, Texas, who described his life as "rebellion against poverty, ignorance and black-boy-enter-the-back-door white superiority," was among the thousands of men and women who relocated to the Pacific Northwest during wartime.[14] Unlike most people who flowed west to work in shipyards and munitions plants or came as soldiers, Evans spent his time in the region at a remote camp for conscientious objectors. Civilian Public Service (CPS) Camp 56 near Waldport, Oregon, opened in 1943, one of 152 camps, units, and projects across the nation providing conscripted conscientious objectors the opportunity for "alternative service" to military duty. The Church of the Brethren, one of three traditional peace churches, administered the daily activity at the Waldport camp, where at any given time 120 conscientious objectors worked under federal supervision in the Siuslaw National Forest.

Evans, who had earned a master's degree in ceramics and had taught crafts on Indian reservations in Wisconsin, requested a transfer to the camp sometime after 1944 after he heard that the camp was starting a fine arts program. The program at the Waldport camp attracted professional musicians, print makers, artists, actors, and writers who were also conscientious objectors from around the country. California poet William Everson directed the program. When painter and sculptor Clayton James arrived at the camp from Massachusetts, he invited Morris Graves, a Washington painter who had been discharged from the army for noncompliance, to visit the camp. Graves spent two months living on a nearby beach, painting, and visiting with the conscripted artists. When he returned home, he invited James and his wife, Barbara, also an artist, to stay with him during a furlough. James never returned to the Waldport camp, instead relocating to Washington's Puget Sound, where he became an important member of the state's postwar art scene.[15]

In setting up remote CPS camps, the federal government sought to remove conscientious objectors from civilian populations that might be inspired or offended by their "witnessing for peace." The government also used conscientious objectors as laborers, replacing the men in the

Civilian Conservation Corps who left for military service with young men who refused to fight for religious reasons. An unintended outcome of the camps was the convening of creative pacifists—men like Everson, James, and Graves—who had the time and predilection to imagine a more peaceful and just future that had at its center the creation of art. After the war dozens of the young men who had been housed at Camp 56 traveled south to California and participated in a postwar San Francisco aesthetic and literary renaissance that included the burgeoning Beat movement to see that vision to reality; a few found their way north to Puget Sound.

The availability of post–high school education and the growth of college and university systems in the postwar era created a significant economic and cultural transformation, fueling, among other things, an interest in and willingness to support the arts. Throughout the early twentieth century, the number of students who continued their education after graduating from high school expanded with each decade. At the turn of the twentieth century, only 4 percent of Americans between the ages of eighteen and twenty-one attended a college or university; by 1920 twice as many men and women were going to college; and at the dawn of World War Two, 18 percent of college-aged Americans were in school.[16]

While the enrollment of male college students declined significantly during the war, female students reached their highest percentage of enrollment during this period, comprising 57 percent of all students. Following the war, the American GI Bill and Canadian educational support for its veterans accelerated the already established trend of rising college enrollment. Between 1940 and 1950, enrollment in American colleges increased by nearly 80 percent and would continue to rise at phenomenal rates through the 1970s. In British Columbia, university enrollment grew from three thousand in 1944 to nine thousand three years later.[17]

The expansion of secondary schools in the nineteenth and early twentieth centuries led to a national "commitment to mass higher education" in both the United States and Canada. Just as important, the U.S. GI Bill put into practice ideas about higher education that had been gaining traction since the opening of the twentieth century. Educators, politicians, and boosters argued that broad access to a college education would create the knowledgeable and active citizenry necessary in a modern democracy. Access to universities and colleges, then, was not merely a way to better one's economic standing. In fact, even in the 1930s "a college degree was more pedigree than a meal ticket." In 1946 President Harry Truman appointed the Commission on Higher Education (often referred to as the Zook Commission), which argued for an expansion of higher education, recommending that "economic, ethnic, and geographical barriers be lowered and the curriculum broadened." The Zook Commission called for "a common cultural heritage towards a common citizenship."[18]

Veterans expressed their agreement with their feet, enrolling at campuses across both countries in record numbers, surpassing even the highest estimates projected by policy makers. The region's colleges and universities exploded with new students in the postwar period. The Oregon State System of Higher Education used a program of extension centers to funnel new students into classes held in places other than the state's primary campuses, which quickly reached capacity. One site was located in the wartime housing neighborhood of Vanport, originally built to house shipyard employees. Veterans comprised 94 percent of the Vanport Extension Center's student body in its first year, and students were more likely to be married and older than college students of the previous decade. They were also more likely to be male; of 221 students, only 8 were women. Eventually, the extension center became Portland State University.[19]

Although the federal support for veterans' education is celebrated for bringing more people into an educated middle class, historian Lizabeth Cohen points out that that support was uneven. Of course, veterans' benefits were limited to those who supported the war effort through conscription and excluded those who were not conscripted or who protested conscription. Moreover, universities and colleges, bursting at the seams with new students, limited female enrollment, eliminating women from some professional programs altogether. Throughout Canada and the United States, female enrollment as a percentage of overall enrollment declined in the postwar years. In Seattle the number of college-aged women in school declined from 20 to 14 percent between 1940 and 1947. Scholars also agree that African Americans faced myriad disadvantages when it came to taking advantage of the GI Bill. Hilary Herbold points out that "although in the abstract the government would pay tuition, that was of little help to blacks who could not enter college, either because of overcrowding at black colleges or inadequate preparation for college-level work." Moreover, many colleges in the northern and western United States used de facto segregation to limit the number of African American students.[20]

The war had other unintended outcomes—the development of a robust postwar economy, the emergence of a military-industrial complex in Washington State, and new populations that remained in the region after the conclusion of the conflict. It was not altogether clear, however, to scholars at the region's first writers' conference held in 1946 at Portland's Reed College that a vibrant regional literature would develop. In titles that suggest their uncertainty of the existence of a dynamic regional culture, Ernest Haycox wondered, "Is There a Pacific Northwest?" Harold G. Merriam asked, "Does the Northwest Believe in Itself?" And Allis McKay exclaimed, "Let's Build Ourselves a 'Great Tradition.'" Peter Odegard, Reed's president, declared that residents "need to discover our own cultural heritage and to encourage our own youth to look about in their own back yard to find inspiration and employment for their creative talents." Little did Odegard know that Don Berry (*Trask*, 1960) and Garry Snyder (*Turtle Island*, 1975 Pulitzer Prize for poetry), two Reed College graduates and housemates, would do just that in the near future. Much of the region's postwar cultural growth can be attributed to the expansion of local universities and colleges, which became incubators of artistic work in every corner of the region.[21]

In their essay about the literary Pacific Northwest, scholars John Findlay and Dan Lamberton describe public institutions of higher education as the "nuclei of the literary region" after the Second World War. Newly hired faculty members such as poets Theodore Roethke and William Stafford and novelist Bernard Malamud founded or reinvigorated creative writing programs at the University of Washington, Lewis and Clark College, the University of Montana, Oregon State University, and the University of British Columbia. Those college programs attracted nationally recognized writers who fostered budding talent and a regional appreciation for literary endeavor.[22]

The University of Washington and the University of Montana comprised two focal points for the "nuclei of the literary region." A teaching position brought poet Theodore Roethke, who won the Pulitzer Prize for poetry in 1954, to the University of Washington in 1947. "When I came out to Seattle," Roethke wrote in his journal, "the head of my department said 'Ted, we don't quite know what to do with you: you're the only serious practicing poet within 1,500 miles.'" Poet and novelist David Wagoner followed his mentor west in 1954. By the 1960s and 1970s, their efforts had seeded an impressive field of writers, magazines and journals, presses, and readers. Wagoner described the success of the university's writing program: "Gradually, there was a kind of saturation of more intense reading in contemporary poetry, and a rise in skills in writing. People came from all over the country to take the writing courses at the University of Washington and then didn't go away."[23]

Seattle native Richard Hugo was among the thousands of Second World War veterans who enrolled at the University of Washington. He studied under Theodore Roethke, earning a master of arts degree in 1952. After graduation, the Seattle aircraft giant, Boeing, hired Hugo as a technical writer; he worked for the company for more than a decade. He wrote poems in his off hours, publishing his first collection, *A Run of Jacks*, in 1961. Hugo wrote that the Northwest "triggered" his poems, which often addressed the region's great scenic beauty as well as social and environmental decay. *A Run of Jacks* begins with the poem "Trout," leading one literary critic to state that the book "proceeds from the very first poem as if the proper study of mankind was fish." Despite a frequent regional focus, Hugo became nationally recognized for his work, with two nominations for a National Book Award (for *The Lady in Kicking Horse Reservoir* in 1973 and *What Thou Lovest Well, Remains American* in 1975) and a Guggenheim Fellowship in 1977.[24]

Hugo began his academic career as a visiting lecturer at the University of Montana in Missoula, eventually becoming a professor and director of its writing program. Hugo never shrank from his working-class roots and celebrated the struggles and riches of ordinary life even as he inspired his students and colleagues to craft the region's literature. When memoir and essay writer William Kittridge initially met Hugo, Kittridge was newly arrived in Missoula set to begin his first teaching job. He climbed Hugo's doorstep unannounced and quite drunk. Hugo, a heavy drinker himself, joined Kittridge, forming a friendship that lasted for years. Kittridge later wrote that "so many of us in the West felt deprived and driven to the contrary idea that the things we know are worthless, or at least of no interest to anybody else, because they are so private. Dick Hugo helped disabuse ourselves of such notions." Among Wagoner's writers who "didn't go away," Hugo returned briefly to the University of Washington in the summer of 1971 as the Roethke Chair.[25]

While Richard Hugo documented ordinary Northwest life in his poetry from his university post, Viola Gale simply wanted more people in the Northwest to read poetry. Originally from Sweden, Gale's family moved to Clatskanie, where her father worked as a logger, when she was six. Vi Gale published her first book of poems, *Several Houses*, in 1959; it was later named to the Oregon Cultural Heritage Commission's one hundred best Oregon books. Armed with a business sense as well as a love of writing poetry, Vi Gale founded the Prescott Street Press in Portland in 1974 and began to publish translations and regional writers, often using local artists to illustrate their books. Like Gale, Barbara Wilson and Rachel da Silva founded a regional press, this time with a focus on feminist writers. When they published their first books in 1976 using da Silva's parents' Seattle home as their production center, Seal Press was born.

Like university writing programs, regional presses were crucial to the creation of a supportive network of writers and readers. Prescott Street Press in Portland, Copper Canyon Press in Port Townsend, Beach Holme Press in Vancouver, British Columbia, and Seattle's feminist Seal Press wrested some control from the publishing houses on the East Coast and provided regional writers with a way to disseminate their work. By not limiting themselves to local talent, these presses extended their own literary reach and highlighted the region's importance to a broad publishing world. In a 1987 essay, Gale claimed, "Visitors to the past few American Booksellers Association conventions have been lavish in praise for the books and periodicals from Northwest presses. Excellent work is coming from small literary houses in Idaho, Seattle, Port Townsend and Portland. The quality of the writing is high, the production outstanding. As one reporter put it, 'Eyes are looking west in a way they haven't since the beats came out of California.'"[26]

Cultural expression in the postwar period took on many issues. In some instances, popular culture reflected society's desire to return to "normalcy" after the disruption of war. One of the most popular books to come out of the region was Betty MacDonald's *The Egg and I* (1945), a satirical look at life on an egg farm in Washington's Chimacum Valley. It was "received by an American public exhausted by the war effort and parched for laughter." The book, MacDonald's first, rocketed up the national best-seller list. MacDonald's humorous account of her four years living on an egg farm (translated into thirty languages) provided the inspiration for more than ten movies (most of them about Ma and Pa Kettle, characters from the book). Her artistry became a short-lived television show and instigated more books, including a series of children's books highlighting the character Mrs. Piggle-Wiggle. She also wrote *The Plague and I* (1948) about a year she spent in a sanatorium sick with tuberculosis and *Anybody Can Do Anything* (1950) about living through the Depression as the single mother of two girls.[27]

While most of her books are devoted to telling humorous stories about neighbors, friends, and family, MacDonald specifically addressed the Pacific Northwest region in *The Egg and I.* In the Chimacum Valley "every window of our house framed a vista so magnificent that our ruffled curtains were as inappropriate frames as tatted edges on a Van Gogh."[28] In an apt description of Seattle she wrote, "The seasons ran together like the stained-glass-window paintings we did at school where we wet the drawing paper first, all over, then dropped on blobs of different colors which ran into each other so that it was impossible to tell where one began and the other left off."[29] Most of MacDonald's descriptions celebrate the natural beauty that surrounded her, but she also remarked on the clear-cutting of timber in the valley: "The only ugliness we saw was the devastation left by the logging companies. Whole mountains left naked and embarrassed, their every scar visible for miles."[30]

The neighbors who inspired MacDonald's characters complained that she turned them into caricatures. She insisted that her characters were composites of people she met in Chimacum Valley, but neighbors recognized themselves in her narrative, which often painted them as country bumpkins and ne'er-do-wells. An effort to sue the author was unsuccessful. MacDonald was hard on many of her neighbors, but she reserved her most caustic remarks for a single chapter, "With Bow and Arrow." In it she describes a picnic that her husband's Indian fishing and hunting buddies, Geoduck, Clamface, and Crowbar Swensen, invited them to attend. MacDonald finds nothing to like about her Indian hosts, depicting them as dirty, poorly educated, negligent of their children, and generally drunken and rowdy. MacDonald concludes her most troubling chapter by writing, "Little red brothers or not, I didn't like Indians, and the more I saw of them the more I thought what an excellent thing it was to take that beautiful country away from them."[31] Twenty-first-century readers who left reviews at the Seattle-based online bookseller amazon.com were divided about how to interpret the overt racism found in an otherwise entertaining book, with some arguing that the book should no longer be widely read and others that MacDonald was still funny and only reflected the tenor of her time.

Artistic endeavors addressed political and social concerns that captured the postwar region. British Columbia's Hubert Evans published important books that featured Asian Canadian and Native characters at their center. His examination of the expulsion of Asian immigrants and their Canadian-born children from the coast, *No More Islands,* was published in 1942. In 1954 he followed up with a novel about Indian people living near Vancouver, *Mist on the River*, considered a classic of Canadian fiction today. Evans received accolades for writing about British Columbia's Native people realistically and with sympathy. Evans made a living as a journalist, a fish hatchery attendant, and a short-story writer, publishing his work in numerous Canadian and American periodicals. By the 1930s, he had become known for his juvenile fiction, much of which focused on animals and wilderness adventures. "In those days," he recalled, "if you could put a short story together, you could sell it. But you couldn't make a living just by writing for Canada. So I wrote pulp stories. The most popular kind back then were war stories by American guys who'd never even been there." Evans had served in the First World War but later became a Quaker. Unlike his contemporaries, he "couldn't write about violence," choosing instead to write "outdoor stories. Animal stories."[32]

In response to the Second World War era internment of Japanese Americans and Japanese Canadians, Evans published a ten-part serial in two denominational magazines titled "No More Islands," "a sympathetic portrayal of the effects of internment on both Japanese Canadians and the people who knew them." Molly Kujomura wrote a fan letter to Evans from Idaho's Minidoka War Relocation Center, telling of her anger at the policy of internment: "I have ranted and stormed but your story 'No More Islands' gave me new hope. It is one of the few articles that I have read that seemed to understand us."[33]

Hubert Evans's 1954 adult novel, *Mist on the River*, drew on his experiences living in Kitimat and Hazelton in northwestern British Columbia while his wife taught children in Kitimat Village on the Haisla Reserve. The novel, which takes place in a Gitskan village on the Skeena River and at a fish cannery in Prince Rupert, focuses on several young aboriginal people who struggle with the traditional ways of their parents and grandparents and the non-Native culture that surrounds them and demands their assimilation. As the title suggests, resolution is not easy. After publication, Evans reported, "People say to me, 'Do you like Indians?' Well, I like some Indians and there are some Indians I don't like. The same with white people." Described as a work of "unlimited understanding and compassion" by Evans's biographer, the novel secured Evans's prominence among British Columbia writers.[34]

After the Second World War, a number of Native, Asian American, and Asian Canadian writers rose to prominence. Monica Sone's *Issei Daughter*

(1953) examined the effects of internment on her Seattle family. John Okada's 1957 novel, *No-No Boy*, was the Seattle writer's only book. In it Okada explored the effects of internment on Japanese and Japanese Americans as they returned to Seattle after the war. The main character, Ichiro Yamada, replied "no" to two questions on a loyalty form that the federal government used to identify potential traitors, hence the title *No-No Boy*. Yamada's answers led to a stint in federal prison, and the novel examines the postwar identity crisis many people suffered after internment. The novel fell into obscurity shortly after it was written, and Okada died at age forty-seven. The novel was reissued in 1976 and is now considered an important nascent publication in Asian American literature.

Novelist Joy Kogawa also wrote about Canadian internment in *Obasan*, which was published in 1981. Unlike Okada's novel, Kogawa's became immediately successful and was part of the impetus for Canadian reparations to internees in the late 1980s. Canadian and American writers of Asian descent have tackled a variety of topics and themes in various forms, from Shawn Wong, whose first novel, *Homebase* (1979), won a Pacific Northwest Booksellers Award and the 15th Annual Governor's Writers Day Award of Washington, to Lawson Fusao Inada, the recipient of a Guggenheim Fellowship who became Oregon's poet laureate in 2006. Because of the concentration of Asian immigrants on the West Coast and the historic waves of Asian immigration in the nineteenth and twentieth centuries, the Pacific Northwest has been an important locus of Asian American literature, second only to California. According to literary critic Laurie Ricou, "Asian ancestors and ancestry blossom as the most visible—after the Native peoples—un-British other in British Columbia." Similarly, Asians and Asian Americans pose a counterpoint to the overwhelming narrative of Anglo settlement in the American Northwest.[35]

Works by Native American and First Nations writers became more prevalent in the Pacific Northwest in the last quarter of the twentieth century. Writers such as James Welch, Janet Campbell Hale, Sherman Alexie, Elizabeth Woody, and George Clutesi gained regional and national prominence. Because he studied under Richard Hugo at the University of Montana, Welch (Blackfeet/Gros Ventre) provides a link back to the flourishing of Pacific Northwest literature and poetry at the University of Washington under Theodore Roethke. Welch, who eventually taught at the University of Washington, grew up in Montana, alternately living on Indian reservations and his family's farm. He was both a poet and a novelist, and his novels *Winter in the Blood* (1974) and *The Death of Jim Loney*

(1979) launched Welch to national recognition as part of the Native American Renaissance, a term coined by critic Kenneth Lincoln to describe the profusion of literature produced by Native Americans, beginning with N. Scott Momaday's *House Made of Dawn* (Pulitzer Prize, 1969).[36]

According to Samuel Corrigan, a scholar of Native American literature, Canada experienced a less robust explosion of First Nations literature than the United States during the same period. He blames federal policies that kept aboriginal populations rural and the fact that there were fewer publishing houses in Canada than in the United States. Corrigan also points out that live theater thrived among Canada's First Nations, providing a similar outlet that literature did among Indians in the United States. Nonetheless, British Columbia First Nations writers contributed important works after the Second World War. Novelist Jeannette Armstrong (Okanagan) points to the various regional Native magazines and newspapers that flourished during the politically charged decades of the 1960s and 1970s as venues for a burgeoning Native literature. Although much of their writing was directed at educating their readers about contemporary political issues, these magazines and newspapers also published contemporary poetry. Armstrong believes that "these papers were instrumental in engendering a literary movement parallel to or perhaps occurring as one of the vehicles of the 'Indian Movement.'" Armstrong's own novel, *Slash* (1985), was the first published by a First Nations woman.[37]

Although she did not mention him by name, Jeannette Armstrong could have been referring to George Clutesi (Nuu-chal-nuth), who began his writing career in 1947 with submissions to the aboriginal newspaper the *Native Voice*. His writing reached a national audience when he published *Son of Raven, Son of Deer* (1967), a collection of Native stories that he also illustrated. Samuel Corrigan called the book "a sensation," and it was sold nationwide and widely used in British Columbian schools. In 1969 Clutesi followed up the success of his first book with *Potlatch*. It describes a potlatch ceremony, which the Canadian government had banned in the Indian Act in 1885 (revisions to the act in 1951 reversed the ban). Clutesi wrote, "This narrative is not meant to be documentary. In fact it is meant to evade documents. It is meant for the reader to feel and to say I was there and indeed I saw." Today, Clutesi is perhaps better remembered as an artist and film and television actor than as a writer (Emily Carr willed Clutesi her "brushes, oils, and unused canvases"). He was commissioned to create a mural for Montreal's Expo 67 and acted in several films before his death in 1988.[38]

Like George Clutesi, Sherman Alexie (Spokane/Coeur d'Alene) ex-presses himself in a variety of media—in novels and poetry, as a per-former of stand-up comedy, and in film. Winner of a National Book Award in 2007 for his young adult novel *The Absolutely True Diary of a Part-Time Indian*, Alexie began publishing as a poet in 1992 with the release of a book of poems and short stories, *The Business of Fancydancing*. More than previous Northwest Native writers, Alexie became a light-ning rod for the contestation of what it meant to be an Indian artist in the late twentieth century. He has been both praised and criticized for his stark, troubling depictions of reservation and contemporary Native life, for his allusions to pop and non-Native cultures, and for the threads of humor that are a part of all his work.

Non-Native critics have overwhelmingly praised Alexie's work. When Frederick Busch reviewed *Reservation Blues* (1995) for the *New York Times*, he exclaimed that Alexie's "talent is real, and it is very large, and I will gratefully read whatever he writes." Another critic described *Reservation Blues* as "a rueful, salty novel, a harsh, affectionate, deeply moving and densely detailed portrait of present-day life on the Spokane Indian Reservation." But unlike the Tseshaht First Nation Web site, which cele-brates its connection to George Clutesi, the Spokane Indian Reservation Web site makes no mention of Alexie, and the librarian at the Spokane tribal campus of the Salish-Kootenai College reported that "he's very controversial here. . . . What people on the reservation feel is that he's making fun of them." Literary critic Gloria Bird agrees, writing that the novel "contributes to a portrait of an exaggerated version of reservation life, one that perpetuates many of the stereotypes of native people."[39]

Depicting a place and people is fraught with political implications. This is particularly true for artists and writers who represent, explain, conjure, or draw inspiration from the Native Northwest. The narratives that poems, short stories, and films construct and repeat create the envi-ronment in which legal and political contests over land, water, and other material resources are waged between the region's Indian and non-Indian residents. Struggles for social justice such as the African American civil rights movement and the Red Power movement and governmental poli-cies such as school desegregation and Native American self-determination are reflected in the literature of the Northwest. Just as important as postwar political change were the social changes that a rising popula-tion brought. Poet Lawson Inada describes population growth in Ash-land, Oregon: "The region became, not only much more 'livable,' but a fundamentally safer place to be. Plain and simple, what with all the actors and tourists and beardeds around, a guy like me wasn't subject to question anymore."[40]

Artists who reside in the Northwest have produced a literature that attends to the physical environment. Representative examples include David Guterson's claustrophobic depiction of Washington State's rain forest in *Our Lady of the Forest* (2003) and the way in which the Columbia River courses through the novels of Oregon author Craig Lesley (*Winterkill*, 1996, and *Riversong*, 1999). In *Sometimes a Great Notion* (1964), Ken Kesey majestically captured the dawning force of a coastal river: "The first little washes flashing like thick rushing winds through sheep sorrel and clover, ghost fern and nettle, sheering, cutting . . . forming branches. Then, through bearberry and salmonberry, blueberry and blackberry, the branches crashing into creeks, into streams. Finally, in the foothills, through tamarack and sugar pine, shittim bark and silver spruce—and the green and blue mosaic of Douglas fir—the actual river falls five hundred feet . . . and look: opens out upon the fields."[41] Kesey's fictional Wakonda Auga River shapes the action in his story of gyppo loggers (men who worked independently of the region's logging companies) during a flood season. The river makes work possible, creating a water highway that moves timber from forest to mill, but it also destroys what falls into it, including human life.

Ken Kesey's novels *One Flew Over the Cuckoo's Nest* and *Sometimes a Great Notion*, published in quick succession in 1962 and 1964, propelled the Oregonian into the national spotlight. Both novels have aged well. In 2005 *Time* magazine listed *One Flew Over the Cuckoo's Nest* among its top one hundred novels written between 1923 and 2005. John Marshall of the *Seattle Post-Intelligencer* calls *Sometimes a Great Notion* "the quintessential Northwest novel." But it would be nearly twenty years before Kesey would publish his third novel, *Sailor Song*, an effort that was largely panned by critics. Instead, Kesey became increasingly famous for his counterculture exploits, which Tom Wolfe chronicled in *The Electric Kool-Aid Acid Test* (1968). By the time of his death in 2001, appraisal of his body of work was mixed, with the *New York Times* stating, "He never did surpass his first two books."[42]

Despite the successes of regional authors like Ken Kesey, for most of the twentieth century, a regional body of literature seemed in its infancy. By the 1980s and 1990s, the seeds planted after the war had germinated into a flowering of poetry, prose, plays, screenplays, essays, and memoirs that had gained national recognition. Historian John Findlay writes that by this time, "critics, commentators, and the authors themselves increasingly agreed that something worthy of the name 'Pacific Northwest literature' had begun to emerge." What was slim pickings when James Stevens and H. L. Davis wrote their screed against melodrama became an accumulation too large and diverse to properly review here. Writers Ken Kesey, Ivan Doig (*This House of Sky: Landscapes of a Western Mind*, 1979, and a trilogy of novels set between 1889 and 1989 in Montana: *English Creek*, 1984, *Dancing at the Rascal Fair*, 1987, and *Ride with Me, Mariah, Montana*, 1990), Tess Gallagher (*The Lover of Horses*, 1986, and *Moon Crossing Bridge*, 1992), Mary Clearman Blue (*All but the Waltz: Essays on a Montana Family*, 1991, and *Balsamroot: A Memoir*, 2001), and Ursula K. Le Guin (*The Left Hand of Darkness*, 1969, and *The Word for World Is Forest*, 1976, both Hugo Award winners) had collectively created a broad body of regional literature by the end of the twentieth century.[43]

Journalist Thomas Griffith described northwesterners in 1976 as people who "may not know Picasso from Andy Warhol, but are learned in the nuances of color and texture in nature." The first part of his description is an unfair generalization of a people who were as likely to be in tune with popular and elite culture as were residents of other regions, but the second part rings true. In the Pacific Northwest, nature and what literary critic Laurie Ricou calls the region's "greyscape" have pervaded the arts and literary scenes. Not all artists in the region have been inspired to depict the world around them, and they are too varied and diverse to delineate much of a "Northwest style" or "school" of regional art over time. But many did find inspiration in the natural world, creating works that reflect a geography and history specific to the Northwest.[44]

Over the course of nearly six decades, four artists—Kenneth Callahan, Morris Graves, E. J. Hughes, and Lawrence Paul Yuxweluptun—have produced oil and acrylic landscape paintings that depict the region's timber industry. Unlike many landscape paintings of the nineteenth century, these paintings comment on the human impact on the land they render. To ask a handful of artists to shoulder the breadth and depth of the Northwest arts world in the twentieth century is an impossible task. Nonetheless, all four have indelibly and in diverse ways shaped regional art and that fleeting concept, regional identity. The authors of *The Pacific Northwest Landscape: A Painted History* call the timber industry "the most powerful and dramatic landscapist of the Northwest" because it "turned the forested mountainsides into a new kind of wilderness of skid roads, stumps, and slash."[45] Collectively, these artists' timber industry paintings represent themes important to Pacific Northwest art and techniques that are emblematic of artistic trends over the decades.

Kenneth Callahan's *Stump Landscape* (1934–35) and Morris Graves's *Logged Mountains* (1935–43) are similar in style and palette, mountains and stumps rendered almost abstractly in shades of gray, green, and brown. In her book *Iridescent Light: The Emergence of Northwest Art*, Deloris Ament cautions readers against looking for a manifesto or other formal documentation for a Northwest "school" of art. Instead, she describes loose connections and compatible works, art that curators and collectors would organize into a school. According to Ament, the artists that were identified with this school "did more than create art; they looked at the world around them and saw what men were doing to it and, in the process, to themselves—butchering trees, cutting roads through forests, paving rich bottomland."[46]

The lives of Kenneth Callahan (1905–86) and Morris Graves (1910–2001) overlapped in significant ways. Both men became nationally recognized artists, in part because their work reflected the Pacific Northwest. Both worked at the Seattle Art Museum and inspired the work of a generation of regional artists as well as one another. Along with Mark Tobey and Guy Anderson, both were identified in a *Life* magazine article published in 1953 as part of an influential group of "Northwest mystic painters." Kenneth Callahan was born in Spokane and raised in Glasgow, Montana, and in Seattle. In Montana cowboy artist Charles Russell was a frequent guest at the Callahan home. In 1930 he married Margaret Bundy, the editor of *Town Crier*, a literary magazine to which Callahan contributed art critiques. Callahan was offered a part-time job in 1933 when the Seattle Art Museum first opened. He stayed for twenty years at a post that offered him plenty of time to paint. Callahan became a nationally recognized artist when his work was represented in exhibits at the Whitney Museum in 1933 and at the Museum of Modern Art in 1934 and 1935. Callahan had his first one-man exhibit in New York at the American-British Art Center in 1946. Francis Henry Taylor, the director of the Metropolitan Museum of Art, called Callahan "probably the most American painter of our time." Of his own inspiration, Callahan told an interviewer, "Nature is almost without exception the source of all my work."[47]

Morris Graves, "the most eccentric of the 'Northwest Mystics,'" was born in Oregon, but his family moved to Seattle when he was a year old.

Like Martina Gangle Curl, Graves participated in the WPA Federal Art Project (though for only a few months). During the Second World War, Kenneth Callahan received a deferment, although he initially sought conscientious objector status. Graves applied to become a conscientious objector but was eventually drafted. After Graves refused to participate in his duties, an army psychiatrist found him psychologically unable to serve, and he was released with an honorable discharge. After the war, Graves traveled, exhibited his work, built or modified several homes, including one in Ireland, and became widely known for his eccentricity. In the mid-1960s, Graves moved to Humboldt County, California, where he remained until his death. Of the four artists dubbed the Northwest mystics, Graves received the most acclaim and the most criticism, with work that was at times pioneering and at times derivative (Mark Tobey claimed Graves copied his techniques). Promoter Elizabeth Bayley Willis praised his technique, claiming that Graves "developed his style from the minute examination of moss," while the *New Yorker*'s art critic wrote in 1948 that "despite his amazing virtuosity one feels that underneath the surface charm there is only emptiness."[48]

Deloris Ament writes, "It is not enough to care about art. One must also care about artists."[49] Kenneth Callahan and Morris Graves would not have reached critical acclaim without their myriad supporters in the Pacific Northwest. Dr. Robert Fuller, the founder of the Seattle Art Museum in 1933, supported both artists with positions at the museum (Callahan for twenty years, 1933–53, and Graves for just two, from 1940 until he was drafted in 1942). The work provided income while not being so arduous as to eclipse painting. Elizabeth Bayley Willis and Thelma Lehmann bought works and promoted Northwest artists to gallery owners in and beyond the region. Even the 1953 *Life* article that propelled Mark Tobey, Morris Graves, Kenneth Callahan, and Guy Anderson to a national audience came about as a result of a friendship between a local art dealer who represented Tobey, Callahan, and Anderson and a feature writer for *Life*, the most popular periodical of the period.[50]

With more than four decades dividing them, E. J. Hughes's *Logs, Ladysmith Harbour* (1949) and Lawrence Paul Yuxweluptun's *Scorched Earth, Clear-Cut Logging on Native Sovereign Soil, Shaman Coming to Fix* (1991) provide very different views of the timber industry in British Columbia. Much of Hughes's work focuses on the interplay between human communities and their environments, but his images are nearly illustrative and appealingly regional in the same way that Emily Carr's paintings are. As Yuxweluptun's title suggests, his work is pointedly political and often comments on the state of First Nations rights in addition to the environmental impact of British Columbia's industrial economy. Though seemingly divergent, both reflect on the land and people of British Columbia and the Pacific Northwest in evocative ways.

Edward John Hughes (1913–2007) is credited with being one of Canada's great artists, and many critics argue that he is Emily Carr's heir, with paintings that clearly reference the region in much the same way. Jack Shadbolt claimed that Hughes was "the most engaging intuitive painter of the BC landscape since Emily Carr." Hughes might have been intuitive, but he was also learned, having spent several years when he was a teenager at the Vancouver School of Art studying under Frederick H. Varley, one of the founding members of Canada's famed Group of Seven. Hughes made his living as a commercial artist in the 1930s and served as an official war artist during the Second World War. Unlike Carr, Hughes was able to make a living from his paintings.[51]

Hughes said of his own work that he "always painted what [he] wanted," with his subjects including the ferries, fishing boats, and steamers that plied the waters off Vancouver Island. Vancouver Art Museum curator Ian Thom wrote that Hughes "made art out of the raw material of the world," and art critic Sarah Milroy observed, "The landscape, inexorably plied by tourism, mediated by industry, transformed by resource extraction—that was his muse." Jacques Barbeau, who wrote a book with Hughes, declared, "Hughes's art *is* British Columbia."[52]

Although overtly political in a way that Hughes's work is not, Lawrence Paul Yuxweluptun's work is also representative of British Columbia. Born on a Kamloops reserve in 1957, Yuxweluptun (Salish/Okanagan) grew up in Vancouver with parents who were active in First Nations organizations. Yuxweluptun's father served as the president of the North American Indian Brotherhood, and his mother was the director of the Indian Homemakers Association. Yuxweluptun graduated from the Emily Carr College of Art and Design in 1983 and shortly thereafter began to exhibit as a solo artist in museums and galleries throughout Canada and the United States. His work reflects the many aboriginal artists who have labored to sustain the varied works that comprise a category of Native Northwest Coast art as well as the post–Second World War indigenous rights movements that have been part of the political landscape of the

E. J. Hughes, *Logs, Ladysmith Harbour*, Art Gallery of Ontario. Edward John Hughes captured the importance of resource extraction to the economy of British Columbia in paintings like this one.

Greater Pacific Northwest. As an introduction to his work he states, "You have a flag, I have a motherland; you have patronage, I was annexed."[53]

A multimedia and performance artist as well as a painter, Yuxweluptun is probably best known for his surrealistic, colorful, and large paintings that combine Northwest Coast Native and European artistic traditions. His paintings are politically charged, addressing First Nations land claims and the impact of resource extraction on former indigenously managed lands. Charlotte Townsend-Gault calls Yuxweluptun's work "an idiom as hybrid as any in Western twentieth-century art in a deliberate act of reciprocal appropriation." Art critic Annette Schroeter writes that Yuxweluptun's work explores "ideas about the environment, spirituality, social injustice, economics and cultural sharing." Although at first glance his paintings are colorful geometric shapes that evoke forms analogous to traditional Native Coast art, Yuxweluptun's landscapes are ultimately two-dimensional and often animated with spirits and people at the edge of despair "in an environment unable to sustain life."[54]

Both Edward John Hughes and Lawrence Paul Yuxweluptun take the

Lawrence Paul Yuxweluptun, *Scorched Earth, Clear-Cut Logging on Native Sovereign Soil, Shaman Coming to Fix*, National Art Gallery of Canada. Lawrence Paul Yuxweluptun comments on the colonization of the land and the First Nations in Canada in paintings that combine Northwest Coast Native and European artistic traditions.

land as their inspiration, and their paintings are a reflection of the close connection that many in the Pacific Northwest feel to their region, especially to those places where human and nature intersect. Hughes's *Logs, Ladysmith Harbour* captures Laurie Ricou's greyscape in the interplay of dark skies and dark water. A tugboat and the harbor's floating logs stand out in colorful relief as river rats guide the forest's bounty into proper position. Sky and water are also important elements in Yuxweluptun's *Scorched Earth, Clear-Cut Logging on Native Sovereign Soil, Shaman Coming to Fix*. Instead of a greyscape, however, Yuxweluptun uses the browns of stumps and cut-over soil to suggest the aftereffects of the same logging that was Hughes's subject. A soil devoid of the lush vegetation that most identify with the region's forests becomes the legacy of the industrialized timber industry, the devastation that the shaman is "coming to fix." Both artists build upon a tradition of creativity in the region, as the artistry of others—Emily Carr and Haida sculptor Bill Reid among them—sustained their own vision.

In the travel sections of national newspapers, the Pacific Northwest is described as eclectic, high-tech, green, a haven for serious coffee drinkers and for hikers, bicyclists, and windsurfers. Nearly every article references the region's many bookstores and thriving formal and informal arts scenes. The intensity with which northwesterners seem to take their coffee and culture, especially their propensity to buy and borrow books, is often chalked up to the weather. In 1999 Speight Jenkins, executive director of the Seattle Opera, told a *Washington Post* writer, "We do have a remarkable audience. And no one knows why. It rains so much in the winter, people want to go somewhere." Mystery writer J. A. Jance suggested, "Maybe it's the rain, but Seattle has always been a reading town." And journalist Andrea Sachs pointed out in an article titled "In Oregon, Just Readin' in the Rain" that Portland hosted more used and independent bookstores in 2001 than it did the popular Seattle-based Starbucks coffee shops.[55]

Soggy weather aside, the Pacific Northwest has developed an important arts and culture scene with events that range from Seattle's Bumbershoot Festival of arts and music to Portland's celebration of the written word, Wordstock, and Vancouver, British Columbia's International Film Festival. Since the Second World War museums have multiplied across the region, with some of the most recent additions organized and funded by the Northwest's tribes—the Tamástslikt Cultural Institute on the Umatilla Indian Reservation in eastern Oregon and the Makah Cultural and Research Center in Neah Bay, Washington. The region's arid cities also boast important cultural endeavors. Boise, Idaho, counts among its arts organizations the Boise Philharmonic, the Boise Art Museum, and Opera Idaho. In 2008 efforts to establish Ballet Idaho got under way. Town leaders in Helena, Montana, recently opted to "brand" their city as "The West's Learning Center for the Arts," and the Montana Council for the Arts determined in a recent study that more Montanans made their living working as full-time artists than they did in the state's mining or wood-products manufacturing industries.[56]

Growth in arts and culture may not be solely a function of the weather. Twentieth-century population growth, which surged as a result of the Second World War and has continued to the present, and the postwar expansion of the middle class strengthened support for museums, galleries, theaters, independent bookstores, and small publishers. Barbara Johns, a curator at the Tacoma Art Museum, credits the "increased affluence of the middle class" and the GI Bill, which led to the accreditation of many of the region's arts schools, with the increasing popularity of modernism and the success of such painters as Morris Graves and Kenneth Callahan. The *Idaho Statesman* documented the growth of Boise arts organizations at the start of the new century, observing that that growth continues to "keep pace with—and in some respects outpace—the valley's development." According to the *Washington Post*, corporate giving to arts groups in King and Pierce counties in 1997 topped out at $8 million, leading journalist Jacqueline Trescott to argue that in other cities such as Washington, D.C., "Seattle envy abounds." And the *New York Times* pointed out that "though the big publishing houses are still ensconced in New York, the Seattle area is the home of Amazon, Starbucks and Costco, three companies that increasingly influence what America reads" through their marketing policies. Moreover, the high-tech industry in Seattle and, to a lesser extent, Portland has channeled new money into cultural programs—the Experience Music Project, a museum that focuses on the history of popular music, was the brainchild of Microsoft cofounder Paul Allen.[57]

Money alone cannot ensure vital arts and culture communities. Increased wealth and population underwrote twentieth-century cultural endeavors in the Pacific Northwest, but they played no larger a role than did national events or the movements to expand civil rights that consumed much of the late twentieth century.

Epilogue
Regional Identity in a New Century

The twenty-first-century Pacific Northwest would be unrecognizable to Abigail Scott Duniway (1834–1915), John Minto (1822–1915), Samuel Hauser (1833–1914), and James Dunsmuir (1851–1920). Although all four lived into the railroad age, rural living still provided powerful insights to the way citizens thought about the region. The twenty-first-century Northwest stands in sharp contrast, with most people living in an urbanized world of rapid population growth, electronic telecommunications, and access to federal highways and international air travel. That urban veneer of wealth and cultural innovation, however, masks a sizable underclass of service workers and the marginally employed. In rural areas beyond the Interstate 5 metroplex and a few urban centers in the interior, economies are spatially uneven, with a few amenity-rich settings prospering, while declining resource industries have brought hardship to other places. The makeover of amenity-driven New West communities like Ashland, Oregon, and Coeur d'Alene, Idaho, stands in sharp contrast to hardscrabble logging towns in western Montana and the aluminum-dependent Kitimat-Stikine district in interior British Columbia.[1]

The elongated four-hundred-mile urban metroplex from vibrant, innovative, and diverse Vancouver, British Columbia, to Eugene, Oregon, embraced eight million people at the onset of the twenty-first century. If the area were a nation-state, it would rank as the tenth largest global economy. Alan Durning, author of the statistically driven "Cascadia Scorecard," points to problems with the new economy, where the largest incomes derive from investments and retirements. Quality of life and a healthy environment are compatible with the new information age economy and explain the Interstate 5 corridor's success story, where the majority of people share generally good health and economic security. The downside to the Greater Northwest economy is the widening gap between rich and poor. The Puget Sound area—Durning calls it an "urban cybertopia"—has the highest number of billionaires per capita in the world. Its fastest-growing housing arrangements are prisons and gated communities.[2]

The increasing disparities in income and wealth are most obvious between major urban centers and communities in the hinterland. Although these differences are apparent in largely rural states such as Montana and Idaho, they also exist in metropolitan-dominated Oregon, Washington, and British Columbia. Although the region has generated thousands of new jobs, few provide wages adequate to support a single adult with children. The Northwest Federation of Community Organizations reported in 2007 (before the economic collapse of 2008) that 34 percent of available jobs in the American Northwest did not offer wages sufficient to support a single person, while 80 percent failed to provide an income adequate to sustain a single parent with two children. The report defined a living wage as an income sufficient to meet basic needs without relying on some form of welfare. The Northwest Federation applauded state and federal efforts to raise the minimum wage but cited the need to ensure that new jobs paid a living wage.[3]

The trends in regional income inequality reflect neoliberal policies in both Canada and the United States, ideologies centered in the belief that economic liberalism and free-market approaches will promote economic development and contribute to a just society. Critics argue that such policies have enriched the wealthy over the last several decades. The data clearly show that this has been true in Washington and Oregon, where the gap between the wealthiest 20 percent of families and the poorest 20 percent placed the states tenth and eleventh in the nation in increasing income inequality between 1985 and 2005. Globalization, a declining resource economy, expanding low-wage service jobs, regressive minimum-wage structures, and weak and ineffective unions explain these growing inequalities, according to the Center on Budget and Policy Priorities.[4]

The economy of the last two decades is markedly different from that of the period following the Second World War, when prosperity was more broadly distributed. Even with the rise of public-sector unions in the 1960s and 1970s, union membership in the United States had fallen to less than 15 percent of the workforce by the close of the twentieth century. Although public-employee union membership has slowed in the United States, Canada has a much higher percentage of its workers in public-employee unions. The rise of conservative politics in the United States in the late 1970s and economic stagnation powered attacks against unions, including those in the public sector.[5]

Although the statistics for Montana and Idaho place both states toward the bottom in growth of income inequality since the 1970s, the differences reflect proportion and scale rather than substance. When local newspapers reported in 2002 that the wealthiest 20 percent of Montana families ranked last in the nation among all states in average income, economist Thomas Power cautioned that the poorest 20 percent also ranked third lowest nationally. What the data reveal, he argues, is that "family incomes in Montana are low across the board." Using crude cost-of-living adjustments, Power estimates that average incomes for Montana families were about 9 percent below the national average. Low and middle incomes, however, did not disadvantage Montanans from their counterparts in other states because they enjoyed real incomes almost identical to their cohorts in higher income states.[6] Power ignores the fact, however, that Montana residents pay comparatively more for fuel, food, and health care, expenses they confront with incomes well below the national average.

Similar debates over income inequality took place in Idaho, although a *USA Today* article in September 2007 praised the state's economic boom as tops in the nation. The *Idaho Statesman* disagreed, pointing out that Micron Technology had laid off more than a thousand workers earlier that year and that average wages across the state were still among the lowest in the nation. Writing for the *Moscow-Pullman Daily News* in January 2008, economist Judith Brown cited a congressional Joint Economic Committee "fact sheet" for Idaho that reported stagnant household incomes and a median income that lagged far behind national averages. Brown was most critical of the state's abysmal effort to invest in education, a shortcoming that left Idaho among the bottom states in awarding four-year college degrees.[7]

Much of the visible inequality in the Greater Northwest is reflected in the growing gentrification of former logging, mining, ranching, and fishing communities, where a new, contemporary gold-rush ethic has been reshaping economies and landscapes during the last few decades. The influx of highly educated, affluent people who have been remaking former resource-dependent communities is a symbol of new wealth in the outback. Cultural disruption and a marginalized workforce, with low-paying retail and service-sector employment replacing good-paying blue-collar jobs, follow in the wake of new wealth. Put simply, the region's declining primary-production economy has made the Northwest's vast interior an attractive investment arena for people with money to spend. The

transformation of communities into playgrounds and homes for the affluent, however, has not diminished exploitive aspects of the new economy.[8]

Although Aspen, Colorado, may be the most extreme example of gentrification in the West, places such as Leavenworth, Washington; Coeur
d'Alene and Wallace, Idaho; Ashland and Bend, Oregon; and Montana's
Gallatin Valley replicate that experience. William Smith, an investment
analyst who moved to Bend with his family for its mountain trails, rippling trout streams, and spacious golf courses, fits the profile of the highly
mobile professionals who have settled in central Oregon. "We're living
where others are fortunate enough just to visit," he told a reporter for the
Eugene Register-Guard in the summer of 1998. Smith is representative of
the mobile wealthy who have transformed old mill towns, contributing
to escalating real estate and rental costs and otherwise pricing working
people out of the housing market. John Shull, a carpenter and former
resident of Ashland, told a reporter that tradespeople could no longer
afford to live there.[9]

Wage/equity relations for British Columbia parallel conditions in the
American Northwest, with tax and census statistics showing dramatic
increases in inequalities in wealth. Writing for the Canadian Centre for
Policy Alternatives, Marc Lee found that "the rich got richer over the 1990s,
while the poor got poorer." Compared with other Canadian provinces,
however, increases in inequality in British Columbia were less severe.
Since 2001, income tax cuts have also favored the wealthy, while health
premiums and consumption taxes have increased.[10]

Although trends in cross-border income inequality in the Northwest
are similar, there are significant differences. Canadians have historically
intervened in the market to mitigate the conditions of inequality to a
much greater degree than their American counterparts. Those interven-
tions include the support of adequate income levels, equal access to education, publicly funded health-care systems, subsidized housing for the
needy, and assistance for child care. Beyond social support, Canadian
and provincial governments also regularly exercise authority to influence labor markets, establishing minimum wages, creating jobs through
lower interest rates, and supporting labor through collective bargaining.
Although inequality has been widening, historian Jeremy Mouat observes,
"There's still a significant chunk of the welfare state intact in Canada."
He adds that he notices "the more extremes of wealth and poverty when-
ever I visit the U.S."[11] Although activist governments in the United States
forced these issues to the forefront of policy debates in the 1930s and 1940s,

evidence suggests that Canadian governments have been more persistent in addressing the consequences of economic inequality.

The demographic landscape of the Pacific Northwest continues a trend that gained momentum in the 1980s, with Asian (primarily Chinese), Southeast Asian, and Hispanic/Latino communities the fastest-growing groups. The transborder region experienced dramatic population growth in the last half century, providing some of the highest percentage increases in the United States and Canada. British Columbia's population, concentrated on the lower mainland and in Vancouver Island's Capital Regional District, increased from 2 million people in 1971 to approximately 4.3 million in 2007.[12] Census data reveal rapid population growth, especially during the 1990s, when thousands of Chinese left Hong Kong for Vancouver and Victoria at the end of British colonial rule. British Columbia's sharp increase in foreign born reflects a pattern repeated across much of Canada.[13]

Although British society and culture dominated Vancouver's population from its inception through most of the twentieth century, the metropolis has earned a reputation as a "city of neighbourhoods" in recent years, a place of distinct ethnic communities. Chinese are the largest and most diverse group, speaking several dialects. Some city neighborhoods—Chinatown, Punjabi Market, Little Italy, Greektown, Japantown—include sizable concentrations of single ethnic groups. Because of the influx of so many people, the metro area is "high rent," home to Canada's least affordable housing, placing Vancouver in competition with San Francisco as the most expensive place to live on the West Coast.[14]

Burnaby, a Vancouver suburb with the largest concentration of immigrant refugees in British Columbia, provides the most striking example of an ethnic makeover in the Greater Northwest. Burnaby has been transformed from a largely white, middle-class suburb into the region's most diverse community. By the spring of 2007, more than one-third of all government-sponsored refugees destined for British Columbia were settling in Burnaby. Coming from the most war-ravaged areas of the world (Somalia, Sudan, and Afghanistan), the refugees are attempting to recover from incredible hardships in the midst of an alien culture and language. To make matters worse, the Canadian government, responsible for the refugees, has been laggard in providing social and economic support for the immigrants. Their adjustments are enormous, especially for children who have lived through horrific violence, and many of them are illiterate even in their own language.[15]

Burnaby's problems with poverty, housing, education, and cultural adjustment are reflected in contentious debates in the federal parliament. Canada has experienced the fastest population growth among the Group of Eight industrialized nations, and immigrants made up two-thirds of Canada's increase between 2001 and 2006. Those who favor open immigration believe that such policies will augment Canada's aging and static population numbers. Conservative critics, however, point to Burnaby's problems as an example of misguided, unrestrictive immigration. Differing arguments drive the debate in the United States, with open-border opponents citing the social and welfare costs of legal and illegal immigration. Supporters of liberal policies include advocates of racial and cultural diversity as well as powerful corporate groups seeking a ready source of cheap labor.[16]

The American West has been the fastest-growing region in the United States since the Second World War. While California's phenomenal growth has dwarfed that of Oregon and Washington, the latter two have manifested sizable population increases in the last half of the twentieth century.[17] As table 1 indicates, Washington's population more than doubled between 1960 and 2000, while Oregon reached nearly the same percentage increase. Puget Sound's booming high-tech economy was the key factor in Washington's increase of more than one million people between 1990 and 2000. With a lower population base, Oregon's population also increased by about six hundred thousand. Except for Nevada's extraordinary percentage increases, Washington and Oregon have always been among the leading states in population growth during the last half of the twentieth century.[18]

With their urban populations concentrated west of the Cascade Mountains, Washington and Oregon led the American Northwest in percentages

Table 1

Population of the American Northwest

	1960	1970	1980	1990	2000
Washington	2,853,214	3,409,410	4,132,353	4,866,663	5,894,121
Oregon	1,768,687	2,091,533	2,633,156	2,842,321	3,421,399
Idaho	667,191	713,015	944,127	1,006,749	1,293,953
Montana	674,767	694,409	786,690	799,065	902,195

of people living in metropolitan areas. Washington had the largest percentage (80.9 percent in 1985 and 82 percent in 2000). Oregon followed, with 67.2 percent in 1985, increasing to 79 percent in 2000. Although growth rates in Seattle, Tacoma, and Portland have slowed, adjacent counties—Snohomish and Thurston counties in western Washington and Clackamas and Washington counties in western Oregon—have exploded in numbers. Snohomish and Thurston counties increased 443 and 362 percent, respectively, between 1950 and 2000. Oregon's Washington and Clackamas counties have grown at a similar pace, with the Clackamas population increasing from fewer than 100,000 in 1950 to nearly 300,000 in 2000. Washington County increased even more dramatically, from 61,269 in 1950 to 445,342 in 2000. East of the Cascade Range a different scenario unfolded, with several rural counties declining in population. While all of Washington's eastern counties reported net gains, several sparsely populated counties in Idaho and Montana declined in numbers in the early twenty-first century.[19]

Urban clusters are scattered in isolated pockets across the interior Northwest—Bend (Deschutes County) and Medford-Ashland in Oregon, Spokane and the Tri-Cities (Richland, Kennewick, and Pasco) in Washington, Missoula in western Montana, and Boise, Idaho's flourishing metropolis. The upward-trending figures in table 2 tell the story of thriving communities: federal investments in infrastructure support, home to corporate headquarters, local incentives to attract new businesses, and the transformation from natural resource to amenity-driven economies. While west side communities continued to attract new businesses and an educated workforce, the region's interior is sprinkled with enclaves of thriving and vibrant economies.

Table 2
Population for Metropolitan Statistical Areas

Date	Tri-Cities	Spokane	Bend (Deschutes County)	Medford-Ashland	Boise	Missoula
1960	85,412	278,333	23,100	73,962	151,122	44,663
1970	93,356	287,487	30,442	94,533	173, 518	58,263
1980	144,469	341,835	62,142	132,456	256,792	76,016
1990	150,033	361,364	74,958	146,389	295,851	78,687
2000	191,822	417,939	115,367	181,269	432,345	95,802

Source: Based on population-growth estimates in CensusScope (http://www.censusscope.org/us/s53/).

The periodic spikes in the Tri-Cities population reflect activities at the Hanford nuclear facility—sporadic boosts in plutonium production through the 1980s and, beginning in the 1990s, the massive effort to clean up contamination in one of the nation's biggest Superfund sites. Geotechnical firms proliferated in Richland and Kennewick as the federal government funded efforts to control contaminated groundwater and other toxic wastes. The fifty thousand new immigrants to the Tri-Cities during the 1990s provide graphic evidence of that federal investment. Spokane, the titular capital of the Inland Empire, suffered through post–Second World War doldrums with a decaying downtown, divisive local politics, and a "brain drain" of its best and brightest people. With an emerging group of new leaders, however, Spokane turned the corner in the late 1990s, renovating the historic Davenport Hotel, building a new convention center, and attracting professional people into downtown office space and apartments.[20]

The greater Boise area may be the most striking example of metropolitan growth in the interior Northwest. Stretching from Boise to Nampa, the metropolitan district is Idaho's largest metropolitan statistical area (MSA). With 34,393 in 1950, Boise and urban communities to the west grew nearly 15 percent during the 1960s and then exploded with an increase of 48 percent in the 1970s. Although state government employees dominated its workforce, Boise also became corporate headquarters for several large firms—Albertson's (supermarkets), Boise Cascade (wood products), Morrison-Knudsen (engineering and construction), and J. R. Simplot (the "Potato King"). Metropolitan growth soared again during the 1990s by 46 percent, with the Boise MSA reaching a population of more than 432,000 people in 2000.[21] Even with a downturn in the economy beginning in 2007, the metropolitan area has continued to grow apace, with a population of 552,287 in 2008.

By comparison with other Northwest states, Montana has experienced modest population increases. Because agriculture, ranching, mining, and wood products are still its economic mainstays, Montana lacks the attractive employment opportunities of its neighbors. In the last two decades, however, western Montana's economy has expanded, and population growth has far outstripped the eastern side of the state, which has suffered a net out-migration of people. As western Montana's largest urban center, Missoula increased from 44,663 people in 1960 to 95,802 in 2000, its growth reflecting a modestly robust economy. Missoula has prospered as home to the University of Montana, federal employees (the Forest

Service, Bureau of Land Management, and Fish and Wildlife Service), a cyclical wood-products industry, and myriad small businesses. While residents appreciate the area's quality of life, they are also aware that the larger community confronts challenges of low wages and poverty.[22]

In southern Oregon, the fast-growing Medford-Ashland district has diversified its economy beyond growing fruit and milling wood products to include retail sales in musical instruments, the production of maps and atlases marketed in the western states, a computer manufacturing firm, and a film company. Medford is home to two major medical centers employing more than two thousand people. The area is also a destination for retirees searching for reasonable assisted living and senior-service costs. Harry and David, the venerable mail-order house for fresh fruits and packaged snacks, remains the area's largest employer, with a nonharvest workforce of 1,700 people. An expanding viticulture industry adds to the ambience of the upper Rogue Valley. The thriving town of Ashland, with its famous Oregon Shakespeare Festival, provides the chief cultural attraction in the metropolitan district. Like the festival itself, Ashland's hotels, bed and breakfasts, restaurants, and art galleries thrive on tourist-generated revenue.[23] Although its enrollment has declined, Southern Oregon University fleshes out the community's cultural offerings. As table 2 indicates, the Medford-Ashland population increased nearly 28 percent in the 1960s, grew by another 40 percent in the 1970s and close to 24 percent in the 1990s.

The spectacular transformation of the central Oregon community of Bend from a bustling center of sawmilling to a home for telecommuters, wealthy retirees, and tourists provides a striking example of the emergence of a New West community. When Brooks-Scanlon closed its pine sawmill in 1994 after nearly eighty years of unprecedented production, Bend's transition to a home for monied refugees from elsewhere was already well under way. With Deschutes County deemed the metro area, Bend's population exploded from 11,409 in 1950 to more than 52,000 in 2000, or 356 percent in four decades. The county's population grew from 23,100 in 1960 to 115,367 in 2000, an increase of 399 percent. Deschutes County's continuing growth in the twenty-first century to a stunning 160,810 in 2007—another 39 percent increase—is equally astonishing. With Bend's demographic makeover, the community has lost its working-class, rolled-up-sleeve qualities. At the time the national economy went into a tailspin in 2008, Bend was home to two classes of people—the affluent and those who drove busses, worked in restaurants and local stores, or sold their carpentry skills in the construction industry.[24]

Central Oregon's economic transformation is similar to changes taking place elsewhere. Long-time residents of Bozeman, Montana, resent the new money that is remaking the state's vast western valleys. When *Atlantic Monthly's* Robert Kaplan visited the town in the mid-1990s, he interviewed Mike Miles, a former Jesuit priest, who expressed contempt for "the seasonal rich," who were introducing new class divisions in Montana. He told Kaplan, "The yellow pages are full of real estate agents" who were willing to sell Montana at any price. In similar circumstances, residents of Crook County, on the fringe of the central Oregon real estate boom, rejected a proposed destination resort because it threatened water supplies, wildlife habitat, and high-quality farmland and might attract low-wage workers from outside the United States.[25]

Census reports in recent decades offer clear evidence that the ethnic mix of the Greater Northwest, once one of the "whitest" regions in the United States, has dramatically diversified. New immigrants, more accurate census enumerations, and the greater assertiveness of Indian/First Nations people have enriched the cultural makeup of a region that Caucasians dominated for much of the twentieth century. British Columbia's diversity began to shift toward people of Asian origin during the 1980s, when Chinese, East Indian, Filipino, Korean, and other Asian peoples began immigrating to the province in large numbers. Chinese, the most numerous, increased from 3.9 percent of the provincial population in 1986 to 5.6 percent in 1991.[26] The 1996 census records 18.1 percent of the population with an ethnic origin other than European or American, listing a new category, "visible minority," to account for nonwhites. Chinese were by far the largest cohort, comprising 8.5 percent of the population.[27]

British Columbia's minority population increased to 22 percent in 2001, with Chinese and South Asians the largest among the immigrant groups. The census listed separate enumerations for aboriginal people— 2.1 percent in 1986, increasing to 4.8 percent in 2006. With the continued influx of East Asians, Indians, and Pakistanis, British Columbia's diversity advanced further, with the visible minority population increasing to 24.5 percent by 2006, approximately one-quarter of the provincial population. For Vancouver, the visible minority population comprised 51 percent of the 2006 census, with Burnaby counting more than half that number.[28] Nothing in the American Northwest can compare with the brisk pace of demographic change taking place in British Columbia since 1980.

Because of the large influx of African Americans to the Northwest during the Second World War, Oregon and Washington, especially Portland, Seattle, and Tacoma, emerged from the conflict with slightly more diverse populations. Even with the new immigrants, however, Oregon's population remained overwhelmingly white (98.4 percent) in 1950, with Washington only slightly less at 97.4 percent. Even with Idaho's and Montana's sizable Indian numbers, the states' white populations hovered at the high end of 90 percent. Table 3 compares the white and nonwhite populations of the northwestern states in 1960. The states with the highest percentages of "nonwhites," Montana and Washington, also differed sharply in population (674,767 for Montana and 2,853,214 for Washington). Moreover, of Montana's 24,029 nonwhites, approximately 21,000 were American Indians.[29] The American Northwest's demographic profile changed little until the 1970s, when increasing numbers of Hispanics and Southeast Asians migrated to the region.

Table 3
Population in 1960

	Population	Percent
Idaho		
White	657,383	98.5
Nonwhite	9,808	1.5
Total	667,191	
Montana		
White	650,739	96.4
Nonwhite	24,029*	3.6
Total	674,767	
Oregon		
White	1,732,037	97.9
Nonwhite	36,650	2.1
Total	1,768,687	
Washington		
White	2,751,675	96.4
Nonwhite	101,539	3.6
Total	2,853,214	

Source: U.S. Census Bureau, "Census of Population, 1960"
(http://www.census.gov/prod/www/abs/decennial/1960cenpopv1.htm).
*Includes an Indian population of 21,000.

Table 4 shows that Oregon's and Washington's Hispanic and Asian population nearly doubled between 1980 and 1990. Idaho's ethnic mix also indicates a rapidly increasing number of Hispanics, ranking the state fourteenth among the fifty states in the 1990 census. Washington and Oregon followed at eighteenth and nineteenth, respectively. For comparative purposes, New Mexico ranked first, with Hispanics comprising 38.2 percent of its population; California was second at 25.8 percent. With the exception of Montana, the other Northwest states were rapidly increasing in diversity, with Hispanics the largest segment among ethnic minorities.[30] Idaho and Montana both have small numbers of African Americans, with Montana ranked last among the fifty states in 2000. If the two states can make a case for cultural diversity in the twenty-first century, it is vested in Idaho's growing number of Hispanics and Montana's sizable Indian population. With its much larger population, Washington listed 81,483 Indians in the 1990 census, a figure nearly double that for Montana. It is also significant that many of the Indians enumerated in the Washington census had moved to the state since the Second World War.

The new century continues trends that began gathering momentum in the 1980s. As table 5 indicates, the Hispanic population is increasing at

Table 4
Population in 1980 and 1990

	Idaho	Montana	Oregon	Washington
1980				
White	902,000	740,000	2,491,000	3,779,000
Black	3,000	2,000	37,000	106,000
Hispanic origin	37,000	10,000	66,000	120,000
Asian	5,500	2,400	32,600	95,800
American Indian	10,500	37,300	27,300	60,800
Other	23,000	5,200	45,500	90,800
Total	944,000	787,000	2,633,000	4,132,000
1990				
White	950,451	741,111	2,636,787	4,308,937
Black	3,370	2,381	46,178	149,801
Hispanic origin	52,927	12,174	112,707	214,570
Asian	9,365	4,259	69,269	210,958
American Indian	13,780	46,679	38,496	81,483
Total	1,006,451	799,065	2,842,321	4,866,692

Source: "Selected Population Characteristics, in Idaho, the Region, and the U.S., Census Years, 1980–1990" (http://www.webs.uidaho.edu/idstats/chapter01/1-8.htm).

an impressive rate in Idaho, Oregon, and Washington. Oregon (3.2 percent) and Washington (6.4 percent) also have sizable and growing Asian populations. The two states also rank fifth and sixth nationally with people acknowledging "two or more races," a new census category beginning in 1990. With 6.4 percent listed as Indian or Alaska Native, Montana has by far the largest per capita percentage in that cohort, a reflection of the state's seven far-flung Indian reservations. Estimates for 2008 indicate that Hispanics comprised more than 15 percent of the national population and more than 10 percent of Idaho's and Oregon's population, with Washington close behind. While those figures provide evidence that the American Northwest is becoming more racially and ethnically diverse, the American Community Survey of 2006 revealed that the region remained predominantly "white": Idaho, 92.5 percent; Montana, 89.7 percent; Oregon, 86.1 percent; and Washington, 80.5 percent.[31]

What are the larger implications of these changes? A profile of the Greater Northwest's twenty-first-century population raises questions anew about what it means to be a northwesterner. The increasing number of *supermercados* (markets), *panaderías* (bakeries), and *tortillerías* (tortilla companies) on the American side of the border and the proliferation of an amazing array of ethnic restaurants in Vancouver, British Columbia, are symbolic of the region's changing human landscape. Walk the streets of Vancouver or Woodburn, Oregon (home to a factory-outlet mall on Interstate 5), and witness colorful dress, a cacophony of languages, and a truly international medley of voices.

Vancouver, Seattle, Portland, and the Greater Northwest are linked closely to trading patterns with Pacific Rim nations. British Columbia exports 40 percent of its products to Asian markets and 50 percent to the

Table 5

Percentage of Ethnic/Minority Population, 2003

	Hispanic/ Latino	Asian	Black	Indian/ Alaska Native	Two or more races
Idaho	7.9	1.5	0.6	1.8	1.0
Montana	2.0	0.6	0.2	6.4	2.1
Oregon	8.0	3.2	1.7	1.1	3.1
Washington	7.7	6.4	3.3	1.2	3.8

Source: "2006 American Community Survey," American Factfinder, U.S. Census Bureau (http://www.factfinder.census.gov/servlet/GRTTable.html).

United States. Warren Gill, an urban geographer, characterized British Columbia's booming mainland city as a kind of universal metropolis—"Vancouver looks like anywhere: it's a generic, post-modern global place." With its "never-empty streets and . . . interracial couples," it also possesses a certain cohesiveness that is "less evident in Seattle and Portland." With their sizable and increasing Asian populations, Seattle and Portland also reflect oceanic ties to Asia, especially Japan, and a growing volume of trade with China. Because Seattle and Portland emphasize high-tech production, they will continue to be points of destination for Asian immigrants, who will enjoy the amenities of expanding urban light-rail and trolley systems. These immigrants, along with other college-educated newcomers, will also contribute to the further gentrification of older sections of urban cores, a trend that prices older residents out of their communities.[32]

Outsiders tend to identify the Greater Northwest with its wet marine climate, home to wineries, coffee bars, and brew pubs. The heavily populated wet side is also the most culturally and ethnically diverse, with Portland reporting 25 percent of its population and Seattle 30 percent as minorities in the census of 2000. A good representation of the "internationalization" of the two cities is reflected in the sport of *besuboru* and the popularity of Seattle Mariners' outfielder Ichiro Suzuki, the first position player from Japan to play major league baseball. When the Mariners hosted Japanese Baseball Night in 2003, fans were treated to *taiko* drumming before the game, and the public address announcer introduced the players in both English and Japanese. The thousands of Japanese who regularly attend Mariners games also testify to a larger truth—that the Pacific Basin is truly a forum for the exchange of Asian, American, and British Columbian influences in food, entertainment, and sports.[33]

New people—whether migrating from within nation-states or from foreign lands—reshape cultural geographies and challenge regional cohesiveness. The sizable number of immigrants in recent years to Idaho, Oregon, Washington, and British Columbia indicate that more than 50 percent of all residents listed in the 2000 census were born elsewhere. Being a northwesterner in the twenty-first century, therefore, may have multiple meanings, many of them associated with people attempting to find their bearings in a new place. What the Northwest has in abundance—and what newcomers and longtime residents alike value—is social space, social property on a magnificent scale. From Montana and Idaho to the Pacific and north into British Columbia, there is considerable public interest in protecting the health of salmon-bearing streams, preserving the region's rich agricultural and forest lands, and maintaining citizen access to ocean beaches, interior waterways, and state, provincial, and federal lands. This social ownership of nature's endowment provides citizens with a collective sense of commonwealth and holds the potential for developing a polity steeped in the values of a public realm, linking inhabitants to a common landscape.[34]

Notes

Preface. Toward a Regional Narrative

1. Ferris, Levine, and Miller quoted in Peter Applebome, "Out from Under the Nation's Shadow," *New York Times*, February 20, 1999.

2. Garry Wills, "A Reader's Guide to the Century," *New York Review*, July 15, 1999, 28.

3. For a provocative discussion of the terms *transnational, transborder*, and *transboundary*, see Joseph E. Taylor III, "Boundary Terminology," *Environmental History* 13 (July 2008): 454–81.

4. Elizabeth Jameson, "Dancing on the Rim, Tiptoeing Through Minefields: Challenges and Promises of Borderlands," *Pacific Historical Review* 75 (February 2006): 3–5.

5. John Mack Faragher, ed., *Rereading Frederick Jackson Turner: "The Significance of the Frontier" and Other Essays* (New York: Henry Holt, 1994), 21.

6. Matthew Klingle, *Emerald City: An Environmental History of Seattle* (New Haven, Conn.: Yale University Press, 2007), xii.

7. The chain of hydroelectric dams on the Columbia River extends into Canada. The British Columbia government and its agency, BC Hydro, developed the huge Peace River project, with its enormous W. A. C. Bennett Dam. See Richard Maxwell Brown, "The Other Northwest: The Regional Identity of a Canadian Province," in *Many Wests: Place, Culture, and Regional Identity*, ed. David M. Wrobel and Michael C. Steiner (Lawrence: University Press of Kansas, 1997), 281.

8. For an excellent discussion of the historical complexities of the western U.S.–Canadian border, see Elizabeth Jameson and Jeremy Mouat, "Telling Differences: The Forty-Ninth Parallel and Historiographies of the West and Nation," *Pacific Historical Review* 75 (May 2006): 183–230. For a recent book that bridges the Canadian and American Wests, see Andrew R. Graybill, *Policing the Great Plains: Rangers, Mounties, and the North American Frontier, 1875–1910* (Lincoln: University of Nebraska Press, 2007). A useful article that compares enforcement at the Canadian and Mexican borders is Patrick Ettinger, "'We sometimes wonder what they will spring on us next': Immigrants and Border Enforcement in the American West, 1882–1930," *Western Historical Quarterly* 37 (Summer 2006): 159–82.

9. Elizabeth Jameson and Jeremy Mouat contend that the U.S.–Canadian border "remained peripheral in most New West histories, because the 1846 treaty

securing the boundary was arranged through mutual agreement" ("Telling Differences," 220–21).

10. These ideas were shared as part of a panel discussion, "Defining the Region: Is There a Pacific Northwest?" Pacific Northwest History Conference, Bellingham, Washington, March 24–26, 1994.

11. "In climate and topography," Richard Maxwell Brown observes, "the Canadian province is simply a northward extension of Oregon and Washington or vice versa" ("The Other Northwest," 280).

12. For the Far West as a land of immigrants, see Walter Nugent, *Into the West: The Story of Its People* (New York: Alfred A. Knopf, 1999), 4.

13. Carl Abbott, *How Cities Won the West: Four Centuries of Urban Change in Western North America* (Albuquerque: University of New Mexico Press, 2008), 4; and Nugent, *Into the West*, 78.

14. Michael B. Katz and Mark J. Stern, *One Nation Divisible: What America Was and What It Is Becoming* (New York: Russell Sage Foundation, 2006), 2–4.

15. Ibid., 5.

16. Ibid., 171–72.

17. Wills, "A Reader's Guide," 24.

Introduction. Mapping the Greater Northwest

1. For a brief discussion of the problems with defining place and region, see William L. Lang, "Series Editor's Preface," in *The Great Northwest: The Search for Regional Identity*, ed. William G. Robbins (Corvallis: Oregon State University Press, 2001), v.

2. The best account of the Lewis and Clark trek down and up the Columbia River is James Ronda, *Lewis and Clark Among the Indians* (Lincoln: University of Nebraska Press, 1984).

3. These quotations can be found in William G. Robbins, *Landscapes of Promise: The Oregon Story, 1800–1940* (Seattle: University of Washington Press, 1997), 50–52, 206–7.

4. For an account of North West Company exploration in the North American West, see Dorothy O. Johansen, *Empire of the Columbia: A History of the Pacific Northwest* (New York: Harper and Row, 1967), 91–107.

5. Gary E. Moulton, ed., *The Journals of Lewis and Clark*, vol. 5 (Lincoln: University of Nebraska Press, 1988), 327.

6. William L. Lang, "Beavers, Firs, Salmon, and Falling Water: Pacific Northwest Regionalism and the Environment," *Oregon Historical Quarterly* 104 (Summer 2003): 156.

7. David Johnson made these remarks at the panel discussion "Defining the Region: Is There a Pacific Northwest?" Pacific Northwest History Conference, Bellingham, Washington, March 24–26, 1994.

8. These ideas are adapted from Cole Harris, banquet address, Pacific Northwest History Conference, Victoria, British Columbia, April 16, 1999. For new insights to historical research that crosses national borders, see Marcus Graser, "World History in a Nation-State: The Transnational Disposition in Historical Writing in the United States," *Journal of American History* 95 (March 2009): 1038.

9. Bancroft is cited in Allan Pritchard, "The Shapes of History in British Columbia Writing," *BC Studies: The British Columbia Quarterly*, no. 93 (Spring 1992): 50–51.

10. See Elizabeth Jameson and Jeremy Mouat, "Telling Differences: The Forty-ninth Parallel and Historiographies of the West and Nation," *Pacific Historical Review* 75 (May 2006): 183–230; Sterling Evans, ed., *The Borderlands of the American and Canadian Wests: Essays on Regional History of the 49th Parallel* (Lincoln: University of Nebraska Press, 2006); and Andrew Graybill, *Policing the Great Plains: Rangers, Mounties, and the North American Frontier, 1875–1910* (Lincoln: University of Nebraska Press, 2007). Also see Ken S. Coates, "Border Crossings: Pattern and Processes along the Canada–United States Boundary West of the Rockies," in *Parallel Destinies: Canadian-American Relations West of the Rockies*, ed. John M. Findlay and Ken S. Coates (Seattle: University of Washington Press, 2002).

11. Cole Harris, *The Resettlement of British Columbia: Essays on Colonialism and Geographical Change* (Vancouver: University of British Columbia Press, 1997), xi.

12. For the ethnic mix in Astoria and Butte, see Paul George Hummasti, *Finnish Radicals in Astoria, Oregon, 1904–1940* (New York: Arno Press, 1979); and Michael P. Malone, *The Battle for Butte: Mining and Politics on the Northern Frontier, 1864–1906* (Seattle: University of Washington Press, 1981).

13. Earl Pomeroy, *The American Far West in the Twentieth Century* (New Haven, Conn.: Yale University Press, 2008), xx.

14. Fay G. Cohen, *Treaties on Trial: The Continuing Controversy over Northwest Indian Fishing Rights* (Seattle: University of Washington Press, 1986).

15. For a general discussion of the *Calder* and other pertinent British Columbia cases, see Paul Tennant, *Aboriginal Peoples and Politics: The Indian Land Question in British Columbia, 1849–1989* (Vancouver: University of British Columbia Press, 1990); and Robert J. Muckle, *The First Nations of British Columbia* (Vancouver: University of British Columbia Press, 1998), 77–81.

16. Dorothy Johansen, "Oregon's Role in American History: An Old Theme Recast," *Pacific Northwest Quarterly* 38 (April 1949): 86.

17. Jensen is quoted in Glen E. Lich, ed., *Regional Studies: The Interplay of Land and People* (College Station: Texas A & M University Press, 1992), x.

18. These ideas are adapted from William Cronon's talk to the conference "Power and Place in the North American West," Seattle, November 3–5, 1994.

19. Allan Smith, "The Writing of British Columbia History," in *British*

Columbia: Historical Readings, ed. W. Peter Ward and Robert A. J. McDonald (Vancouver: Douglas and McIntyre, 1981), 25; and Robert A. J. McDonald, *Making Vancouver: Class, Status, and Social Boundaries, 1863–1913* (Vancouver: University of British Columbia Press, 1996), 232–36.

20. See Dana Frank, *Purchasing Power: Consumer Organizing, Gender, and the Seattle Labor Movement, 1919–1929* (New York: Cambridge University Press, 1994).

21. Kenneth S. Coates, "A Matter of Context: The Pacific Northwest in World History," in *Terra Pacific: People and Place in the Northwest States and Canada*, ed. Paul W. Hirt (Pullman: Washington State University Press, 1998), 112, 114.

22. See Thomas Bender, "Review Essay: Strategies of Narrative Synthesis in American History," *American Historical Review* 107 (February 2002): 129–53; and Bender, "Historians, the Nation and the Plentitude of Narratives," in *Rethinking American History in the Global Age*, ed. Thomas Bender (Berkeley: University of California Press, 2002), 1.

23. Johansen, "Oregon's Role," 89.

24. Richard White, "Contested Terrain: The Business of Land in the American West," in *Land in the American West: Private Claims and the Common Good*, ed. William G. Robbins and James C. Foster (Seattle: University of Washington Press, 1999), 7.

25. Robert Cail, *Land, Man, and the Law: The Disposal of Crown Lands in British Columbia, 1871–1913* (Vancouver: University of British Columbia Press, 1974), 13–15; and Allen Seager, "The Resource Economy, 1871–1921," in *The Pacific Province: A History of British Columbia*, ed. Hugh J. M. Johnston (Vancouver: Douglas & McIntyre, 1996), 220.

26. M. Allerdale Grainger, *Woodsmen of the West* (1908; Toronto: McClelland and Stewart, 1964), 34; and Jean Barman, *The West Beyond the West: A History of British Columbia* (Toronto: University of Toronto Press, 1991), 182–83.

27. Pomeroy, *The American Far West*, 7–10.

28. See Frank, *Purchasing Power*, 97–104.

29. For British Columbia, see John Douglas Belshaw and David J. Mitchell, "The Economy since the Great War," in Johnston, *The Pacific Province*, 333.

30. *This Place on Earth 2002* (Seattle: Northwest Environment Watch, 2002), 13.

Chapter 1. The Years of "Exuberant Optimism"

1. Ruth Barnes Moynihan, "Of Women's Rights and Freedom: Abigail Scott Duniway," in *Women in Pacific Northwest History*, ed. Karen J. Blair, rev. ed. (1988; Seattle: University of Washington Press, 2001), 28–33; and Dorothy Johansen, *Empire of the Columbia: A History of the Pacific Northwest*, 2nd ed. (New York: Harper and Row, 1967), 296, 298, 358.

2. Moynihan, "Of Women's Rights," 35–40.

3. John Minto, "From Youth to Age as an American," *Oregon Historical Quarterly* 9 (1908): 127–73.

4. Ibid.

5. This brief summary of Samuel Hauser's career is from William G. Robbins, *Colony and Empire: The Capitalist Transformation of the American West* (Lawrence: University Press of Kansas, 1994), 103–20.

6. Ibid.

7. Allen Seager, "The Resource Economy, 1871–1921," in *The Pacific Province: A History of British Columbia*, ed. Hugh J. M. Johnston (Vancouver: Douglas & McIntyre, 1996), 123, 144–45, 217; and "James Dunsmuir," *Dictionary of Canadian Biography On Line*, http://www.biographi.ca/EN/index.html.

8. "James Dunsmuir," *Dictionary of Canadian Biography On Line*.

9. Cole Harris, *The Resettlement of British Columbia: Essays on Colonialism and Geographical Change* (Vancouver: University of British Columbia Press, 1997), xii; and Earl Pomeroy, *The American Far West in the Twentieth Century* (New Haven, Conn.: Yale University Press, 2008), 12.

10. For a summary of these events, see Carlos A. Schwantes, *Railroad Signatures across the Pacific Northwest* (Seattle: University of Washington Press, 1993), 60; and Randall Mills, "A History of Transportation in the Pacific Northwest," *Oregon Historical Quarterly* 45 (1946): 291–92.

11. *Portland Oregonian*, September 12, 1883.

12. For Villard's financial machinations and judgments of his character, see E. Kimbark MacColl, *Merchants, Money, and Power: The Portland Establishment, 1843–1913* (Portland: Georgian Press, 1988), 220–25.

13. Johansen, *Empire of the Columbia*, 302, 313.

14. Donald W. Meinig, *The Great Columbia Plain: A Historical Geography, 1805–1910* (Seattle: University of Washington Press, 1968), 271.

15. Katherine G. Morrissey, *Mental Territories: Mapping the Inland Empire* (Ithaca, N.Y.: Cornell University Press, 1997), 41–43, 179.

16. William Cronon, *Nature's Metropolis: Chicago and the Great West* (New York: W. W. Norton, 1991), 55.

17. Morrissey, *Mental Territories*, 3, 23.

18. Johansen, *Empire of the Columbia*, 310–11; and Murray Morgan, *Puget's Sound: A Narrative of Early Tacoma and the Southern Sound* (Seattle: University of Washington Press, 1979), 183–87.

19. Morgan, *Puget's Sound*, 188–94; and Morgan, *The Mill on the Boot: The Story of the St. Paul and Tacoma Lumber Company* (Seattle: University of Washington Press, 1982), 62, 163.

20. *Seattle Post-Intelligencer*, November 11, 2001; and Roger Sale, *Seattle, Past to Present* (Seattle: University of Washington Press, 1976), 34–35.

21. Sale, *Seattle*, 32–35, 62–63.

22. Ibid., 64–67. Thomas Burke is quoted in Michael P. Malone, *James J. Hill: Empire Builder of the Northwest* (Norman: University of Oklahoma Press, 1996).

23. Malone, *James J. Hill*, 142. For Hill's influence with the political world, see W. Thomas White, "A Gilded-Age Businessman in Politics: James J. Hill, the Northwest, and the American Presidency, 1884–1912," *Pacific Historical Review* 57 (1988): 439–56.

24. Malone, *James J. Hill*, 149–50, 183–84; and Sale, *Seattle*, 67–68.

25. Jean Barman, *The West Beyond the West: A History of British Columbia* (Toronto: University of Toronto Press, 1991), 106.

26. Norbert MacDonald, "The Canadian Pacific Railway and Vancouver's Development to 1900," in *British Columbia: Historical Readings*, ed. W. Peter Ward and Robert A. J. McDonald (Vancouver: Douglas & McIntyre, 1981), 398–99.

27. Ibid., 400–409; Robert A. J. McDonald, *Making Vancouver: Class, Status, and Social Boundaries, 1863–1913* (Vancouver: University of British Columbia Press, 1996), xi–xii, 37–39; and Richard Maxwell Brown, "The Other Northwest: The Regional Identity of a Canadian Province," in *Many Wests: Place, Culture, and Regional Identity*, ed. David M. Wrobel and Michael C. Steiner (Lawrence: University Press of Kansas, 1997), 299.

28. For a description of the great Columbia Plain, see Meinig, *The Great Columbia Plain*, 4.

29. Symons is quoted in ibid., 264.

30. Ibid., 160–64; Johansen, *Empire of the Columbia*, 316–17; and John Fahey, *The Inland Empire: Unfolding Years, 1879–1929* (Seattle: University of Washington Press, 1986), 23–33. For an environmental history of the Palouse, see Andrew P. Duffin, *Plowed Under: Agriculture and Environment in the Palouse* (Seattle: University of Washington Press, 2007).

31. Meinig, *The Great Columbia Plain*, 269–70; Wayne D. Rasmussen, "A Century of Farming in the Inland Empire," in *Spokane and the Inland Empire: An Interior Pacific Northwest Anthology*, ed. David H. Stratton (Pullman: Washington State University Press, 1991), 39; and Helmut K. Buechner, "Some Biotic Changes in the State of Washington, Particularly During the Century 1853–1953," *Research Studies of the State College of Washington* 21 (1953): 168–69.

32. On Idaho's geography and history, see Earl Pomeroy, *The Pacific Slope: A History of California, Oregon, Washington, Idaho, Utah, and Nevada* (New York: Alfred A. Knopf, 1965), 64; Carlos A. Schwantes, *In Mountain Shadows: A History of Idaho* (Lincoln: University of Nebraska Press, 1991), 1; and J. Anthony Lukas, *Big Trouble: A Murder in a Small Western Town Sets Off a Struggle for the Soul of America* (New York: Simon and Schuster, 1997), 98.

33. Mark Fiege, *Irrigated Eden: The Making of an Agricultural Landscape in the American West* (Seattle: University of Washington Press, 1999). The population figures are from Robbins's files.

34. Ibid., 18–19, 23, 24, 52, 86.

35. E. A. Schwartz, *The Rogue River Indian War and Its Aftermath, 1850–1890* (Norman: University of Oklahoma Press, 1997), 161–213; and Stephen Dow Beckham, "Federal-Indian Relations," in *The First Oregonians: An Illustrated Collection of Essays on Traditional Lifeways, Federal-Indian Relations, and the State's Native People Today*, ed. Carolyn M. Buan and Richard Lewis (Portland: Oregon Council for the Humanities, 1991), 47–48.

36. Schwartz, *The Rogue River Indian War*, 216–17; Beckham, "Federal-Indian Relations," 49; and Richard White, *"It's Your Misfortune and None of My Own": A New History of the American West* (Norman: University of Oklahoma Press, 1991), 115–16.

37. http://www.u-s-history.com/pages/h1588.html; Laura Woodworth-Ney, *Mapping Identity: The Creation of the Coeur d'Alene Indian Reservation* (Boulder: University of Colorado Press, 2004); and http://www.cradleboard.org/sites/coeur.html.

38. Ronald J. Paul and Daniel W. Hester, "Through Change and Transition: Treaty Commitments Made and Broken," in *Wiaxayxt/wiyaakaa'awn/As Days Go By: Our Land, Our People—The Cayuse, Umatilla, and Walla Walla*, ed. Jennifer Karson (Pendleton, Ore.: Tamastslikt Cultural Institute and Oregon Historical Society Press, Portland, 2006), 102–13.

39. Coll Thrush, *Native Seattle: Histories from the Crossing-Over Place* (Seattle: University of Washington Press, 2007), 4–5, 11.

40. Paul Tennant, *Aboriginal Peoples and Politics: The Indian Land Question in British Columbia, 1849–1989* (Vancouver: University of British Columbia Press, 1990), 17, 26–29, 52–53.

41. Robert J. Muckle, *The First Nations of British Columbia* (Vancouver: University of British Columbia Press, 1998), 71–77.

42. Peter Boag points out that reformers across the Pacific Northwest reacted strongly against same-sex affairs, strengthening laws when conventional sexuality was violated. See Boag, *Same-Sex Affairs: Constructing and Controlling Homosexuality in the Pacific Northwest* (Berkeley: University of California Press, 2003), 1–3.

43. Patricia E. Roy, *The White Man's Province: British Columbia Politicians and Chinese and Japanese Immigrants, 1858–1914* (Vancouver: University of British Columbia Press, 1989), xiv–xvii, 54–55; Wing Chung Ng, *The Chinese in Vancouver, 1945–1980: The Pursuit of Identity and Power* (Vancouver: University of British Columbia Press, 1999), 11–13; and Hugh Johnston, "Native People, Settlers, and Sojourners, 1871–1916," in Johnston, *The Pacific Province*, 191–92.

44. *Roseburg Plaindealer*, April 1, 1870. For historical background to the Chinese experience in the United States, see Roger Daniels, *Asian America: Chinese and Japanese in the United States since 1850* (Seattle: University of Washington Press, 1988); Sucheng Chan, *Asian Americans: An Interpretive History* (Boston: Twayne Publishers, 1991), 25–34; and White, *It's Your Misfortune*, 321–22.

45. Michael P. Malone, Richard B. Roeder, and William L. Lang, *Montana:*

A History of Two Centuries (Seattle: University of Washington Press, 1991), 85; Schwantes, *In Mountain Shadows*, 128–30; and R. Gregory Nokes, "'A Most Daring Outrage,' Murders at Chinese Massacre Cove, 1887," *Oregon Historical Quarterly* 107 (Fall 2006): 326–53.

46. Carlos A. Schwantes, *The Pacific Northwest: An Interpretive History* (Lincoln: University of Nebraska Press, 1996), 156–57; and Daniels, *Asian America*, 60–63.

47. Daniels, *Asian America*, 63–64; and MacColl, *Merchants*, 238–40.

48. Abigail Scott Duniway, *Path Breaking: An Autobiographical History of the Equal Suffrage Movement in the Pacific Coast States* (Portland: James, Kerris and Abbott, 1914); Moynihan, "Of Women's Rights," 28–42; Daniels, *Asian America*, 56–66; and Stanford Lyman, "The Oriental in America," typescript of broadcast on University of California Radio, January 17, 1962 (copy in Robbins's possession).

49. The Web site http://www.jimcrowhistory.org/scripts/jimcrow/lawsoutside .cgi?state=Oregon includes a brief summary of each state's Jim Crow laws. See also *Salem Statesman-Journal*, January 3, 2003; and Cheryl A. Brooks, "Politics of Forgetting: How Oregon Forgot to Ratify the Fourteenth Amendment," *Oregon Humanities*, Fall–Winter 2006, 1–9.

50. Stefanie Johnson, "Blocking Racial Intermarriage Laws in 1935 and 1937: Seattle's First Civil Rights Coalition," in Seattle Civil Rights Labor History Project, http://www.civilrights.washington.edu. My thanks to British Columbia historians Patricia Roy, Jean Barman, and Robert A. J. McDonald for their information on the province's lack of miscegenation legislation.

51. Sharon Meen, "Colonial Society and Economy," in Johnston, *The Pacific Province*, 123, 135, 154–56.

52. G. Thomas Edwards, *Sowing Good Seeds: The Northwest Suffrage Campaigns of Susan B. Anthony* (Portland: Oregon Historical Society Press, 1990), xx–xxii; and Schwantes, *In Mountain Shadows*, 134.

53. Robert E. Ficken and Charles P. LeWarne, *Washington: A Centennial History* (Seattle: University of Washington Press, 1989), 82, 88; Schwantes, *The Pacific Northwest*, 163–65; and William G. Robbins, *Oregon, This Storied Land* (Portland: Oregon Historical Society Press, 2005), 78–80.

54. Malone, Roeder, and Lang, *Montana*, 218, 262–63.

Chapter 2. Reformers, Radicals, and the New Order

1. Melvyn Dubofsky, *We Shall Be All: A History of the Industrial Workers of the World* (Chicago: Quadrangle Books, 1969), 237–41; and Richard White, *"It's Your Misfortune and None of My Own": A History of the American West* (Norman: University of Oklahoma Press, 1991), 293.

2. White, *It's Your Misfortune*, 293–96; Dubofsky, *We Shall Be All*, 238; and Michael P. Malone and F. Ross Peterson, "Politics and Protests," in *The Oxford*

History of the American West, ed. Clyde A. Milner II, Carol A. O'Conner, and Martha A. Sandweiss (New York: Oxford University Press, 1994), 502.

3. J. Anthony Lukas, *Big Trouble: A Murder in a Small Western Town Sets Off a Struggle for the Soul of America* (New York: Simon and Schuster, 1997), 13–15.

4. David B. Danbom, *Born in the Country: A History of Rural America* (Baltimore, Md.: Johns Hopkins University Press, 1995), 132–34.

5. Malone and Peterson, "Politics and Protests," 503; and Marilyn P. Watkins, *Rural Democracy: Family Farmers and Politics in Western Washington, 1890–1925* (Ithaca, N.Y.: Cornell University Press, 1995), 12.

6. Watkins, *Rural Democracy*, 4, 67; Lawrence M. Lipin, "'Cast Aside the Automobile Enthusiast': Class Conflict, Tax Policy, and the Preservation of Nature in Progressive-Era Oregon," *Oregon Historical Quarterly* 107 (Summer 2006): 166; and Jeffrey M. LaLande, "'It Can't Happen Here' in Oregon: The Jackson County Rebellion, 1932–1933, and Its 1890s–1920s Background" (Ph.D. dissertation, University of Oregon, 1993), 21, 29, 36, 45.

7. E. Kimbark MacColl, *Merchants, Money, and Power: The Portland Establishment, 1843–1913* (Portland: Georgian Press, 1988), 259–82; and Gordon B. Dodds, *Oregon: A History* (New York: W. W. Norton, 1977), 157–62. For two interpretive works on U'Ren, see Robert D. Johnston, *The Radical Middle Class: Populist Democracy and the Question of Capitalism in Progressive Era Portland, Oregon* (Princeton, N.J.: Princeton University Press, 2003); and Lawrence M. Lipin, *Workers and the Wild: Conservation, Consumerism, and Labor in Oregon, 1910–30* (Urbana: University of Illinois Press, 2007).

8. Watkins, *Rural Democracy*, 68, 85; and Robert E. Ficken and Charles P. LeWarne, *Washington: A Centennial History* (Seattle: University of Washington Press, 1989), 74–77.

9. Michael P. Malone, Richard B. Roeder, and William L. Lang, *Montana: A History of Two Centuries* (Seattle: University of Washington Press, 1991), 214–18.

10. F. Ross Peterson, *Idaho: A History* (New York: W. W. Norton, 1976), 160–61; Carlos A. Schwantes, *In Mountain Shadows: A History of Idaho* (Lincoln: University of Nebraska Press, 1991), 149–50; and *Idaho Blue Book, 1995–1996* (Caldwell, Idaho: Caxton Printers, 1996), 22–23.

11. Kenneth S. Coates, "The Matter of Context: The Pacific Northwest in World History," in *Terra Pacifica: People and Place in the Northwest States and Canada*, ed. Paul W. Hirt (Pullman: Washington State University Press, 1998), 114.

12. Jeremy Mouat, *Roaring Days: Rossland's Mines and the History of British Columbia* (Vancouver: University of British Columbia Press, 1995), 123–24. Studies that reference cross-border union organizing include Carlos A. Schwantes, *Radical Heritage: Labor, Socialism, and Reform in Washington and British Columbia, 1885–1979* (Seattle: University of Washington Press, 1979); and Allen Seager, "The Resource Economy, 1871–1921," in *The Pacific Province: A History of British Columbia*, ed. Hugh M. Johnston (Vancouver: Douglas & McIntyre, 1996), 216–20.

13. F. Ross McCormack, *Reformers, Rebels, and Revolutionaries: The Western Canadian Radical Movement, 1899–1919* (Toronto: University of Toronto Press, 1977), 14–15; and John Douglas Belshaw, *Colonization and Community: The Vancouver Island Coalfield and the Making of the British Columbia Working Class* (Montreal: McGill-Queen's University Press, 2002), 136. For the complexities of population movements in the North American West, see Elizabeth Jameson and Jeremy Mouat, "Telling Differences: The Forty-ninth Parallel and Historiographies of the West and Nation," *Pacific Historical Review* 75 (May 2006): 184.

14. Jean Barman, *The West Beyond the West: A History of British Columbia* (Toronto: University of Toronto Press, 1991), 121–22; Seager, "The Resource Economy," 217; John Douglas Belshaw, "Provincial Politics, 1871–1916," in Johnston, *The Pacific Province*, 156–57; and Allan Smith, "The Writing of British Columbia History," in *British Columbia: Historical Readings*, ed. W. Peter Ward and Robert A. J. McDonald (Vancouver: Douglas & McIntyre, 1981), 23–25.

15. Dubofsky, *We Shall Be All*, 175–84; and W. Thomas White, "Railroad Labor Protests, 1894–1917," *Pacific Northwest Quarterly* 75 (1984): 13–14.

16. This well-known story is summarized in Lukas, *Big Trouble*, 100–104.

17. Ibid., 111–15, 140–53.

18. Katherine G. Aiken, *Idaho's Bunker Hill: The Rise and Fall of a Great Mining Company, 1885–1981* (Norman: University of Oklahoma Press, 2005), 32–37.

19. William G. Robbins, "The Social Context of Forestry: The Pacific Northwest in the Twentieth Century," *Western Historical Quarterly* 16 (1985): 413–15; and Robert E. Ficken, "Weyerhaeuser and the Pacific Northwest Timber Industry, 1899–1903," *Pacific Northwest Quarterly* 70 (October 1979): 146–54.

20. William G. Robbins, "The Western Lumber Industry: A Twentieth-Century Perspective," in *The Twentieth-Century West: Historical Interpretations*, ed. Gerald D. Nash and Richard W. Etulain (Albuquerque: University of New Mexico Press, 1989), 234–35.

21. A good summary of these conditions is Robert E. Ficken, *The Forested Land: A History of Lumbering in Western Washington* (Seattle: University of Washington Press, 1987). Also see Robbins, "The Social Context," 415–20; and Robbins, *Hard Times in Paradise: Coos Bay, Oregon, 1850–1986*, rev. 2nd ed. (1988; Seattle: University of Washington Press, 2006), 122–37.

22. Thomas R. Cox, "Trade, Development, and Environmental Change: The Utilization of North America's Pacific Coast Forests to 1914 and Its Consequences," in *Global Deforestation and the Nineteenth Century World Economy*, ed. Richard P. Tucker and John F. Richards (Durham, N.C.: Duke University Press, 1983), 18.

23. Charles E. Twining, *Phil Weyerhaeuser: Lumberman* (Seattle: University of Washington Press, 1985), 36–92; Michael P. Malone and Richard B. Roeder, *Montana: A History of Two Centuries* (Seattle: University of Washington Press, 1976), 253–54; and John Fahey, *The Inland Empire: Unfolding Years, 1879–1929* (Seattle: University of Washington Press, 1986), 188–213.

24. William G. Robbins, *Landscapes of Promise: The Oregon Story, 1800–1940* (Seattle: University of Washington Press, 1997), 171–72, 202–3, 230–34.

25. Seager, "The Resource Economy," 220–22; and Margaret A. Ormsby, *British Columbia: A History* (Toronto: Macmillan of Canada, 1958), 307.

26. Seager, "The Resource Economy," 220–22; and Ormsby, *British Columbia*, 330, 357.

27. Norman Clark, *Mill Town: A Social History of Everett, Washington* (Seattle: University of Washington Press, 1970), 66, 233.

28. Richard Rajala, *Up-Coast: Forests and Industry on British Columbia's North Coast, 1870–2005* (Victoria: Royal British Columbia Museum, 2006), 72–75.

29. Dubofsky, *We Shall Be All*, 9; Chris Friday, *Asian American Labor: The Pacific Coast Canned-Salmon Industry, 1870–1942* (Philadelphia: Temple University Press, 1994), 1–6; and Maurine Weiner Greenwald, "Working-Class Feminism and the Family Wage Ideal: The Seattle Debate on Married Women's Right to Work, 1914–1920," in *Women in Pacific Northwest History*, ed. Karen J. Blair (Seattle: University of Washington Press, 2001), 100.

30. Dubofsky, *We Shall Be All*, 36–38. Also see Richard Maxwell Brown, "The Other Northwest: The Regional Identity of a Canadian Province," in *Many Wests: Place, Culture, and Regional Identity*, ed. David M. Wrobel and Michael C. Steiner (Lawrence: University Press of Kansas, 1997), 285.

31. McCormack, *Reformers*, 15–39; and Mouat, *Roaring Days*, 96–100. Mouat argues that mining was the quintessential western American industry, "*the* metaphor for the settlement of the West" (*Roaring Days*, xii).

32. Russell Thornton, *American Indian Holocaust and Survival: A Population History since 1492* (Norman: University of Oklahoma Press, 1987), 133, 159–63, 172–75.

33. Jennifer Karson, ed., *Wiaxayxt/wiyaakaa'awn/As Days Go By: Our Land, Our People—The Cayuse, Umatilla, and Walla Walla* (Pendleton, Ore.: Tamastslikt Cultural Institute and Oregon Historical Society Press, Portland, 2006), 115.

34. Ibid., 117–22.

35. Paige Raibmon, *Authentic Indians: Episodes of Encounter from the Late-Nineteenth-Century Northwest Coast* (Durham, N.C.: Duke University Press, 2005), 75–81.

36. Cary C. Collins, "Subsistence and Survival: The Makah Indian Reservation, 1855–1933," *Pacific Northwest Quarterly* 87 (Fall 1996): 182–91.

37. Daniel L. Boxberger, *To Fish in Common: The Ethnohistory of Lummi Indian Salmon Fishing* (1989; Seattle: University of Washington Press, 2000), 48–62.

38. Hugh Johnston, "Native People, Settlers, and Sojourners, 1871–1916," in Johnston, *The Pacific Province*, 169–72.

39. Ibid., 175–76; and Paul Tennant, *Aboriginal Peoples and Politics: The Indian Land Question in British Columbia, 1849–1989* (Vancouver: University of British Columbia Press, 1990), 79–83.

40. Carl Abbott, *How Cities Won the West: Four Centuries of Urban Change in Western North America* (Albuquerque: University of New Mexico Press, 2008), 141; Johnston, *The Radical Middle Class*, 120–21; and Dorothy O. Johansen, *Empire of the Columbia: A History of the Pacific Northwest* (New York: Harper and Row, 1967), 456.

41. Johnston, *The Radical Middle Class*, 128–29. U'Ren is quoted in Johansen, *Empire of the Columbia*, 451.

42. Johnston, *The Radical Middle Class*, 129–33; and Johansen, *Empire of the Columbia*, 450–56.

43. Ficken and LeWarne, *Washington*, 81; Richard C. Berner, *Seattle 1900–1920: From Boomtown, Urban Turbulence, to Restoration* (Seattle: Charles Press, 1991), 110; and Johansen, *Empire of the Columbia*, 465, 471.

44. Ficken and LeWarne, *Washington*, 81; Berner, *Seattle 1900–1920*, 118; and Roger Sale, *Seattle, Past to Present* (Seattle: University of Washington Press, 1976), 71. Also see Dale E. Soden, *The Reverend Mark Matthews: An Activist in the Progressive Era* (Seattle: University of Washington Press, 2001).

45. Schwantes, *In Mountain Shadows*, 162; and F. Ross Peterson, *Idaho: A Bicentennial History* (New York: W. W. Norton, 1976), 161–63.

46. Malone, Roeder, and Lang, *Montana*, 256–57.

47. Ibid., 258–60; and Michael P. Malone and Dianne G. Dougherty, "Montana's Political Culture: A Century of Evolution," in *The Montana Heritage: An Anthology of Historical Essays*, ed. Robert R. Swartout, Jr., and Harry W. Fritz (Helena: Montana Historical Society Press, 1992), 179–80.

48. Malone, Roeder, and Lang, *Montana*, 259–66.

49. Johansen, *Empire of the Columbia*, 464, 470–72; and Ficken and LeWarne, *Washington*, 81. For a biography of Poindexter, see Howard W. Allen, *Poindexter of Washington: A Study in Progressive Politics* (Carbondale: Southern Illinois University Press, 1981).

50. Malone, Roeder, and Lang, *Montana*, 262–64, 289–90, 307; and Earl Pomeroy, *The American Far West in the Twentieth Century* (New Haven, Conn.: Yale University Press, 2008), 366. Also see Hannah Josephson, *Jeannette Rankin, First Lady in Congress: A Biography* (Indianapolis: Bobbs-Merrill, 1974); and James J. Lopach and Jean A. Luckowski, *Jeannette Rankin: A Political Woman* (Boulder: University Press of Colorado, 2005).

51. Jackson is quoted in Marshall N. Dana, *Newspaper Story: Fifty Years of the Oregon Journal, 1902–1952* (Portland: Binfords and Mort, 1951), 132.

52. Robert E. Burton, *Democrats of Oregon: The Pattern of Minority Politics, 1900–1956* (Eugene: University of Oregon Press, 1970), 25, 33–35, 43; Jewel Lansing, *Portland: People, Politics, and Power, 1851–2001* (Corvallis: Oregon State University Press, 2003), 260–74; and Johansen, *Empire of the Columbia*, 462–63.

53. Schwantes, *Radical Heritage*, 189–93; Barman, *The West Beyond the West*, 204–7, 217–18; and Belshaw, "Provincial Politics," 156–58.

54. Ormsby, *British Columbia*, 375–85.

Chapter 3. War and Peace: The Politics of Reaction

1. Carl Abbott, "The Federal Presence," in *The Oxford History of the American West*, ed. Clyde A. Milner II, Carol A. O'Conner, and Martha A. Sandweiss (New York: Oxford University Press, 1994), 474.

2. Michael P. Malone and F. Ross Peterson, "Politics and Protests," in Milner, O'Conner, and Sandweiss, *The Oxford History of the American West*, 510–12.

3. Earl Pomeroy, *The Pacific Slope: A History of California, Oregon, Washington, Idaho, Utah, and Nevada* (New York: Alfred A. Knopf, 1965), 216–17, 223–25.

4. Roger Sale, *Seattle, Past to Present* (Seattle: University of Washington Press, 1976), 116–17.

5. Richard C. Berner, *Seattle 1900–1920: From Boomtown, Urban Turbulence, to Restoration* (Seattle: Charles Press, 1991), 178, 186–87, 211, 214–15.

6. Margaret A. Ormsby, *British Columbia: A History* (Toronto: Macmillan of Canada, 1958), 377, 384–85, 406; and Jean Barman, *The West Beyond the West: A History of British Columbia* (Toronto: University of Toronto Press, 1991), 198–99, 219.

7. Michael P. Malone, Richard B. Roeder, and William L. Lang, *Montana: A History of Two Centuries* (Seattle: University of Washington Press, 1991), 268; Malone and Peterson, "Politics and Protests," 511; and Christopher Capozzola, "The Only Badge Needed Is Your Patriotic Fervor: Vigilance, Coercion, and the Law in World War I America," *Journal of American History* 89 (March 2002): 1355.

8. Malone, Roeder, and Lang, *Montana*, 275–79.

9. Despite its 1969 publication date, the best account of the IWW in the Pacific Northwest is Melvyn Dubofsky's *We Shall Be All: A History of the Industrial Workers of the World* (Chicago: Quadrangle Books, 1969).

10. William G. Robbins, *Oregon, This Storied Land* (Portland: Oregon Historical Society Press, 2005), 105.

11. Ibid.; Dubofsky, *We Shall Be All*, 361–65; and William G. Robbins, *Hard Times in Paradise: Coos Bay, Oregon, 1850–1986*, rev. 2nd ed. (1988; Seattle: University of Washington Press, 2006), 50–51.

12. Berner, *Seattle 1900–1920*, 241–42. Parker is quoted in Robert E. Ficken, *The Forested Land: A History of Lumbering in Western Washington* (Seattle: University of Washington Press, 1987), 143–44.

13. Dubofsky, *We Shall Be All*, 413–14; Victor Stevens, *The Powers Story* (North Bend, Ore.: Wegford Publications, 1979), 94; and Robbins, *Hard Times*, 51.

14. Dubofsky, *We Shall Be All*, 379–81.

15. Ibid., 381–84; Joseph R. Conlin, *Bread and Roses Too: Studies of the Wobblies* (Westport, Conn.: Greenwood Publishing, 1969), 140–43; and Carlos A. Schwantes, *The Pacific Northwest: An Interpretive History* (Lincoln: University of Nebraska Press, 1996), 355.

16. Malone, Roeder, and Lang, *Montana*, 275–76; and Clemens P. Work, *Darkest*

Before Dawn: Sedition and Free Speech in the American West (Albuquerque: University of New Mexico Press, 2005), 120–23, 137.

17. Work, *Darkest Before Dawn*, 143–48, 181–83; and *Billings (Mont.) Gazette*, May 4, 2006.

18. Robert E. Ficken and Charles P. LeWarne, *Washington: A Centennial History* (Seattle: University of Washington Press, 1989), 86–87; and Dorothy O. Johansen, *Empire of the Columbia: A History of the Pacific Northwest* (New York: Harper and Row, 1967), 485–86. For an account of Seattle's shipbuilding industry during the First World War, see William J. Williams, "Accommodating American Shipyard Workers, 1917–1918: The Pacific Coast and the Federal Government's First Public Housing and Transit Programs," *Pacific Northwest Quarterly* 84 (April 1993): 51–59.

19. Dana Frank, *Purchasing Power: Consumer Organizing, Gender, and the Seattle Labor Movement, 1919–1929* (New York: Cambridge University Press, 1994), 39, 45–46.

20. Ficken and LeWarne, *Washington*, 86–87; and H. C. Peterson and Gilbert C. Fite, *Opponents of War, 1917–1918* (Seattle: University of Washington Press, 1968), 286–87.

21. John Douglas Belshaw and David J. Mitchell, "The Economy since the Great War," in *The Pacific Province: A History of British Columbia*, ed. Hugh J. M. Johnston (Vancouver: Douglas & McIntyre, 1996), 313; F. Ross McCormack, *Reformers, Rebels, and Revolutionaries: The Western Canadian Radical Movement, 1899–1919* (Toronto: University of Toronto Press, 1977), 158–61, 165–71; and Margaret A. Ormsby, *British Columbia: A History* (Toronto: Macmillan of Canada, 1958), 400, 408–10.

22. "Labour's Revolt: The Winnipeg General Strike," http://www.civilization.ca/hist/labour/labh22e.html; Norman Penner, ed., *Winnipeg 1919: The Strikers' Own History of the Winnipeg General Strike* (Toronto: James Lewis and Samuel, 1973), ix; Barman, *The West Beyond the West*, 223–24; and Ormsby, *British Columbia*, 408–10.

23. E. A. Schwartz, *The Rogue River Indian War and Its Aftermath, 1850–1980* (Norman: University of Oklahoma Press, 1997), 226–29; and Brian W. Dippie, *The Vanishing American: White Attitudes and U.S. Indian Policy* (Lawrence: University Press of Kansas, 1982), 195–96.

24. Alexandra Harmon, *Indians in the Making: Ethnic Relations and Indian Identities around Puget Sound* (Berkeley: University of California Press, 1998), 174–82.

25. Schwartz, *The Rogue River Indian War*, 233–35, 242–44.

26. Malone, Roeder, and Lang, *Montana*, 355–56.

27. Laurie Arnold, "The Paradox of a House Divided: The Colville Tribes and Termination" (Ph.D. dissertation, Arizona State University, 2006), 4–5, 23–24.

28. Ibid., 25–26; and http://www.colvilletribes.com/past3.html, 3–5.

29. Paul Tennant, *Aboriginal Peoples and Politics: The Indian Land Question in British Columbia, 1849–1989* (Vancouver: University of British Columbia Press, 1990), 80–81, 84–90. Native leaders Peter Kelly and Andrew Paull attended missionary schools with the unintentional consequence of contributing to pan-Indianism.

30. Ibid., 92–113.

31. Earl Pomeroy, *The American Far West in the Twentieth Century* (New Haven, Conn.: Yale University Press, 2008), 112–13; and F. Ross Peterson, *Idaho: A History* (New York: W. W. Norton, 1976), 139–41.

32. Malone, Roeder, and Lang, *Montana*, 280–81; and Joseph Kinsey Howard, *Montana High, Wide, and Handsome* (1943; Lincoln: University of Nebraska Press, 1983), 197–204, 208.

33. Malone, Roeder, and Lang, *Montana*, 283–84.

34. Ficken and LeWarne, *Washington*, 98.

35. George Case, "A History of the Port of Coos Bay" (M.A. thesis, Pan American University, 1983), 82–83. Also see William G. Robbins, *Hard Times in Paradise: Coos Bay, Oregon, 1850–1986* (Seattle: University of Washington Press, 2007), 68–79.

36. Belshaw and Mitchell, "The Economy," 317–19; and Barman, *The West Beyond the West*, 222–25, 236–39.

37. Belshaw and Mitchell, "The Economy," 313–15.

38. Pomeroy, *The Pacific Slope*, 216, 227–28; Lawrence M. Lipin, *Workers and the Wild: Conservation, Consumerism, and Labor in Oregon, 1910–30* (Urbana: University of Illinois Press, 2007), 125; Malone and Peterson, "Politics and Protests," 513; Eckard V. Toy, Jr., "Hoods across the Border: The Ku Klux Klan and the Far Right in the American and Canadian Wests," in *The Borderlands of the American and Canadian Wests*, ed. Sterling Evans (Lincoln: University of Nebraska Press, 2006), 262–65; and Evelyn A. Schlatter, *Aryan Cowboys: White Supremacists and the Search for a New Frontier, 1970–2000* (Austin: University of Texas Press, 2006), x, 2, 26.

39. Kenneth T. Jackson, *The Ku Klux Klan in the City, 1915–1930* (New York: Oxford University Press, 1967), 237. See also Toy, "Hoods across the Border," 264.

40. For a broad, general survey of nativism, see Malcolm Clark, "The Bigot Disclosed: 90 Years of Nativism," *Oregon Historical Quarterly* 75 (1974): 109–90; and Lipin, *Workers and the Wild*, 68–69.

41. Clark, "The Bigot Disclosed," 120–50; Johansen, *Empire of the Columbia*, 496–97; and Walter M. Pierce, *Oregon Cattleman, Governor, Congressman: Memoirs and Times of Walter M. Pierce*, ed. Arthur H. Bone (Portland: Oregon Historical Society Press, 1981). For evidence that Pierce was at least a fellow traveler and friend of the Klan, see David A. Horowitz, "Order, Solidarity, and Vigilance: The Ku Klux Klan in Oregon," in *The Invisible Empire in the West: Toward a New Historical Appraisal of the Ku Klux Klan of the 1920s*, ed. Shawn Lay (Urbana: University of Illinois Press, 1992), 185, 199–200.

42. Johansen, *Empire of the Columbia*, 494–95; Horowitz, "Order, Solidarity, and Vigilance," 192; and Schwantes, *The Pacific Northwest*, 374–75.

43. Lipin, *Workers and the Wild*, 125–27; Johansen, *Empire of the Columbia*, 495; and E. Kimbark MacColl, *The Growth of a City: Power and Politics in Portland, Oregon, 1915–1950* (Portland: Georgian Press, 1979), 162–72.

44. "Lesson Nineteen, Economic and Political Change Between the Wars, 1919–1939," in *History of Washington State and the Pacific Northwest*, Center for the Study of the Pacific Northwest, University of Washington, http://www.washington.edu/uwired/outreach/cspn/Website/index.html.

45. I am indebted to William L. Lang for explaining the weakness of the Ku Klux Klan in Montana. Also see Michael P. Malone, *The Battle for Butte: Mining and Politics on the Northern Frontier, 1864–1906* (Seattle: University of Washington Press, 1981), 64–65; and Christine K. Erickson, "'Kluxer Blues': The Klan Confronts Catholics in Butte, Montana, 1923–1929," *Montana: The Magazine of Western History* 53 (Spring 2003): 1–3, 8.

46. For the influence of the Klan on the Canadian prairies, see Gerald Friesen, *The Canadian Prairies: A History* (Toronto: University of Toronto Press, 1984), 404–7, 451, 465.

47. Toy, "Hoods across the Border," 263–65; and "Letter to Thomas Mulvey from A. M. Manson Regarding KKK," http://canadianmysteries.ca/sites/verigin/suspects/kkk/1742en.html.

48. Ficken and LeWarne, *Washington*, 96; and Richard C. Berner, *Seattle 1921–1940: From Boom to Bust* (Seattle: Charles Press, 1992), 132–36.

49. Norman H. Clark, *Mill Town: A Social History of Everett, Washington* (Seattle: University of Washington Press, 1970), 163–64, 238–39; and Richard White, *"It's Your Misfortune and None of My Own": A New History of the American West* (Norman: University of Oklahoma Press, 1991), 467.

50. Pierce, *Oregon Cattleman*, 264–78, 322–23; and Johansen, *Empire of the Columbia*, 498.

51. Schwantes, *In Mountain Shadows*, 197–99; and Malone, Roeder, and Lang, *Montana*, 288–91.

52. Robin Fisher and David J. Mitchell, "Patterns of Provincial Politics since 1916," in Johnston, *The Pacific Province*, 254–58.

53. David M. Kennedy, *Freedom from Fear: The American People in Depression and War, 1929–1945* (New York: Oxford University Press, 1999), 10–18.

54. Ibid., 21–25; and White, *It's Your Misfortune*.

Chapter 4. Shaping a Regional Culture, 1900–1930

1. Sara Ellen Paulson, "The Oaks in the Progressive Era: Consumer Culture in a Portland, Oregon Amusement Park, 1905–1925" (M.A. thesis, Portland State University, 2005).

2. Carl Abbott, *Great Extravaganza: Portland & the Lewis & Clark Exposition* (Darby, Pa.: Diane Publishing Company, 1981), 15, 39.

3. All Lewis and Clark Exposition attendance figures are from ibid., 54.

4. Ibid., 11.

5. Digital Collections, "Alaska-Yukon-Pacific Exposition," University of Washington Libraries, n.d., http://content.lib.washington.edu/aypweb/context.html (accessed September 15, 2008); Kate C. Duncan, *1001 Curious Things: Ye Olde Curiosity Shop and Native American Art* (Seattle: University of Washington Press, 2001), 63; Abbott, *Great Extravaganza,* 76.

6. Lisa Blee, "Exhibiting a History of Empire at the 1905 Portland World's Fair," *Oregon Historical Quarterly* 106 (Summer 2005): par. 16, http://www.historycooperative.org.proxy.lib.pdx.edu/journals/ohq/106.2/blee.html (accessed September 15, 2008).

7. Cheryl Gunselman, "Cornelia Marvin and Mary Frances Isom: Leaders of Oregon's Library Movement," *Library Trends* (Spring 2004): 6, 7, http://findarticles.com/p/articles/mi_m1387/is_4_52/ai_n7074035/ (accessed September 15, 2008).

8. Jean Barman, *The West Beyond the West: A History of British Columbia,* rev. ed. (1991; Toronto: University of Toronto Press, 1996), 246.

9. Sidney Warren, *Farthest Frontier: The Pacific Northwest* (New York: Macmillan, 1949), 235; Carlos A. Schwantes, *The Pacific Northwest: An Interpretive History* (1996; University of Nebraska Press, 2000), 281; Dye quoted in Sheri Bartlett Browne, *Eva Emery Dye: Romance with the West* (Corvallis: Oregon State University Press, 2004), 70–71.

10. Sandra Haarsager, *Organized Womanhood: Cultural Politics in the Pacific Northwest, 1840–1920,* new ed. (Norman: University of Oklahoma Press, 1997); J. E. Passet, *Cultural Crusaders: Women Librarians in the American West, 1900–1917* (Albuquerque: University of New Mexico Press, 1994), quoted in Gunselman, "Cornelia Marvin and Mary Frances Isom," 8.

11. Haarsager, *Organized Womanhood,* 162.

12. Thomas Augst and Kenneth Carpenter, *Institutions of Reading: The Social Life of Libraries in the United States* (Amherst: University of Massachusetts Press, 2007), 15.

13. Pacific Northwest Library Association, *Pacific Northwest Libraries: History of Their Early Development in Washington, Oregon and British Columbia. Papers Prepared for the Seventeenth Annual Conference of the Pacific Northwest Library Association, 1926* (Seattle: University of Washington Press, 1926), 7; Jim Scheppke, "The Origins of the Oregon State Library," *Oregon Historical Quarterly* 107 (Spring 2006): 5; Wikipedia contributors, "Carnegie Library" (encyclopedia entry), in *Wikipedia, the Free Encyclopedia* (accessed September 24, 2008), http://en.wikipedia.org/w/index.php?title=Carnegie_library&oldid=240662519 (accessed September 26, 2008); Dr. Ann Curry, "A Grand Old Sandstone Lady: Vancouver's

Carnegie Library," School of Library, Archival and Information Studies, University of British Columbia, http://www.slais.ubc.ca/PEOPLE/faculty/curry-p/pdf/Carnegie.pdf, 2.

14. Timothy A. Dunn, "The Rise of Mass Public Schooling in British Columbia, 1900–1929," in *Schooling and Society in Twentieth Century British Columbia*, ed. J. Donald Wilson (Calgary, Alberta: Detselig Enterprises, 1980), 24.

15. Thomas Fleming, "'Our Boys in the Field': Inspectors, Superintendents, and the Changing Character of School Leadership in British Columbia," in *Schools in the West: Essays in Canadian Educational History*, ed. Nancy M. Sheehan, J. Donald Wilson, and David C. Jones (Calgary, Alberta: Detselig Enterprises, 1986), 287; Leonard J. Arrington, *History of Idaho*, vol. 2 (Moscow: University of Idaho Press, 1994); Michael P. Malone, Richard B. Roeder, and William L. Lang, *Montana: A History of Two Centuries* (Seattle: University of Washington Press, 1991), 361; Barman, *The West Beyond the West* (1996), 227.

16. Malone, Roeder, and Lang, *Montana*, 360; Elizabeth McLagan, *Peculiar Paradise: A History of Blacks in Oregon, 1788–1940* (Portland: Georgian Press, 1980), 140–41.

17. E. Brian Titley, "Indian Industrial Schools in Western Canada," in Sheehan, Wilson, and Jones, *Schools in the West*, 146–47; Roger L. Nichols, *Indians in the United States and Canada: A Comparative History* (Lincoln: University of Nebraska Press, 1999), 246–47.

18. Lorna Farrell-Ward, "Tradition/Transition: The Keys to Change," in *Vancouver: Art and Artists, 1931–1983* (Vancouver: Vancouver Art Gallery, 1983), 23; Barman, *The West Beyond the West* (1996), 245.

19. Ginny Allen and Jody Klevit, *Oregon Painters: The First Hundred Years (1859–1959): Index and Biographical Dictionary* (Portland: Oregon Historical Society Press, 1999).

20. David M. Wrobel, *Promised Lands: Promotion, Memory, and the Creation of the American West* (Lawrence: University Press of Kansas, 2002).

21. Kathleen S. Fine-Dare, *Grave Injustice: The American Indian Repatriation Movement and NAGPRA* (Lincoln: University of Nebraska Press, 2002), 20.

22. Duncan, *1001 Curious Things*, 22.

23. Steven Ross Evans, *Voice of the Old Wolf: Lucullus Virgil McWhorter and the Nez Perce Indians* (Pullman: Washington State University Press, 1996).

24. Dexter Fisher quoted in Mourning Dove, *Cogewea, the Half Blood: A Depiction of the Great Montana Cattle Range* (Lincoln: University of Nebraska Press, 1981), xxvi.

25. Steven L. Grafe and Lee Moorhouse, *Peoples of the Plateau: The Indian Photographs of Lee Moorhouse, 1898–1915* (Norman: University of Oklahoma Press, 2005), 4, 56, 30.

26. Ibid., 32.

27. Brian W. Dippie, *Looking at Russell* (Fort Worth, Tex.: Amon Carter

Museum, 1987), 68, 12; unnamed critic, *Victoria Colonist*, March 6, 1930, quoted in Gerta Moray, *Unsettling Encounters: First Nations Imagery in the Art of Emily Carr* (Vancouver: University of British Columbia Press, 2006), 12.

28. Lawrence Kreisman and Glenn Mason, *The Arts and Crafts Movement in the Pacific Northwest* (Portland: Timber Press, 2007), 28.

29. Sharon Anne Cook, Lorna R. McLean, and Kate O'Rourke, *Framing Our Past: Canadian Women's History in the 20th Century* (Montreal: McGill-Queen's University Press, 2001), 46.

30. Barman, *The West Beyond the West* (1996), 246.

31. Parker quoted in John Findlay and Dan Lamberton, "Aggressive Regionalism, 1920s–," in *History and Literature in the Pacific Northwest*, Center for the Study of the Pacific Northwest, University of Washington, n.d., http://www.washington.edu/uwired/outreach/cspn/Website/Hist%20n%20Lit/Part%20Four/Aggressive%20Essay.html (accessed September 15, 2008). See also "The 25 Best Northwest Books," *Pacific Northwest*, December 1981, 46–51.

32. Warren, *Farthest Frontier*, 265, 264.

33. Ibid., 271; James Stevens and H. L. Davis, "Status Rerum: A Manifesto, Upon the Present Condition of Northwestern Literature Containing Several Near-Libelous Utterances, Upon Persons in the Public Eye," in *History and Literature in the Pacific Northwest*, Center for the Study of the Pacific Northwest, University of Washington, n.d., http://www.washington.edu/uwired/outreach/cspn/Website/Hist%20n%20Lit/Part%20Four/Texts/Status%20Rerum.html (accessed September 19, 2008).

34. Harold P. Simonson, "Pacific Northwest Literature—Its Coming of Age," *Pacific Northwest Quarterly* 71 (October 1980): 149; Arrington, *History of Idaho*, 2:246.

35. Doug Marx, "We Are the World," *Oregon Focus*, February 1988, 9.

36. Simonson, "Pacific Northwest Literature," 149; Marx, "We Are the World," 9; Howard Brier, *Sawdust Empire: The Pacific Northwest* (New York: Alfred A. Knopf, 1957).

37. Findlay and Lamberton, "Aggressive Regionalism."

38. H. G. Merriam, *"The Frontier" and the Frontier [and] Midland* (Missoula: University of Montana Press, 1964), 3.

39. Hugh J. M. Johnston, ed., *The Pacific Province: A History of British Columbia* (Vancouver: Douglas & McIntyre, 1996), 8.

40. Allen and Klevit, *Oregon Painters*; Browne, *Eva Emery Dye*, 107.

41. Paulson, "The Oaks," 46; Gloria E. Myers, *A Municipal Mother: Portland's Lola Greene Baldwin, America's First Policewoman* (Corvallis: Oregon State University Press, 1995).

42. Paulson, "The Oaks," 46; Jim Kershner, "Segregation in Spokane," *Columbia Magazine* 14 (Winter 2000–2001), http://washingtonhistory.org/wshs/columbia/articles/0400-a2.htm (accessed September 15, 2008).

Chapter 5. Descent into Despair and War

1. Norman H. Clark, *The Dry Years: Prohibition and Social Change in Washington* (Seattle: University of Washington Press, 1988), 216–18.

2. Ibid., 218; and Richard C. Berner, *Seattle 1921–1940: From Boom to Bust* (Seattle: Charles Press, 1992), 293–95, 301–3, 313–14.

3. E. Kimbark MacColl, *The Growth of a City: Power and Politics in Portland, Oregon, 1915–1950* (Portland: Georgian Press, 1979), 453, 487.

4. Carl Abbott, *Portland: Planning, Politics, and Growth in a Twentieth-Century City* (Lincoln: University of Nebraska Press, 1983), 109–11. For Scott's meeting with the Unemployed Citizens' League, see MacColl, *The Growth of a City*, 453–57.

5. John Douglas Belshaw and David J. Mitchell, "The Economy since the Great War," in *The Pacific Province: A History of British Columbia*, ed. Hugh J. M. Johnston (Vancouver: Douglas & McIntyre, 1996), 313, 320; and Pierre Berton, *The Great Depression, 1929–1939* (1990; East Mississauga, Ontario: Anchor Canada, 2001), 12.

6. Jean Barman, *The West Beyond the West: A History of British Columbia* (Toronto: University of Toronto Press, 1991), 247–48.

7. Livesay is quoted in Brenda Lea White, ed., *British Columbia: Visions of the Promised Land* (Vancouver: Flight Press, 1986), 46–47.

8. Earl Pomeroy, *The Pacific Slope: A History of California, Oregon, Washington, Idaho, Utah, and Nevada* (New York: Alfred A. Knopf, 1965), 294–95; and Carlos A. Schwantes, *In Mountain Shadows: A History of Idaho* (Lincoln: University of Nebraska Press, 1991), 201–3.

9. Michael P. Malone, Richard B. Roeder, and William L. Lang, *Montana: A History of Two Centuries* (Seattle: University of Washington Press, 1991), 292–95; and Joseph Kinsey Howard, *Montana: High, Wide, and Handsome* (1943; Lincoln: University of Nebraska Press, 1983), 285.

10. Laurie Mercier, *Anaconda: Labor, Community, and Culture in Montana's Smelter City* (Urbana: University of Illinois Press, 2001), 45–49.

11. Jennifer Karson, ed., *Wiaxayxt/wiyaakaa'awn/As Days Go By: Our Land, Our People—The Cayuse, Umatilla, and Walla Walla* (Pendleton, Ore.: Tamastslikt Cultural Institute and Oregon Historical Society Press, Portland, 2006), 139; Daniel L. Boxberger, *To Fish in Common: The Ethnohistory of Lummi Indian Salmon Fishing* (1989; Seattle: University of Washington Press, 2000), 107; and Alexandra Harmon, *Indians in the Making: Ethnic Relations and Indian Identities around Puget Sound* (Berkeley: University of California Press, 1998), 191.

12. Harmon, *Indians in the Making*, 191–92; and Coll Thrush, *Native Seattle: Histories from the Crossing-Over Place* (Seattle: University of Washington Press, 2007), 152–59.

13. Boxberger, *To Fish in Common*, 61–63, 98–102.

14. Ibid., 98–111, 118–19.

15. Barman, *The West Beyond the West*, 251; and Ronald W. Hawker, *Tales of Ghosts: First Nations Art in British Columbia* (Vancouver: University of British Columbia Press, 2003).

16. Paul Tennant, *Aboriginal Peoples and Politics: The Indian Land Question in British Columbia, 1849–1989* (Vancouver: University of British Columbia Press, 1990), 115–19.

17. For much of this argument, I have drawn extensively from the following article: William G. Robbins, "Franklin D. Roosevelt and the Emergence of the Modern West," *Journal of the West* 34 (April 1995): 43–48. For the giant Fort Peck project, see Malone, Roeder, and Lang, *Montana*, 300–302.

18. William F. Willingham, *Army Engineers and the Development of Oregon: A History of the Portland District U.S. Army Corps of Engineers* (Washington, D.C.: Government Printing Office, 1983), 93–100; and Richard White, *"It's Your Misfortune and None of My Own": A New History of the American West* (Norman: University of Oklahoma Press, 1991), 484–85.

19. White, *It's Your Misfortune*, 485–87.

20. Ibid., 472–73; and Robbins, "Franklin D. Roosevelt," 46.

21. Malone, Roeder, and Lang, *Montana*, 297–99; Schwantes, *In Mountain Shadows*, 204–5; Walter Nugent, *Into the West: The Story of Its People* (New York: Alfred A. Knopf, 1999), 251; and Howard, *Montana*, 315.

22. Malone, Roeder, and Lang, *Montana*, 296–300; Schwantes, *In Mountain Shadows*, 204–5; and William G. Robbins, *Oregon, This Storied Land* (Portland: Oregon Historical Society Press, 2005), 116–20.

23. Malone, Roeder, and Lang, *Montana*, 299; and F. Ross Peterson, *Idaho: A History* (New York: W. W. Norton, 1976), 157.

24. Lauren Graham, "Who They Were and What They Did: Washington State's CCC Boys," http://www.academic.evergreen.edu/g/gralau30/CCC.htm; and "Civilian Conservation Corps Heritage Sites," Washington State Parks and Recreation Commission, http://www.parks.wa.gov/.

25. "Unemployment and the WPA in Seattle," http://clerk.ci.seattle.wa.us/~public/doclibrary/wpa/wpa_intro.html; and "King County Land Use Survey—a Remarkable WPA Project of the Great Depression," http://www.historylink.org.htm.

26. Martha H. Swain, "Women's Work Relief in the Great Depression," *Mississippi History Now*, http://mshistory.k12.ms.us/features/feature49/women.htm; and Neil Barker, "Portland's Works Progress Administration," *Oregon Historical Quarterly* 101 (2000): 427–28.

27. Barker, "Portland's Works Progress Administration," 428–29. A WPA administrator reported in 1939 that the WPA spent 10 percent of its funding on sewing and canning projects, with sewing-related work employing more than

half the women hired by the agency. See "WPA Project," Gjenvick-Gjenvick Archives, http://www.wpaproject.com/QandA-WPA/GeneralQuestions.html.

28. For an overview of Collier's Indian policies, see Kenneth R. Philp, *John Collier's Crusade for Indian Reform, 1920–1954* (Tucson: University of Arizona Press, 1977). Also see Stephen Dow Beckham, "Federal-Indian Relations," in *The First Oregonians: An Illustrated Collection of Essays on Traditional Lifeways, Federal-Indian Relations, and the State's Native People Today*, ed. Carolyn M. Buan and Richard Lewis (Portland: Oregon Council for the Humanities, 1991), 50; and Nugent, *Into the West*, 252.

29. Beckham, "Federal-Indian Relations," 50; Patrick Haynal, "Termination and Tribal Survival: The Klamath Tribes of Oregon," *Oregon Historical Quarterly* 101 (2000): 275–76; Karson, *As Days Go By*, 139; Malone, Roeder, and Lang, *Montana*, 356; and Theodore H. Haas, *Ten Years of Tribal Government under N.R.A.* (1947), http://thorpe.ou.edu/IRA/IRAbook/tblB2.htm.

30. Barman, *The West Beyond the West*, 253–54.

31. Berton, *The Great Depression*, 209.

32. Ibid., 256–59; and "The Great Depression and the Development of Social Programs by the Government of MacKenzie King," Parks Canada—Laurier House National Historic Site of Canada, http://www.pc.gc.ca/lhn-nhs/on/laurier/edu/edu3b_e.asp.

33. Robbins's vivid memories of a long-ago conversation with Ian MacSwan, a native of British Columbia and a colleague in Plant Pathology at Oregon State University.

34. Emily Carr, *Hundreds and Thousands: The Journals of Emily Carr* (Toronto: Clarke and Irwin, 1966); and David M. Kennedy, *Freedom from Fear: The American People in Depression and War, 1929–1945* (New York: Oxford University Press, 1999), 425–26.

35. Barman, *The West Beyond the West*, 261–62; and William G. Robbins, *Landscapes of Conflict: The Oregon Story, 1940–2000* (Seattle: University of Washington Press, 2004), 7–8.

36. Malone, Roeder, and Lang, *Montana*, 308–11; and Mercier, *Anaconda*, 64.

37. *The Idaho Home Front: World War II*, Idaho Public Television, http://www.idahoptv.org/productions/specials/homefront/wwii/axtell.cfm.

38. Schwantes, *In Mountain Shadows*, 213–14.

39. Ibid., 214–15; and http://www.mariannelove.com/Farragut.html.

40. White, *It's Your Misfortune*, 496.

41. Pomeroy, *The American Far West*, 112, 117; and White, *It's Your Misfortune*, 496–97.

42. Pomeroy, *The American Far West*, 121–22. See the articles in Carlos A. Schwantes, ed., *The Pacific Northwest in World War II* (Manhattan, Kans.: Sunflower University Press, 1986).

43. Carl Abbott, "Planning for the Home Front in Seattle and Portland,

1940–45," in *The Martial Metropolis: U.S. Cities in War and Peace*, ed. Roger W. Lotchin (New York: Praeger, 1984), 165–66; Robert E. Ficken and Charles P. LeWarne, *Washington: A Centennial History* (Seattle: University of Washington Press, 1989), 130; and Richard C. Berner, *Seattle Transformed: World War II to Cold War* (Seattle: Charles Press, 1999), 93–94.

44. Carl Abbott, *How Cities Won the West: Four Centuries of Urban Change in Western North America* (Albuquerque: University of New Mexico Press, 2008), 174–78; Carlos A. Schwantes, *The Pacific Northwest: An Interpretive History* (Lincoln: University of Nebraska Press, 1996), 331–32; and Manly Maben, *Vanport* (Portland: Oregon Historical Society Press, 1987), 1–12.

45. Maben, *Vanport*, 87–93; Schwantes, *The Pacific Northwest*, 419; Pomeroy, *The American Far West*, 222; and Ellen Stroud, "A Slough of Troubles: An Environmental and Social History of the Columbia Slough" (M.A. thesis, University of Oregon, 1995), 1–3, 12–13.

46. Berner, *Seattle Transformed*, 50–51, 119–21. For a more detailed study, see Quintard Taylor, Jr., *The Forging of a Black Community: A History of Seattle's Central District, 1870 Through the Civil Rights Era* (Seattle: University of Washington Press, 1994).

47. Harmon, *Indians in the Making*, 205–6; Thrush, *Native Seattle*, 164; and White, *It's Your Misfortune*, 507.

48. Kennedy, *Freedom from Fear*, 778–79; Barman, *The West Beyond the West*, 262; Abbott, *How Cities Won the West*; and "World War II Transformed the Canadian Economy," http://www.canadianeconomy.gc.ca/english/economy/1939ww2 .html.

49. Ficken and LeWarne, *Washington*, 131–32; Karen Beck Skold, "The Job He Left Behind: Women in the Shipyards During World War II," in *Women in Pacific Northwest History*, ed. Karen J. Blair (Seattle: University of Washington Press, 2001), 158–64; and Schwantes, *The Pacific Northwest*, 415–16.

50. Skold, "The Job He Left Behind," 166–76.

51. Roger Daniels, *Asian America: Chinese and Japanese in the United States since 1850* (Seattle: University of Washington Press, 1988), 160–85; Kennedy, *Freedom from Fear*, 401–3; and Ficken and LeWarne, *Washington*, 132–33.

52. Dorothy O. Johansen, *Empire of the Columbia* (New York: Harper and Row, 1967), 608–9; and Ficken and LeWarne, *Washington*, 133–34. DeWitt is quoted in Kennedy, *Freedom from Fear*, 750–52.

53. Kennedy, *Freedom from Fear*, 752–53; and Robbins, *Oregon, This Storied Land*, 129–30.

54. "Oregon's Japanese Americans Learn Their Fate," http://arcweb.sos.state .or.us/exhibits/ww2/threat/eo9066.html; and Kennedy, *Freedom from Fear*, 753–56.

55. James T. Patterson, *Grand Expectations: The United States, 1945–1964* (New York: Oxford University Press, 1996), 6.

56. Casey J. Pallister, "George 'Montana' Oiye: The Journey of a Japanese

American from the Big Sky to the Battlefields of Europe," *Montana: The Magazine of Western History* 57 (Autumn 2007): 21–33.

57. Patricia E. Roy, *The White Man's Province: British Columbia Politicians and Chinese and Japanese Immigrants, 1858–1914* (Vancouver: University of British Columbia Press, 1989), 266.

58. Patricia E. Roy, *The Oriental Question: Consolidating the White Man's Province, 1914–41* (Vancouver: University of British Columbia Press, 2003), 237–39.

59. Ken Adachi, *The Enemy That Never Was* (Toronto: McClelland and Stewart, 1976), ii–iii.

60. Kennedy, *Freedom from Fear*, 852–58; and "Military History of Canada During the Second World War," http://en.wikipedia.org/wiki/Main_Page.

Chapter 6. The Great Boom

1. Henry R. Luce, *The American Century* (New York: Farrar and Rinehart, 1941), 27, 30.

2. Walter Lippmann quoted in James T. Patterson, *Grand Expectations: The United States, 1945–1964* (New York: Oxford University Press, 1996), 7–8.

3. Richard Neuberger is quoted in the *Portland Oregonian*, August 26, 1945. Also see John Douglas Belshaw and David J. Mitchell, "The Economy since the Great War," in *The Pacific Province: A History of British Columbia*, ed. Hugh J. M. Johnston (Vancouver: Douglas & McIntyre, 1996), 320–21; and Richard C. Berner, *Seattle Transformed: World War II to Cold War* (Seattle: Charles Press, 1999), 171.

4. Gerald D. Nash, *The American West Transformed: The Impact of the Second World War* (Bloomington: Indiana University Press, 1985), 204; "Progress Report of Postwar Readjustment and Development Commission of the State of Oregon," no. 14 (August 1944): 1–2; Berner, *Seattle Transformed*, 171–72, 196–97; and Carlos A. Schwantes, *The Pacific Northwest: An Interpretive History* (Lincoln: University of Nebraska Press, 1996), 421.

5. *Reno Gazette*, February 8, 1945; Schwantes, *The Pacific Northwest*, 421–22; and Karen Beck Skold, "The Job He Left Behind: Women in the Shipyards During World War II," in *Women in Pacific Northwest History*, ed. Karen J. Blair (Seattle: University of Washington Press, 2001), 173, 176.

6. Belshaw and Mitchell, "The Economy," 320; Robert E. Ficken and Charles P. LeWarne, *Washington: A Centennial History* (Seattle: University of Washington Press, 1989), 144–45; Berner, *Seattle Transformed*, 174–77; and Jewel Lansing, *Portland: People, Politics, and Power, 1851–2001* (Corvallis: Oregon State University Press, 2003), 347.

7. Berner, *Seattle Transformed*, 192–94.

8. Earl Pomeroy, *The Pacific Slope: A History of California, Oregon, Washington, Idaho, Utah, and Nevada* (New York: Alfred A. Knopf, 1965), 301–2.

9. Michael P. Malone, Richard B. Roeder, and William L. Lang, *Montana: A*

History of Two Centuries (Seattle: University of Washington Press, 1991), 309–11; http://en.wikipedia.org/wiki/Malmstrom_Air_Force_Base; and Laurie Mercier, *Anaconda: Labor, Community, and Culture in Montana's Smelter City* (Urbana: University of Illinois Press, 2001), 73.

10. "The Economy," Montana Historical Society, http://www.his.state.mt .us/education/studentguide/economy.asp; http://www.usbr.gov/dataweb/html/ bitterrt.html#Post; and Mercier, *Anaconda*, 78.

11. Carlos A. Schwantes, *In Mountain Shadows: A History of Idaho* (Lincoln: University of Nebraska Press, 1991), 216–19; and "SAC Bases: Mountain Home Air Force Base," http://www.mountainhome.af.mil/.

12. Schwantes, *In Mountain Shadows*, 218–19; and "Idaho National Laboratory," http://www.inl.gov/history/.

13. Mark Fiege, *Irrigated Eden: The Making of an Agricultural Landscape in the American West* (Seattle: University of Washington Press, 1999), 75; and Leonard Arrington, *History of Idaho* (Moscow: University of Idaho Press, 1994), 2:131–32.

14. Walter M. Pierce, *Oregon Cattleman, Governor, Congressman: Memoirs and Times of Walter M. Pierce*, ed. Arthur H. Bone (Portland: Oregon Historical Society Press, 1981), 395–97.

15. Lauren Kessler, *Stubborn Twig: Three Generations in the Life of a Japanese American Family* (New York: Random House, 1993), 235–54; and Linda Tamura, *The Hood River Issei: An Oral History of Japanese Settlers in Oregon's Hood River Valley* (Urbana: University of Illinois Press, 1993), 224–33.

16. Berner, *Seattle Transformed*, 124–27.

17. Ibid., 129–30. The government study *People in Motion: The Postwar Adjustment of the Evacuated Japanese Americans* is quoted in Berner.

18. Patricia E. Roy, "Lessons in Citizenship, 1945–1949: The Delayed Return of the Japanese to Canada's Pacific Coast," *Pacific Northwest Quarterly* 93 (Spring 2002): 69–76; and Roy, *The Oriental Question: Consolidating the White Man's Province, 1914–41* (Vancouver: University of British Columbia Press, 2003), 238.

19. A Department of Energy study conducted in 1990 determined that more than three thousand people were exposed to radiation doses seventy times above exposures under normal conditions. For this and other information about Hanford, see Bruce Hevly, "Introduction to the Nuclear Northwest," and Daniel Grossman, "Hanford and Its Early Radioactive Atmospheric Releases," *Pacific Northwest Quarterly* 85 (January 1994): 4–14. Also see *Tri-City Herald*, http://archive.tri-city herald.com/thyroid/history.html.

20. Ficken and LeWarne, *Washington*, 145–46.

21. Richard S. Kirkendall, "The Boeing Company and the Military-Metropolitan-Industrial Complex, 1945–1953," *Pacific Northwest Quarterly* 85 (October 1994): 137–49.

22. Roger Sale, *Seattle, Past to Present* (Seattle: University of Washington Press, 1976), 183–84.

23. Carl Abbott, "Regional City and Network City: Portland and Seattle in the Twentieth Century," *Western Historical Quarterly* 23 (August 1992): 305, 314.

24. Sale, *Seattle*, 186–89.

25. Pomeroy, *The Pacific Slope*, 150–51; "Spokane—Thumbnail History," http://www.historylink.org/essays/output.cfm?file_id=7686, 8–9; "Spokane and Fairchild Air Force Base," http://public.fairchild.amc.af.mil/library/factsheets/factsheet.asp?id=4303; and http://www.spokanecity.org/services/about/spokane/history/economy/.

26. Malone, Roeder, and Lang, *Montana*, 356; and Alexandra Harmon, *Indians in the Making: Ethnic Relations and Indian Identities around Puget Sound* (Berkeley: University of California Press, 1998), 205.

27. Brian W. Dippie, *The Vanishing American: White Attitudes and U.S. Indian Policy* (Lawrence: University Press of Kansas, 1982), 336–41; and Harmon, *Indians in the Making*, 206.

28. Paul C. Rosier, "'They Are Ancestral Homelands': Race, Place, and Politics in Cold War Native America, 1945–1961," *Journal of American History* 93 (March 2006): 1301–2.

29. Stephen Dow Beckham, "Federal-Indian Relations," in *The First Oregonians: An Illustrated Collection of Essays on Traditional Lifeways, Federal-Indian Relations, and the State's Native People Today*, ed. Carolyn M. Buan and Richard Lewis (Portland: Oregon Council for the Humanities, 1991), 51–52.

30. "Termination of the Tribes," http://www.klamathtribes.org/TerminationStatement.html.

31. Harmon, *Indians in the Making*, 207–13.

32. Laurie Arnold, "The Paradox of a House Divided: The Colville Tribes and Termination" (Ph.D. dissertation, Arizona State University, 2006), 25–27.

33. Ibid., 36–37; Mel Tonasket, "Termination: The Colville Situation," Washington State University, October 30, 1970, http://www.cwis.org/fwdp/Americas/terminat.txt; and Rosier, "They Are Ancestral Homelands," 1302.

34. Jean Barman, *The West Beyond the West: A History of British Columbia* (Toronto: University of Toronto Press, 1991), 175, 307–9; and Paul Tennant, *Aboriginal Peoples and Politics: The Indian Land Question in British Columbia, 1849–1989* (Vancouver: University of British Columbia Press, 1990), 121–38.

35. Quintard Taylor, Jr., *The Forging of a Black Community: A History of Seattle's Central District, 1870 Through the Civil Rights Era* (Seattle: University of Washington Press, 1994), 154–56, 187–89.

36. Berner, *Seattle Transformed*, 164–65; and Taylor, *The Forging of a Black Community*, 175.

37. E. Kimbark MacColl, *The Growth of a City: Power and Politics in Portland, Oregon, 1915–1950* (Portland: Georgian Press, 1979), 580–85, 593.

38. Ibid., 596–602.

39. Timothy Egan, "The Lives They Lived: Carl Maxey; Type-A Gandhi," *New*

York Times, November 19, 2007; and Jim Kershner, "Longtime Black Residents Recount the Injustices and the Victories," *Columbia Magazine* 14 (Winter 2000–2001): 1–10. Also see Kershner, *Carl Maxey: A Fighting Life* (Seattle: University of Washington Press, 2008).

40. Schwantes, *The Pacific Northwest*, 228–29.

41. Erasmo Gamboa, *Mexican Labor and World War II: Braceros in the Pacific Northwest, 1942–1947* (Seattle: University of Washington Press, 1990), vii, 128–29; and Richard W. Etulain, *Beyond the Missouri: The Story of the American West* (Albuquerque: University of New Mexico Press, 2006), 369–70.

42. "Mexican Americans in the Columbia Basin: Historical Overview," http://www.vancouver.wsu.edu/crbeha/ma/ma.htm, 2; and Gamboa, *Mexican Labor*, 128–29.

43. "Mexican Americans in the Columbia Basin," 3–4; and Gamboa, *Mexican Labor*, 130–31.

44. Carl Abbott, "The Federal Presence," in *The Oxford History of the American West*, ed. Clyde A. Milner II, Carol A. O'Connor, and Martha A. Sandweiss (New York: Oxford University Press, 1994), 487–90; and William G. Robbins, "The Western Lumber Industry: A Twentieth-Century Perspective," in *The Twentieth-Century West: Historical Interpretations*, ed. Gerald D. Nash and Richard W. Etulain (Albuquerque: University of New Mexico Press, 1989), 246.

45. Robbins, "The Western Lumber Industry," 246–47; and Ken Drushka, *Stumped: The Forest Industry in Transition* (Toronto: Douglas & McIntyre, 1985), 81.

46. Belshaw and Mitchell, "The Economy," 323; Dennis C. LeMaster, *Mergers Among the Largest Forest Products Firms, 1950–1970*, College of Agriculture Research Bulletin 854 (Pullman: Washington State University, 1977), 1; and Robbins, "The Western Lumber Industry," 247–48.

47. Belshaw and Mitchell, "The Economy," 324–25.

48. Ibid., 329; and *Frontier to Freeway: A Short Illustrated History of the Roads of British Columbia* (British Columbia: Ministry of Transportation and Highways, n.d.), 16–30 http://www.gov.bc.ca/th.

Chapter 7. Remaking Northwest Landscapes

1. "Columbia River History," Center for Columbia River History, http://www.ccrh.org/river/history.php.

2. Ibid.; Jim Lichatowich, *Salmon Without Rivers: A History of the Pacific Salmon Crisis* (Washington, D.C.: Island Press, 1999), 170–71; Joseph E. Taylor III, *Making Salmon: An Environmental History of the Northwest Fisheries Crisis* (Seattle: University of Washington Press, 1999), 174–77; and "Dams of the Columbia Basin and Their Effects on the Native Fishery," Center for Columbia River History, http://www.ccrh.org/river/history.php.

3. For a more detailed discussion of jetty construction and the two upriver

projects, see William G. Robbins, *Landscapes of Promise: The Oregon Story, 1800–1940* (Seattle: University of Washington Press, 1997), 192–95, 242–44.

4. William F. Willingham, *Army Engineers and the Development of Oregon: A History of the Portland District U.S. Army Corps of Engineers* (Washington, D.C.: Government Printing Office, 1983), 93–95; and 308 Report, document, http://www.ccrh.org/comm/umatilla/primary/308rprt.htm.

5. Willingham, *Army Engineers*, 93–95; Robbins, *Landscapes of Promise*, 280–81; Lichatowich, *Salmon Without Rivers*, 222; and Taylor, *Making Salmon*, 225–29.

6. During the presidential campaign of 1932 a *New York Times* reporter referred to Franklin Roosevelt's small group of advisors as the "Brains Trust." See David M. Kennedy, *Freedom from Fear: The American People in Depression and War, 1929–1945* (New York: Oxford University Press, 1999), 119–20.

7. Roosevelt's speeches are quoted in Richard Neuberger, *Our Promised Land* (1939; Moscow: University of Idaho Press, 1989), 3.

8. Keith C. Peterson, *River of Life, Channel of Death: Fish and Dams on the Lower Snake* (Lewiston, Idaho: Confluence Press, 1995), 113; and Anthony Netboy, *Columbia River Salmon and Steelhead Trout* (Seattle: University of Washington Press, 1980), 82.

9. Willingham, *Army Engineers*, 152–58; and Manly Maben, *Vanport* (Portland: Oregon Historical Society Press, 1987), 104–5.

10. Richard White, *The Organic Machine: The Remaking of the Columbia River* (New York: Hill and Wang, 1995), 74–75. The Guthrie quote is on page 75.

11. William G. Robbins, *Landscapes of Conflict: The Oregon Story, 1940–2000* (Seattle: University of Washington Press, 2004), 67–70.

12. Richard L. Neuberger, "The Columbia," *Holiday*, June 1949, reprinted in Steve Neal, ed., *They Never Go Back to Pocatello: The Selected Essays of Richard Neuberger* (Portland: Oregon Historical Society Press, 1988), 30–45.

13. Willingham, *Army Engineers*, 158–59; Gus Norwood, *Columbia River Power for the People: A History of the Bonneville Power Administration* (Portland: Bonneville Power Administration, 1981), 160; and Robbins, *Landscapes of Conflict*, 71.

14. *Columbia River and Tributaries, Northwestern United States*, 81st Cong., 2nd sess., 1950, H. Doc. 531, 1:74–75; and Willingham, *Army Engineers*, 158.

15. Willingham, *Army Engineers*, 117–19.

16. The quotation is in William L. Lang, "What Has Happened to the Columbia? A Great River's Fate in the Twentieth Century," in *Great River of the West: Essays on the Columbia River*, ed. William L. Lang and Robert C. Carriker (Seattle: University of Washington Press, 1999), 150.

17. Katrine Barber, *Death of Celilo Falls* (Seattle: University of Washington Press, 2005), 3–13.

18. The quotation is in Murray Morgan, *The Columbia: Powerhouse of the West* (Seattle: Superior Publishing Company, 1949), 283.

19. Charles Wilkinson, "Celilo Falls: Forever at the Center of Western History," keynote address at the conference "Celilo Stories: New Conversations about an Ancient Place," Columbia Gorge Discovery Center, The Dalles, Oregon, March 17, 2007. Lang's remarks were made at the same conference.

20. Roberta Ulrich, *Empty Nets: Indians, Dams, and the Columbia River* (Corvallis: Oregon State University Press, 1999), 1–3; and "Cascade Fisheries: Bonneville Dam and Native American Fishing Rights," Center for Columbia River History, http://www.ccrh.org/comm/camas/fishing.htm.

21. The U.S. Army Corps of Engineers' account of this story is at http://windsurf.gorge.net/cgwa/sites/in_lieu_sites.html.

22. Paul C. Pitzer, *Grand Coulee: Harnessing a Dream* (Pullman: Washington State University Press, 1994), 221–22, 372; and "Native Americans Begin 'Ceremony of Tears' for Kettle Falls on June 14, 1940," http://www.historylink.org/essays/output.cfm?file_id=7276.

23. Pitzer, *Grand Coulee*, 221–22; and http://www.nps.gov/history/online_books/laro/adhi/adhi1.htm.

24. Lichatowich, *Salmon Without Rivers*, 170; and http://www.chrs.ca/Rivers/Fraser/Fraser-F_e.htm, 1–2.

25. Lichatowich, *Salmon Without Rivers*, 194–95.

26. Ibid., 195–96.

27. Ibid., 197–201; and Jeff Crane, review of Matthew D. Evenden, *Fish versus Power: An Environmental History of the Fraser River*, in *H-Environment*, June 2005, http://www.hnet.org/reviews/showrev.cgi?path=320201122324066.

28. M. Anita Tozer (née Bennett), "William Andrew Cecil Bennett," http://sunnyokanagan.com/wacbennett/index.html; and John Douglas Belshaw and David J. Mitchell, "The Economy since the Great War," in *The Pacific Province: A History of British Columbia*, ed. Hugh J. M. Johnston (Vancouver: Douglas & McIntyre, 1996), 327–28.

29. "Dams of the Columbia Basin and Their Effects on the Native Fishery," Center for Columbia River History, http://www.ccrh.org/comm/river/dams9.htm; and "History of BC Dams," http://www.recovery.bcit.ca/history.html.

30. Jean Barman, *The West Beyond the West: A History of British Columbia* (Toronto: University of Toronto Press, 1991), 283–85; and "W. A. C. Bennett Dam," http://www.en.wikipedia.org/wiki/W._A._C._Bennett_Dam. Also see Karl Froschauer, *White Gold: Hydroelectric Power in Canada* (Vancouver: University of British Columbia Press, 1997).

31. Scott Simpson, "A Dam Never Forgotten: First Nations Demand Redress for Bennett Dam before They Will Agree to Another," *Vancouver Sun*, October 28, 2005, http://www.canada.com/components/print.aspx; and "Tsay Keh Dene Band—Aboriginal Relations and Reconciliation," http://www.gov.bc.ca/arr/first nation/tsaykeh_dene/default.html.

262 Notes to Pages 160–165

32. For a detailed explanation of Klamath Basin issues, see Robbins, *Landscapes of Conflict*, 104–5; and Robbins, *Landscapes of Promise*, 250–54.

33. William Kittredge, *Balancing Water: Restoring the Klamath Basin* (Berkeley: University of California Press, 2000), 77–79; and Doug Foster, "Refuges and Reclamation: Conflicts in the Klamath Basin, 1904–1964," *Oregon Historical Quarterly* 103 (Summer 2002): 163.

34. Kittredge, *Balancing Water*, 85–86; and Foster, "Refuges and Reclamation," 180.

35. Robbins, *Landscapes of Conflict*, 106; and Foster, "Refuges and Reclamation," 164, 183.

36. Harry H. Stein, *Gus J. Solomon: Liberal Politics, Jews, and the Federal Courts* (Portland: Oregon Historical Society Press, 2006), 188–90; and Patrick Haynal, "Termination and Tribal Survival: The Klamath Tribes of Oregon," *Oregon Historical Quarterly* 101 (Fall 2000): 290–94; and Kittredge, *Balancing Water*, 89–90.

37. Kittredge, *Balancing Water*, 91; and Robbins, *Landscapes of Conflict*, 106–7.

38. Mark Fiege, *Irrigated Eden: The Making of an Agricultural Landscape in the American West* (Seattle: University of Washington Press, 1999), 15–16, 31, 52–53; and "The Eastern Snake River Plain Aquifer," http://imnh.isu.edu/digital atlas/hydr/snakervr/esrpa.htm.

39. Bureau of Reclamation, "Minidoka Project, Idaho," http://www.usbr.gov/dataweb/html/pnminprjdata.html; and Fiege, *Irrigated Eden*, 95.

40. Robert E. Bonner, "Local Experience and National Policy in Federal Reclamation: The Shoshone Project, 1909–1953," *Journal of Policy History* 15 (2003): 307; and Fiege, *Irrigated Eden*, 29–31.

41. Fiege, *Irrigated Eden*, 38–40.

42. "The Eastern Snake River Plain," http://www.uidaho.edu/~johnson/ifiwrri/sr3/esna.html; "The Eastern Snake River Plain Aquifer," http://imnh.isu.edu/digitalatlas/hydr/snakervr/esrpa.htm; and Fiege, *Irrigated Eden*, 40.

43. Eric A. Stene, "The Teton Basin Project," http://www.usbr.gov/dataweb/html/teton.html; Marc Reisner, *Cadillac Desert: The American West and Its Disappearing Water* (New York: Viking, 1986), 399–404; and Cecil Andrus, *Cecil Andrus: Politics Western Style* (Seattle: Sasquatch Books, 1998).

44. Reisner, *Cadillac Desert*, 406; and Andrus, *Cecil Andrus*.

45. Eric A. Stene, *The Umatilla Project* (Denver: Bureau of Reclamation DataWeb, Bureau of Reclamation History Program, 1993), 2–7; and Christopher W. Shelley, "The Resurrection of a River: Re-watering the Umatilla Basin," (Vancouver, Wash. Center for Columbia River History, 1999), 1–2.

46. Shelley, "The Resurrection of a River," 5–6; and Jennifer Karson, ed., *Wiaxayxt/wiyaakaa'awn/As Days Go By: Our Land, Our People—The Cayuse, Umatilla, and Walla Walla* (Pendleton, Ore.: Tamastslikt Cultural Institute and Oregon Historical Society Press, Portland, 2006), 230–31.

47. Shelley, "The Resurrection of a River," 6–7; and Karson, *As Days Go By*, 231–32.

48. "Hungry Horse Project," http://www.usbr.gov/dataweb/html/hungryho .html; and "Libby Dam," http://en.wikipedia.org/wiki/Libby_Dam.

49. William F. Willingham, *Northwest Passages: History of the Seattle District U.S. Army Corps of Engineers, 1920–1970* (Seattle: U.S. Army Corps of Engineers, 2006), 78–82.

50. Martin Reuss, "The Pick-Sloan Plan," www.usace.army.mil/publications/ eng-pamphlets/ep870-1-42/c-4-2, 233–34, 242–43.

51. Eric A. Stene, "Pick-Sloan Missouri Basin Program, Canyon Ferry Unit," http://www.usbr.gov/dataweb/html/canyonferryh.html.

52. Ibid., 10–11; and http://yosemite.epa.gov/water/surfnote.nsf/11ef47e42e21 77af85256392006c244e/7c1fbc7ad8d4befd852566b800567288!OpenDocument.

53. Willingham, *Northwest Passages*, 75–77.

54. Ibid., 77–78.

55. "History of BC Dams."

56. Edward Goldsmith and Nicholas Hildyard, http://www.idsnet.org/ Resources/Dams/Development/Impact.html.

57. White, *The Organic Machine*, 112–13.<\>

Chapter 8. The Conflicted Politics of Environmentalism

1. Brent Walth, *Fire at Eden's Gate: Tom McCall and the Oregon Story* (Portland: Oregon Historical Society Press, 1994), 3–4.

2. Ibid., 141–46.

3. Ibid., 147–48.

4. Ted Steinberg, *Down to Earth: Nature's Role in American History* (New York: Oxford University Press, 2002), 246–47.

5. John Opie, *Nature's Nation: An Environmental History of the United States* (New York: Harcourt Brace, 1998), 415–17; and William G. Robbins, *Landscapes of Conflict: The Oregon Story, 1940–2000* (Seattle: University of Washington Press, 2004), 188–205.

6. Robbins, *Landscapes of Conflict*, 239; and http://www.geog.ucsb.edu/~ jeff/sb_69oilspill/69oilspill_articles2.html.

7. See Kathryn Harrison, *Passing the Buck: Federalism and Canadian Environmental Policy* (Vancouver: University of British Columbia Press, 1996), 3–6, 29, 33.

8. Graeme Wynn, "Introduction: Environmental Perspectives on British Columbia," in "On the Environment," special issue, *BC Studies: The British Columbia Quarterly*, nos. 142–43 (Summer–Autumn 2004): 17–20; and Jean Barman, *The West Beyond the West: A History of British Columbia* (Toronto: University of Toronto Press, 1991), 279–85.

9. Arn Keeling and Robert McDonald, "The Profligate Province: Roderick Haig-Brown and the Modernizing of British Columbia," *Journal of Canadian Studies* 36 (Autumn 2001): 12–14, 18–19.

10. Robin Fisher and David J. Mitchell, "Patterns of Provincial Politics since 1916," in *The Pacific Province: A History of British Columbia*, ed. Hugh J. M. Johnston (Vancouver: Douglas & McIntyre, 1996), 260–62.

11. David Mitchell, *W. A. C. Bennett and the Rise of British Columbia* (Vancouver: Douglas & McIntyre, 1983), 258; and Robert McDonald, "'Variants of Liberalism' and the Liberal Order Framework in British Columbia," manuscript in the authors' possession.

12. Frank Zelko, "Making Greenpeace: The Development of Direct Action Environmentalism in British Columbia," in "On the Environment," special issue, *BC Studies: The British Columbia Quarterly*, nos. 142–43 (Summer–Autumn 2004): 197–239.

13. Wynn, "Introduction," 20–21; Arn Keeling, "Sink or Swim: Water Pollution and Environmental Politics in Vancouver, 1889–1975," in "On the Environment," special issue, *BC Studies: The British Columbia Quarterly*, nos. 142–43 (Summer–Autumn 2004): 94–101; "BC Ignored Evidence in Approving Victoria's Sewage Plan," http://www.georgiastrait.org/?q=node/327/print; and Joel Connelly, "Victoria Flushing Away Its Image," *Seattle Post-Intelligencer*, July 12, 2006.

14. Steinberg, *Down to Earth*, 250–51.

15. For McCall and the cleanup of the Willamette River, see Robbins, *Landscapes of Conflict*, chap. 8. Also see Ethel A. Starbird, "River Restored: Oregon's Willamette," *National Geographic* 141 (June 1972): 816–35.

16. Robbins, *Landscapes of Conflict*, 294–95.

17. Ibid., 286–313; and personal conversation with Charles Wilkinson, January 31, 2008.

18. Michael P. Malone, Richard B. Roeder, and William L. Lang, *Montana: A History of Two Centuries* (Seattle: University of Washington Press, 1991), 391–94.

19. Ibid., 394; and John Mundinger and Todd Everts, *A Guide to the Montana Environmental Policy Act*, rev. Larry Mitchell (Helena: Legislative Environmental Policy Office, 2004), iii, 1.

20. Malone, Roeder, and Lang, *Montana*, 395; and Bob Campbell for the *Missoulian*, "1972 Constitutional Convention," http://www.missoulian.com/specials/100montanans/list/002.html.

21. Malone, Roeder, and Lang, *Montana*, 395; and Mundinger and Everts, *A Guide*, 2.

22. Malone, Roeder, and Lang, *Montana*, 398–400.

23. Harry W. Fritz, "Montana in the Twenty-first Century," in *Montana Legacy: Essays on History, People, and Place*, ed. Harry W. Fritz, Mary Murphy, and Robert R. Swartout, Jr. (Helena: Montana Historical Society Press, 2002), 342–45.

24. National Research Council, *Superfund and Mining Megasites: Lessons*

from the Coeur d'Alene River Basin (Washington, D.C.: National Academy Press, 2005), 27, 33–36.

25. Ibid., 37–41.

26. Ibid., 42–43; and Leonard J. Arrington, *History of Idaho* (Moscow: University of Idaho Press, 1994), 2:156–57.

27. Arrington, *History of Idaho*, 2:111, 147–49.

28. LeRoy Ashby, "Frank Church Goes to the Senate: The Idaho Election of 1956," *Pacific Northwest Quarterly* 78 (January–April 1987): 17–29; and Cecil D. Andrus, *Cecil Andrus: Politics Western Style* (Seattle: Sasquatch Books, 1998), 148.

29. Arrington, *History of Idaho*, 2:150–51; and Sara Dant Ewart, "Evolution of an Environmentalist: Senator Frank Church and the Hells Canyon Controversy," *Montana: The Magazine of Western History* 51 (Spring 2001): 45–50.

30. Arrington, *History of Idaho*, 2:151–53; Ewart, "Evolution of an Environmentalist," 50–51; LeRoy Ashby and Rod Gramer, *Fighting the Odds: The Life of Senator Frank Church* (Pullman: Washington State University Press, 1994), 350–51; and Andrus, *Politics Western Style*, 165. For a description of the background to the Sawtooth National Recreation Area, see Erica Jensen, "'Hysterical Preservationists' and 'Gouge-and-Run Bulldozer Boys': The Land-Use Controversy in Idaho's White Cloud Mountains, 1968–1972" (M.S. thesis, Oregon State University, 2007).

31. Richard White, *The Organic Machine: The Remaking of the Columbia River* (New York: Hill and Wang, 1995), 79–81; and Robert J. Kaufman, *Henry M. Jackson: A Life in Politics* (Seattle: University of Washington Press, 2000), 32–33.

32. Kaufman, *Henry M. Jackson*, 32–33, 164, 201–5. For a recent study that includes North Cascades Park, see David Louter, *Windshield Wilderness: Cars, Roads, and Nature in Washington's National Parks* (Seattle: University of Washington Press, 2006).

33. "Warren G. Magnuson (1905–1989)," http://www.historylink.org/essays/printer_friendly/index.cfm?file_id=5569, 1–7; and Daniel Jack Chasan, *The Water Link: A History of Puget Sound as a Resource* (Seattle: University of Washington Press, 1981), 152.

34. Kaufman, *Henry M. Jackson*, 53, 108, 207; John Strang, "1944–1951: 727,900 Curies of Radioactive Iodine Released," *Tri-City Herald*.com (1999), http://archive.tri-cityherald.com/thyroid/history.html; and *Spokesman-Review*, December 7, 1991.

35. United States, Environmental Protection Agency, "NPL Site Narrative for Hanford 100-Area (USDOE)," *Federal Register Notice*, October 4, 1989.

36. Washington State Department of Health, Environmental Health Programs, Hanford Health Information Network, Office of Radiation Protection; and *Seattle Post-Intelligencer*, January 5, 2003.

37. Chasan, *The Water Link*, 61–65, 105.

38. Ibid., 105–15.

39. Ibid., 108–9; and Matthew Klingle, *Emerald City: An Environmental History of Seattle* (New Haven, Conn.: Yale University Press, 2007), 211–22.

40. This information is gleaned from several sources. See especially http://www.psat.wa.gov/About_Sound/AboutPS.htm; http://www.en.wikipedia.org/wiki/Puget_Sound_environmental_issues; and http://www.seattlepi.nwsource.com/specials/sound/.

41. Paul Tennant, *Aboriginal Peoples and Politics: The Indian Land Question in British Columbia, 1849–1989* (Vancouver: University of British Columbia Press, 1990), 216–18; and Donald Sampson, "Epilogue: Asserting Sovereignty into the Future," in *Wiaxayxt/wiyaakaa'awn/As Days Go By: Our Land, Our People—The Cayuse, Umatilla, and Walla Walla*, ed. Jennifer Karson (Pendleton, Ore.: Tamástslikt Cultural Institute and Oregon Historical Society Press, Portland, 2006), 247.

42. Alexandra Harmon, *Indians in the Making: Ethnic Relations and Indian Identities around Puget Sound* (Berkeley: University of California Press, 1998), 228; and Charles Wilkinson, *Messages from Frank's Landing: A Story of Salmon and the Indian Way* (Seattle: University of Washington Press, 2000), 49.

43. Joseph E. Taylor III, *Making Salmon: An Environmental History of the Northwest Fisheries Crisis* (Seattle: University of Washington Press, 1999), 242; Harmon, *Indians in the Making*, 229; and Fay G. Cohen, *Treaties on Trial: The Continuing Controversy over Northwest Indian Fishing Rights* (Seattle: University of Washington Press, 1986), 70–71.

44. Cohen, *Treaties on Trial*, 76–79; Taylor, *Making Salmon*, 243; and Wilkinson, *Messages from Frank's Landing*, 50.

45. Cohen, *Treaties on Trial*, 80; and Harmon, *Indians in the Making*, 230.

46. Cohen, *Treaties on Trial*, 11–12, 80–82; Harmon, *Indians in the Making*, 230–31; Coll Thrush, *Native Seattle: Histories from the Crossing-Over Place* (Seattle: University of Washington Press, 2007), 190, 192. Also see Alvin J. Ziontz, *A Lawyer in Indian Country: A Memoir* (Seattle: University of Washington Press, 2009). Ziontz was one of the principal litigants for the treaty tribes.

47. Cohen, *Treaties on Trial*, 90–106, 154–76; and Wilkinson, *Messages from Frank's Landing*, 59–60.

48. Harmon, *Indians in the Making*, 231; Wilkinson, *Messages from Frank's Landing*, 62; and Cohen, *Treaties on Trial*, 38.

49. Cohen, *Treaties on Trial*; and Connie Sue Martin, "'Go Fish': State Told Not to Build Culverts That May Hinder Fish Passage," Martin Law Group, Environmental News, http://www.martinlaw.com/news/?20071010-fish-passage-hindrance.

50. Martin, "Go Fish."

51. http://www.abcbookworld.com/?state=view_author&author_id=4284; and Tennant, *Aboriginal Peoples*, 210–11. For Sewid's autobiography, see James P. Spradley, ed., *Guests Never Leave Hungry: The Autobiography of James Sewid, a Kwakiutl Indian* (New Haven, Conn.: Yale University Press, 1969).

52. Tennant, *Aboriginal Peoples*, 213–21.

53. Robert J. Muckle, *The First Nations of British Columbia* (Vancouver: University of British Columbia Press, 1998), 77–78; and Tennant, *Aboriginal Peoples*, 222–25.

54. Muckle, *The First Nations*, 79; and Tennant, *Aboriginal Peoples*, 225.

55. Tennant, *Aboriginal Peoples*, 228–37.

56. Muckle, *The First Nations*, 80–87.

57. Paul W. Hirt, *A Conspiracy of Optimism: Management of the National Forests since World War Two* (Lincoln: University of Nebraska Press, 1994), 272; Catherine Caufield, "The Ancient Forest," *New Yorker*, May 14, 1990, 82–83; and M. Lynn Corn, "Spotted Owls and Northwest Forests," *Congressional Research Service Issue Brief* (Library of Congress), January 14, 1993, 1–2.

58. John Douglas Belshaw and David J. Mitchell, "The Economy since the Great War," in Johnston, *The Pacific Province*, 336–38; *Eugene Register-Guard*, April 27, 1995; *Portland Oregonian*, July 25, 1999; and *This Place on Earth, 2002* (Seattle: Northwest Environment Watch, 2002), 13.

Chapter 9. Culture Works, 1930–2000

1. Ronald W. Taber, "Vardis Fisher and the 'Idaho Guide,'" *Pacific Northwest Quarterly*, April 1968, as quoted in Tim Woodward, *Tiger on the Road: The Life of Vardis Fisher* (Caldwell, Idaho: Caxton Printers, 1989), 217, 142.

2. David A. Horowitz, *Martina Gangle Curl—People's Art and the Mothering of Humanity* (Portland: Oregon Cultural Heritage Commission, 2004), 2, 5.

3. Carolyn Howe and Portland State University, *The Production of Culture on the Oregon Federal Arts Project of the Works Progress Administration*, 1980, 22; Elizabeth Mentzer, "Made in Montana: Montana's Post Office Murals," *Montana Magazine* 53 (Autumn 2003), http://www.visitmt.com/history/Montana_the _Magazine_of_Western_History/fall2003/madeinmontana.htm (accessed September 15, 2008).

4. Carlos A. Schwantes, *The Pacific Northwest: An Interpretive History*, rev. ed. (1996; Lincoln: University of Nebraska Press, 2000), 363.

5. Jean Barman, *The West Beyond the West: A History of British Columbia*, rev. ed. (Toronto: University of Toronto Press, 1996), 243; Patricia E. Roy and John Herd Thompson, *British Columbia: Land of Promises* (New York: Oxford University Press, 2005), 116; Schwantes, *The Pacific Northwest* (2000), 370; Barman, *The West Beyond the West*, 281; Leonard J. Arrington, *History of Idaho* (Moscow: University of Idaho Press, 1994), 2:25.

6. Barman, *The West Beyond the West*, 260; Arrington, *History of Idaho*, 2:26; Michael P. Malone, Richard B. Roeder, and William L. Lang, *Montana: A History of Two Centuries* (Seattle: University of Washington Press, 1991), 369.

7. Nard Jones, *Oregon Detour* (Corvallis: Oregon State University Press,

1990), 108; Mildred Walker, *Winter Wheat* (Lincoln: University of Nebraska Press, 1993), 167–68.

8. Thomas Fleming, "'Our Boys in the Field': School Inspectors, Superintendents, and the Changing Character of School Leadership in British Columbia," in *Schools in the West: Essays in Canadian Educational History*, ed. Nancy M. Sheehan, J. Donald Wilson, and David C. Jones (Calgary, Alberta: Detselig Enterprises, 1986), 295; Arrington, *History of Idaho*, 2:168.

9. William F. Willingham, *Starting Over: Community Building on the Eastern Oregon Frontier* (Portland: Oregon Historical Society Press, 2006), 160; Barman, *The West Beyond the West*, 290–91.

10. Horowitz, *Martina Gangle Curl*, 10; Bullock quoted in Chauncey Del French, *Waging War on the Home Front* (Corvallis: Oregon State University Press, 2007), xxiv.

11. Emily Carr, *Hundreds and Thousands: The Journals of Emily Carr* (Toronto: Clarke, Irwin, 1966), 233.

12. Robert Dietsche, *Jumptown: The Golden Years of Portland Jazz, 1942–1957* (Corvallis: Oregon State University Press, 2005), 107; Paul de Barros, *Jackson Street after Hours: The Roots of Jazz in Seattle* (Seattle: Sasquatch Books, 1993), vii.

13. Dietsche, *Jumptown*, 55; Cassandra Tate, "Rhythm & Roots: Birth of Seattle's First Sound," November 25, 2001, http://www.historylink.org/essays/output .cfm?file_id=3641 (accessed September 15, 2008); see also Barros, *Jackson Street after Hours*.

14. *Compass*, Summer–Fall 1944, 43, box 9, folder 5, Camp Waldport Records 1943–45, University of Oregon Libraries, Special Collections and University Archives, Eugene, Oregon. See also Katrine Barber and Eliza Elkins Jones, "'The Utmost Human Consequence': Art and Peace on the Oregon Coast, 1942–1946," *Oregon Historical Quarterly*, Winter 2006, http://www.historycooperative.org/ journals/ohq/107.4/barber.html (accessed December 28, 2009); and Eliza Elkins Jones, "'All Done as a Real Pacifist': Manche Langley's Recollections of Peace and Art in America's Mid-Twentieth-Century Far West" (M.A. thesis, Portland State University, 2005).

15. Deloris Tarzan Ament, *Iridescent Light: The Emergence of Northwest Art* (Seattle: University of Washington Press, 2002), 184–85.

16. John Seiler Brubacher, *Higher Education in Transition: A History of American Colleges and Universities*, 4th ed., Foundations of Higher Education (New Brunswick, N.J.: Transaction Publishers, 1997), 257.

17. Paula S. Fass, "The Female Paradox: Higher Education for Women, 1945–1963," in *The History of Higher Education*, 2nd ed., ed. Lester Goodchild and Harold Wechsler (Needham Heights, Mass.: Simon & Schuster Custom Publisher, 1997), 705; John R. Thelin, *A History of American Higher Education* (Baltimore, Md.: Johns Hopkins University Press, 2004), 261; F. Henry Johnson, *A Brief History of Canadian Education* (Ontario: McGraw-Hill of Canada, 1968), 187.

18. Thelin, *A History of American Higher Education*, 205, 253; Hugh Hawkins, "The Making of the Liberal Arts College Identity," *Daedalus* 28, no. 1 (1999): 14; Richard M. Freeland, "The World Transformed: A Golden Age for American Universities, 1945–1970," in Goodchild and Wechsler, *The History of Higher Education*, 593.

19. Gordon B. Dodds, *The College That Would Not Die: The First 50 Years of Portland State University, 1946–1996* (Portland: Oregon Historical Society Press, 1999), 10.

20. Lizabeth Cohen, *A Consumers' Republic: The Politics of Mass Consumption in Postwar America* (New York: Vintage, 2003), 140; Hilary Herbold, "Never a Level Playing Field: Blacks and the GI Bill," *Journal of Blacks in Higher Education* 6 (Winter 1994–95): 106.

21. Victor Lovitt Oakes Chittick, ed., *Northwest Harvest: A Regional Stock Taking* (New York: Macmillan, 1948), 14.

22. John Findlay and Dan Lamberton, "Aggressive Regionalism, 1920s–," in *History and Literature in the Pacific Northwest*, Center for the Study of the Pacific Northwest, University of Washington, n.d., http://www.washington.edu/uwired/outreach/cspn/Website/Hist%20n%20Lit/Part%20Four/Aggressive%20Essay.html (accessed September 15, 2008).

23. Ibid.

24. Patrick McRoberts, "Hugo, Richard (1923–1982)," January 20, 2003, http://historylink.org/essays/output.cfm?file_id=5082 (accessed September 15, 2008); Stanford Pinsker, *Three Pacific Northwest Poets: William Stafford, Richard Hugo, and David Wagoner* (Boston: Twayne Publishers, 1987), 66.

25. Lex Runciman and Steven Sher, *Northwest Variety: Personal Essays by 14 Regional Authors* (Corvallis, Ore.: Arrowood Books, 1987), 75.

26. Ibid., 55.

27. Mildred Andrews, "MacDonald, Betty (1908–1958)," November 4, 1998, http://www.historylink.org/essays/output.cfm?file_id=156 (accessed September 15, 2008); Wikipedia contributors, "The Egg and I," in *Wikipedia: The Free Encyclopedia*, September 10, 2008, http://en.wikipedia.org/w/index.php?title=The_Egg_and_I&oldid=237437537 (accessed September 15, 2008).

28. Betty Bard MacDonald, *The Egg and I* (Philadelphia: J. B. Lippincott Company, 1946), 91.

29. Ibid., 105.

30. Ibid., 91.

31. Ibid., 220.

32. Alan Twigg, *Hubert Evans: The First Ninety-three Years* (Madeira Park, British Columbia: Harbour, 1984), 13.

33. "Hubert Evans," in *BC Author Bank* (BC Bookworld), http://www.abcbookworld.com/view_author.php?id=147 (accessed September 15, 2008); Twigg, *Hubert Evans*, 25–26.

34. Alan Twigg, *Vancouver and Its Writers* (Madeira Park, British Columbia: Harbour, 1986), 6; Twigg, *Hubert Evans*, 31, 114.

35. Laurie Ricou, *The Arbutus/Madrone Files: Reading the Pacific Northwest* (Corvallis: Oregon State University Press, 2002), 79.

36. Kenneth Lincoln, *Native American Renaissance* (Berkeley: University of California Press, 1985).

37. Samuel Corrigan, "One People, Two Paths: Aboriginal Literature in Canada and the United States," 2002 Sequoyah Research Center Symposium—First Nations Literature, Sequoyah Research Center, University of Arkansas at Little Rock, November 2002, http://anpa.ualr.edu/symposia/2002_symposium/Samuel_Corrigan.htm (accessed September 15, 2008); Jeannette Armstrong and Lally Grauer, *Native Poetry in Canada* (Peterborough, Ontario: Broadview Press, 2001), xviii. Armstrong's grand-aunt Mourning Dove was the first Native American to write a novel when she published *Cogewa* in 1927.

38. Corrigan, "One People, Two Paths"; George Clutesi, *Potlatch* (Sidney, British Columbia: Gray's Publishing, 1969); "George Clutesi," in BC Archives, Royal British Columbia Museum, October 18, 2007, http://www.bcarchives.gov.bc.ca/exhibits/timemach/galler03/frames/clutesi.htm (accessed September 15, 2008).

39. Frederick Busch, "Longing for Magic," *New York Times*, July 16, 1995, late ed., sec. 7; Richard Nicholls, "Skin Games," *New York Times*, November 24, 1996, late ed., sec. 7; Timothy Egan, "An Indian Without Reservations," *New York Times*, January 18, 1998, late ed., sec. 6; Gloria Bird, "The Exaggeration of Despair in Sherman Alexie's *Reservation Blues*," *Wicazo Sa* 11 (Autumn 1995): 47.

40. Runciman and Sher, *Northwest Variety*, 106.

41. Ken Kesey, *Sometimes a Great Notion* (New York: Viking Press, 1964), 1, ellipses in original.

42. Lev Grossman and Richard Lacayo, "The Complete List—All-Time 100 Novels," October 16, 2005, http://www.time.com/time/2005/100books/the_complete_list.html (accessed September 15, 2008); John Marshall, "Ken Kesey's True Legacy Is 'Sometimes a Great Notion,'" *Seattle Post-Intelligencer*, November 16, 2001, http://seattlepi.nwsource.com/books/46819_book16.shtml; Christopher Lehmann-Haupt, "Ken Kesey, Author of 'Cuckoo's Nest,' Who Defined the Psychedelic Era, Dies at 66," *New York Times*, November 11, 2001, http://query.nytimes.com/gst/fullpage.html?res=9D02EFDC1238F932A25752C1A9679C8B63&sec=&spon=&pagewanted=3.

43. John Findlay, "Something in the Soil?: Literature and Regional Identity in the 20th-Century Pacific Northwest," *Pacific Northwest Quarterly* 97 (Fall 2006): 182.

44. Thomas Griffith, "The Pacific Northwest," *Atlantic Monthly*, April 1976, 58; Ricou, *The Arbutus/Madrone Files*, 17.

45. Harmon and Raban, *The Pacific Northwest Landscape*, 18.

46. Ament, *Iridescent Light*, 3.

47. Ibid., 68; Kenneth Callahan, *Kenneth Callahan: Universal Voyage*, Index of Art in the Pacific Northwest no. 6 (Seattle: Published for the Henry Art Gallery by the University of Washington Press, 1973); Sheryl Conkelton and Tacoma Art Museum, *Northwest Mythologies: The Interactions of Mark Tobey, Morris Graves, Kenneth Callahan, and Guy Anderson* (Tacoma: Tacoma Art Museum, 2003); Thelma Lehmann, "Masters of Northwest Art: Kenneth Callahan—A Creative Mix of Family and Art," October 25, 2001, http://historylink.org/essays/output .cfm?file_id=3616 (accessed September 15, 2008).

48. Deloris Tarzan Ament, "Graves, Morris (1910–2001)," February 15, 2003, http://www.historylink.org/essays/output.cfm?file_id=5205 (accessed September 15, 2008); Ament, *Iridescent Light*; Conkelton and Tacoma Art Museum, *Northwest Mythologies*.

49. Ament, *Iridescent Light*, xvi.

50. Conkelton and Tacoma Art Museum, *Northwest Mythologies*, 27.

51. Jacques Barbeau, *A Journey with E. J. Hughes* (Vancouver, British Columbia: Barbeau Foundation, 2000); Brian Brennan, "The Artist Who Almost Became a Postman Captures the Essence of British Columbia in His Stylized Realist Paintings," in *GalleriesWest* (2006).

52. Brennan, "The Artist Who Almost Became a Postman"; "Artist Heir to Emily Carr; Raw Strength of Coastal Scenes Earned Fame for British Columbia's E. J. Hughes," *Toronto Star*, January 8, 2007, sec. Entertainment.

53. Vancouver Art Gallery Library Canadian Artist Files, "Lawrence Paul Yuxweluptun, the Impending Nisga'a' Deal. Last Stand. Chump Change— Artist's Biography," in *First Nations: Myths and Realities* (Vancouver Art Gallery, 2005), http://projects.vanartgallery.bc.ca/publications/75years/exhibitions/2/1/ artist/43/96.27/biography/44 (accessed September 15, 2008); "Lawrence Paul Yuxweluptun, Welcome," artist's Web site, http://www.lawrencepaulyuxweluptun .com/index.html (accessed September 15, 2008).

54. Charlotte Townsend-Gault, "Northwest Coast Art: The Culture of the Land Claims," *American Indian Quarterly* 18 (Autumn 1994): 464; George Harris, "Confronting Colonialism," in Lawrence Paul Yuxweluptun, in *First Nations: Myths and Realities* (Vancouver Art Gallery, 2005), http://projects.vanartgallery .bc.ca/publications/75years/exhibitions/2/1/artist/43/96.27/bibliography/325 (accessed September 15, 2008).

55. Jacqueline Trescott, "The Arts' Northwest Passage; What Seattle Can Teach D.C. About Support for Culture," *Washington Post*, August 15, 1999, final ed., sec. Arts; Julie Bick, "Book Lovers Ask, What's Seattle's Secret?" *New York Times*, March 9, 2008, late ed., sec. BU; Money and Business/Financial Desk; Andrea Sachs, "In Oregon, Just Readin' in the Rain," *Washington Post*, December 2, 2001, final ed., sec. Travel.

56. Dana Oland, "Ballet Idaho's New Artistic Director to Set Company's Vision:

His Hiring Is a Key Step as Boise's Company Prepares to Split from Eugene Ballet," *Idaho Statesman*, January 19, 2008; John Harrington, "Helena, Mont., Leaders Plan to Brand City as Arts Learning Center," *Independent Record*, March 6, 2008, sec. Business and Financial News; Dr. Ann L. Adair and Kristin S. Wagner, "The Economic Impact of Montana Artists," Montana Arts Council, January 2005, http://art.mt.gov/resources/resources_econartists1.asp (accessed September 15, 2008).

57. Tacoma Art Museum and Douglas F. Cooley Memorial Art Gallery, *Jet Dreams: Art of the Fifties in the Northwest* (Tacoma: Tacoma Art Museum in association with the University of Washington Press, 1995), 61; Dana Oland, "Boise Arts Glow, Grow and Change," *Idaho Statesman*, January 1, 2007; Trescott, "The Arts' Northwest Passage"; Bick, "Book Lovers Ask."

Epilogue: Regional Identity in a New Century

1. For a discussion of the term *New West*, see William Riebsame, ed., *Atlas of the New West: Portrait of a Changing Region* (New York: W. W. Norton, 1997). Philip L. Jackson and Robert Kuhlken, *A Rediscovered Frontier: Land Use and Resource Issues in the New West* (Lanham, Md.: Rowan and Littlefield, 2006), vii–viii, 1–5; and Don Whiteley, "A Tale of Two Cities," *BC Business*, April 1, 2007, http://bcbusinessmagazine.com/bcb/top-stories/2007/04/01/tale-two-towns.

2. "About the Northwest Economy," www.gonorthwest.com/visitor/about/economy.htm; and Alan Durning, "Slow News Is Good News," *Open Spaces* 6, no. 4 (2005): 57–59.

3. *Eugene Register-Guard*, February 7, 2007.

4. Center on Budget and Policy Priorities, *Pulling Apart: A State-by-State Analysis of Income Trends*, January 2000, http://www.cbpp.org; and 2008, http://www.cbpp.org/4-9-08sfp.htm.

5. *Idaho Statesman*, April 9, 2008; "New Data Shows Oregon's Wealthiest Pulling Away from the Rest," Oregon Center for Public Policy, April 8, 2008, http://www.ocpp.org; and Joseph A. McCartin, "'A Wagner Act for Public Employees': Labor's Deferred Dream and the Rise of Conservatism, 1970–1976," *Journal of American History* 95 (June 2008): 124–25, 148.

6. Center on Budget and Policy Priorities, *Pulling Apart: A State-by-State Analysis of Income Trends*, 2005, http://www.cbpp.org/4-9-08sfp.htm; and Thomas M. Power, *Income Inequality in Montana*, KUFM/KGPR, May 5, 2002, http://www.cas.umt.edu/econ/Power/kufm/2002/050602.htm.

7. "Bull's-Eye on the Poor and Middle Class," Emergency Campaign for America's Priorities, February 2006, http://www.usaction.org, 1; *Idaho Statesman*, September 28, 2007; Judith L. Brown, "An Economic Snapshot of Idaho for the 2008 Campaigns," *Moscow-Pullman Daily News*, January 5, 2008; and Huei-Hsia Wu,

"By the Numbers: Demographic Changes, Education and Earnings Gaps between Hispanics and Non-Hispanic Whites in Idaho," http://www.boise state.edu/history/issuesonline/2007spring/7f_numbers.html.

8. For literature addressing these issues, see William G. Robbins, "Creating a 'New West': Big Money Returns to the Hinterland," *Montana: The Magazine of Western History* 46 (Summer 1996): 66–72; and Jim Robbins, *Last Refuge: The Environmental Showdown in Yellowstone and the American West* (New York: William Morrow and Co., 1994).

9. *Eugene Register-Guard*, August 16, 1998; and *Portland Oregonian*, September 27, 1994.

10. Marc Lee, "New Perspectives on Income Inequality in BC," Canadian Centre for Policy Alternatives, BC Office, December 2004, http://www.policy.ca/policy-directory/Detailed/New-Perspectives-on-income-inequality-in-BC-668.html, 4–5; and Jared Bernstein, Elizabeth McNichol, and Andrew Nicholas, Center on Budget and Policy Priorities, *Pulling Apart: A State-by-State Analysis of Income Trends*, April 2008, http://www.cbpp.html.

11. Lee, "New Perspectives," 22; and Jeremy Mouat to William G. Robbins, May 6, 2008.

12. http://www.bcstats.gov.bc.ca/DATA/pop/popstart.asp.

13. The Capital Regional District is the regional government for thirteen municipalities on the southern tip of Vancouver Island. "BC since the 1990s," http://www.heartlandcenter.info/visionssite/fall2000/RUconnection.html; and "Demographics of Vancouver," http://www.en.wikipedia.org/wiki/Vancouver.

14. Thomas R. Berger, *A City of Neighbourhoods: Report of the 2004 Vancouver Electoral Commission* (Vancouver, June 2004); "Demographics of Vancouver"; and http://www.wikipedia.org/wiki/British_Columbia.html.

15. *Ottawa Citizen*, April 8, 2007, http://www.canada.com/topics/news/story.html?id=b6984636-4c50-4068-8c7d-a539ccof3643.

16. Ibid.; and http://www.ctv.ca/servlet/ArticleNews/Story/CTVNews/20070313/census.

17. Richard White, *"It's Your Misfortune and None of My Own": A New History of the American West* (Norman: University of Oklahoma Press, 1991), 503–4.

18. "Historical County Population Change, 1950–2000," Puget Sound Trends, http://psrc.org/publications/pubs/trends/index.htm; and "Resident Population and Apportionment of the U.S. House of Representatives," http://www.quickfacts.census.gov/qfd/states/41000.htm.

19. "Population Growth in Relation to the State's Metropolitan Areas," Washington State Department of Transportation, http://www.wsdot.wa.gov/planning/wtp/datalibrary/population/PopGrowthSMSA.htm; "Oregon: Population Patterns," http://www.encarta.msn.com/encyclopedia_761558216_5/oregon.html; "Washington County Profile, 2006," http://www.washtech.co.washington.or.us/budget

summary/pdf/345-351_County%20Profile_345-351.pdf; "History of Industry and Workforce of Clackamas County," Oregon Department of Employment, 2007, http://www.qualityinfo.org/olmisj/ArticleReader?itemid=00003531; OREGON: Population of Counties by Decennial Census, http://www.censusbureau.biz/population/cencounts/or190090.txt; http://www.npg.org/states/id.htm; http://www.npg.org/states/wa.htm; and http://www.npg.org/states/mt.htm.

20. "Reinventing Spokane," http://www.historylink.org/essays/output.cfm?file_id=7462; and Robert Brewster, Jr., "Sleepy Spokane Awakes to Real Estate Renaissance," http://www.djc.com/news/re/11163671.html.

21. "Boise City and Urban Area Population, 1863–1980," Idaho State Historical Society Reference Series, http://history.idaho.gov/Reference%20Series/0363.pdf; and "Boise: Major Industries and Commercial Activity," http://www.city-data.com/us-cities/The-West/Boise-Economy.html.

22. Ginny Fay and SuzAnne Miller, "Missoula Economic Development Forum, Oct. 20, 2003," December 8, 2003, http://www.crmw.org/MontanaOnTheMove/data/Missoula.pdf, 3–22; and Missoula, Montana, Population Growth, http://www.censusscope.org.

23. "Medford-Ashland," http://en.wikipedia.org/wiki/Medford,_Oregon; and "Harry and David, Medford, Oregon," http://www.bco.com/overview/locations.html; http://www.harryanddavid.com/.

24. "601 Largest US Cities, 2000 Census," http://www.cfweb.cc.yse.edu/psi/census_pdf/census; and Portland State University, Population Research Center, http://www.pdx.edu/prc/.

25. Robert Kaplan, An Empire Wilderness: Travels into America's Future (New York: Random House, 1998), 283–87; and Portland Oregonian, May 27, 2008.

26. The Canadian census, taken in five-year intervals (1986, 1991, 1996, etc.), traditionally sorted people by ethnic/national origin until 1996, when the census employed a new category, "Visible Minorities." People of "Aboriginal identity" (North American Indian, Metis, Inuit) were listed in a separate category. See BC STATS, http://www.bcstats.gov.bc.ca.

27. "1996 Census Facts," BC STATS.

28. Vancouver Sun, April 2, 2008, http://www.canada.com/vancouversun/news/story.html; and "Profile of British Columbia, 2006," http://www.bcstats.gov.bc.ca.

29. Dorothy Johansen, Empire of the Columbia: A History of the Pacific Northwest (New York: Harper and Row, 1967), 608–9.

30. For these comparisons, see Carlos A. Schwantes, The Pacific Northwest: An Interpretive History (Lincoln: University of Nebraska Press, 1996), 529.

31. U.S. Census Bureau, "State and County Quickfacts," http://www.quickfacts.census.gov/qfd/states/53000.html.

32. Robert D. Kaplan, "Travels into America's Future," Atlantic Monthly, August 1998, 50–55.

33. "Quickfacts from the US Census Bureau," http://www.infoplease.com/us/census/data/portland/seattle.html; and Mary L. Hanneman, "The Asianization of America: A New Look at the 'Pacific Basin Frontier,'" *Columbia: The Magazine of Northwest History* (Winter 2006–7): 18–22.

34. This argument is adapted from William Leach, *Country of Exiles: The Destruction of Place in American Life* (New York: Random House, 1999), 16–17.

Illustration Credits

The two maps were created by Robert Hildebrand, Portland State University Center for Spatial Analysis and Research.

Chapter 1. The Years of "Exuberant Optimism"

Abigail Scott Duniway. Courtesy of Oregon Historical Society Research Library, neg. no. 4146.

James Dunsmuir. Courtesy of Royal BC Museum, BC Archives, image B-01949.

Chapter 2. Reformers, Radicals, and the New Order

Roy Bishop, Pendleton Woolen Mills, and Jackson Sundown. Courtesy of Oregon Historical Society Research Library, OrHi 59805.

Jeannette Rankin. Courtesy of Archives & Special Collections, Mansfield Library, University of Montana, Vivian Brooke Collection, photo no. 85.0257.

Chapter 3. War and Peace: The Politics of Reaction

Skinner & Eddy Shipyard, Seattle. Courtesy of the Museum of History & Industry, Seattle; Collection of David Rogers; photo ref. 19137.

Forest Grove Indian Training School. Courtesy of Oregon Historical Society Research Library, OrHi 384s.

Chapter 4. Shaping a Regional Culture, 1900–1930

Lewis and Clark Exposition catalog cover. Courtesy of the Oregon State Library.

Emily Carr, *Totem Poles, Kitseukla*, 1912, Vancouver Art Gallery. Courtesy of Collection of the Vancouver Art Gallery, Founders' Fund; photograph by Trevor Mills, Vancouver Art Gallery.

Charles Russell, *Sun Worship in Montana*, 1907. Opaque and transparent watercolor over graphite underdrawing on paper, 22⅜ × 17½ inches. Courtesy of Amon Carter Museum, Fort Worth, Texas, 1961.150.

Chapter 5. Descent into Despair and War

Vancouver, British Columbia, May Day demonstration. Courtesy of Special Collections, Vancouver Public Library, VPL 13320.

Chapter 6. The Great Boom

V-J Day, Portland. *Oregon Journal.* Courtesy of *The Oregonian,* Oregon Historical Society Research Library, *Oregon Journal* neg. no. CN005931.

Carl Maxey. Courtesy of the Northwest Museum of Arts & Culture/Eastern
Washington State Historical Society, Spokane, Washington; L87.1-1237-59JAG.

Farmworkers at their camp. Courtesy of Photograph Collection, Oregon State
University Archives, Extension Bulletin Illustrations, item no. P20:791.

Chapter 7. Remaking Northwest Landscapes

Lucy Covington. Courtesy of Manuscripts, Archives, and Special Collections,
Washington State University Libraries, Frank Fuller Avery Collection, PC 19,
14-075.

W.A.C. Bennett. Courtesy of Royal BC Museum, BC Archives, image C-06472.

Chapter 8. The Conflicted Politics of Environmentalism

Federal District Judge George Boldt. Courtesy of Oregon Historical Society
Research Library, OrHi 000828.

Chapter 9. Culture Works, 1930–2000

Idaho author Vardis Fisher. Courtesy of Grant Fisher and Boise State University
Library.

E. J. Hughes, *Logs, Ladysmith Harbour,* 1949. Oil on canvas, 76.2 × 101.6 cm. Art
Gallery of Ontario, Gift from the Albert H. Robson Memorial Subscription
Fund, 1950, © 2010AGO.

Lawrence Paul Yuxweluptun, *Scorched Earth, Clear-Cut Logging on Native Sovereign Soil, Shaman Coming to Fix,* 1991. Acrylic on canvas, 195.6 × 275 cm.
Courtesy of National Gallery of Canada, Ottawa.

Index

About the Authors

William G. Robbins, a Connecticut native, earned a B.S. degree from Western Connecticut University and a Ph.D. in history from the University of Oregon (1969). After a two-year stint at Western Oregon University, in 1971 he joined the faculty at Oregon State University, where he taught courses in Pacific Northwest history, history of the American West, and environmental history until his retirement in 2002. He has authored or edited eleven books, most recently *Landscapes of Conflict: The Oregon Story, 1940–2000* (2004) and *Oregon, This Storied Land* (2005). Oregon State University named him Distinguished Professor of History in 1997. He is presently working on a biography of Monroe Sweetland, who was a founder of Portland State University and principal architect of the federal Bilingual Education Act of 1968.

Katrine Barber is an associate professor of history at Portland State University. She teaches Pacific Northwest and western U.S. history as well as public history courses. She is on the Native American Studies faculty and is the director of the Center for Columbia River History, a consortium that includes Portland State University, Washington State University Vancouver, and the Washington State Historical Society (http://www.ccrh.org). Her first book, *Death of Celilo Falls*, was published by the University of Washington Press in 2005.